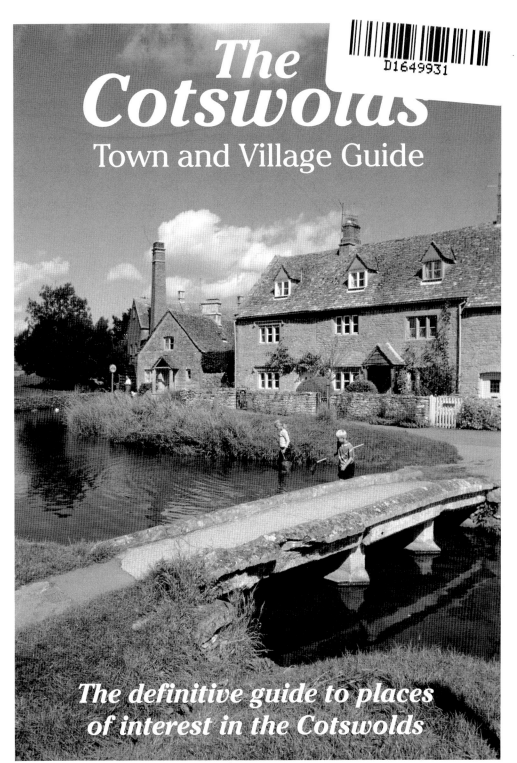

The Cotswolds
Town and Village Guide

The definitive guide to places of interest in the Cotswolds

Published
by
REARDON PUBLISHING
PO Box 919, Cheltenham, Glos, GL50 9AN
Copyright © 2000 Reardon Publishing

Fully Revised
4th Edition 2014

Researched, Written and Compiled
by
Peter Titchmarsh

Layout and Design
by
Nicholas Reardon

ISBN 1 874192782

ISBN(13) 9781874192787

Inner Photographs
by
Peter Titchmarsh

Cover Design & Cover Photographs
by
Nicholas Reardon

Pen and Ink illustrations
by
Peter T Reardon

Introduction

This guidebook is the result of my continuing love affair with the Cotswolds, an area that I have known for most of my life and one that I have been visiting with my camera and notebook for well over fifty years. A glance at the maps on pages 168 - 172 will soon reveal that the area covered extends well beyond the classic Cotswolds, but it never strays far from true limestone country with its typically lovely stone towns and villages. These are enfolded by rolling hills and quiet wooded valleys through which clear streams flow and all have a similar character to the better-known places of pilgrimage like Stow-on-the Wold, Cirencester, Bourton-on-the-Water or Broadway. Of course these favourites have not been ignored!

The Cotswold countryside is as near to perfection as one could wish for, but it is still further enhanced by the treasures to be found within its towns, villages and hamlets. Here are some of Britain's loveliest medieval churches and domestic buildings, almost all of which are built of the marvellous honey-coloured Cotswold stone that here lies so close to the surface.

When setting out on your journeys of discovery, savour each day and do not try to cover too much ground - it has taken me most of a lifetime to get round it all! If possible buy a good map or maps (preferably Ordnance Survey ones) and walk from village to village along a quiet footpath or bridleway, stopping beside a stream for a picnic, or at a pub for lunch.

Good luck with your explorations. I do hope that you enjoy them as much as I have.

Peter Titchmarsh.

How To Use This Guide

All the towns, villages, hamlets of any significance and many other places of interest are described and listed in alphabetical order. In almost every case their location is shown on one or both of the two maps on pages 168 - 171. The relationship of these two maps to each other is shown on the Key Map on page 172, where it will be noted that there is a considerable overlap.

The numbers and letters in brackets after the subject heading are as follows: The first group is the number or numbers of the map or maps on which the place is located. The second group is the map reference which applies to either or both of the maps, the reference letter and number being the same on both maps. This may sound complicated, but try locating a place which is indicated as being on two maps and all will soon become clear!

Place headings are in bold capitals - thus - **ABLINGTON**; while places within the article which are also described elsewhere under a separate heading are in bold small letters - thus - **Winson**.

ABLINGTON (1-2 J9) *1 mi. NW Bibury, 7mi. NE Cirencester.* Enchanting hamlet on the River Coln with a fine manor house, built in the late 16th century by a wealthy Cirencester wool merchant, John Coxwell. This was once the home of J.Arthur Gibbs, the author of *A Cotswold Village*, that classic evocation of life in the area surrounding Ablington in the closing years of the 19th century. Nearby Ablington House, a beautiful 17th-century building, is complete with gateposts surmounted by lions which once graced the Houses of

Barns at Ablington

Parliament, but perhaps the most pleasing buildings in the hamlet are the two great barns at its centre, one dated 1727. It is possible to walk north-westwards up the valley to **Winson** and on to **Coln Rogers,** or south-eastwards to **Burford** and **Coln St Aldwyns.**

ADDERBURY (1 C16) *3 mi. S Banbury.* Handsome ironstone village, much of which is astride the busy Banbury to Oxford road, off which is a quiet tree-lined street leading down to the Sor Brook. The church has a fine spire and tower, and around the tower and beneath the aisle parapets there is a splendid series of nearly a hundred medieval carved figures, ranging from a man ringing handbells, to a boy with dogs on a lead and a dragon with two tails. These carvings are thought to be the work of a mid-l4th-century mason, or group of masons, who also worked at **Alkerton, Bloxham** and Hanwell, a village just to the north of Banbury. Medieval doorways open into an equally fascinating interior, with a fine early-l5th-century chancel-screen, and several interesting monuments. Adderbury House, at the end of a small avenue of trees opposite the green, was the home of John Wilmot, Earl of Rochester, the dissolute l7th-century poet. Walk westwards from here to **Bloxham**, partly along the disused line of the old Banbury and Cheltenham Direct Railway; or northwards over the fields to Bodicote, passing an old windmill at Bloxham Grove.

ADLESTROP (1-2 E12) *3 mi. E Stow-on-the-Wold.* This small village lies between parkland and a belt of trees climbing the hillside to its east. It has several pleasant houses in a cul-de-sac by the church. This stands in a well kept churchyard, but its interior has been over-restored and the only items of any real interest to visitors are various Leigh family monumental tablets. Their presence reminds us that Jane Austen used to come here often to visit her uncle, Theophilus Leigh, at his rectory, a partly 17th-century building now known as Adlestrop House. Theophilus, who was a member of the

Station signboard at Adlestrop

family which owned Adlestrop Park, was also Master of Balliol College, Oxford. He died in 1785. The modest mansion of Adlestrop Park dates back to the 16th century, but its best feature is the south-west front designed in the Gothick style by Sanderson Miller, squire of **Radway** in neighbouring Warwickshire and a talented gentleman-architect in the best 18th-century tradition. Part of the surrounding parkland was laid out by Humphry Repton, and some of this is crossed by a path leading south-westwards to **Oddington,** following the course of the **Macmillan Way.** It is also possible to walk northwards from Adlestrop over the hill to **Chastleton.** There is a useful parking space in front of the Village Hall and users are asked to place money in a collecting box.

This village's name will always be remembered as the subject of Edward Thomas's highly evocative poem *Adlestrop*, the first two verses of which run:

Yes, I remember Adlestrop ...
The name ... because one afternoon
Of heat the express-train drew up there
Unwontedly. It was late June.

The steam hissed. Someone cleared his throat,
No one left and no one came
On the bare platform. What I saw
Was Adlestrop ... only a name.

The station was closed many years ago, but the station sign and station bench now stand in a small shelter in Adlestrop - a tribute to the young poet by the village he immortalised. Sadly Thomas died on active service at Arras in 1917, aged only 39.

AKEMAN STREET (Not shown on map) This important Roman road ran from Cirencester, through Bicester, to St Albans. Unlike several other Roman highways it has not been retained as a part of the Cotswolds' major road network, although several sections in the southern Cotswolds are followed by minor roads, and a few by bridleways and footpaths. Its course passes not far from **Widford** and **North Leigh Villa,** both of which have Roman connections, but it is perhaps best viewed as it crosses the Leach Valley about 1 1/2 miles north of **Eastleach Turville.**

Akeman Street where it crosses the Leach Valley

ALDERLEY (2 M3) *2 mi. SE Wotton-under-Edge.* Rosehill, a house next to the church, was built by the industrious architect, Lewis Vulliamy, in 1860, but there are several much older houses in this small village in lovely valley country below the Cotswold edge. The church, apart from its Perpendicular tower, was rebuilt in 1802, and has an elegant white-painted interior with a series of stylish monuments, one by the celebrated early-19th-century sculptor, Sir Francis Chantrey. There is a pink marble headstone in the churchyard commemorating the noted 19th-century flower illustrator, Marianne North. Alderley lies on the **Cotswold Way** and this can be followed southwards to **Lower Kilcott** and beyond to the **Somerset Monument,** or northwards to **Wotton-under-Edge** and on to the **Tyndale Monument.**

ALDERTON (1 D7) *3 mi. NW Winchcombe.* Lying between the Cotswold edge and the outlying Alderton and Dumbleton Hills, this is a transitional village, as much 'Avon Valley' as 'Cotswold' in character. Some half-timbering is to be seen, as well as some stone, and there are several thatched roofs. The largely 14th-century church looks pleasant enough standing in its tidy churchyard, but its interior was ruthlessly restored in the late 19th century, and is not of great interest to visitors apart from its long iron-bound chest, which is a fine specimen of medieval craftsmanship. There is a pleasant bridleway northwards over wooded hills to Dumbleton.

ALDSWORTH (1-2 H10) *3 mi. NE Bibury.* Thankfully most of this village is just far enough away to escape the fumes and noise of the still busy B4425. Aldsworth's prosperity must have been at its peak when Bibury Racecourse was situated on Upton Down to its immediate south, although no trace of this now remains. The date of Bibury Race Club's foundation is in some doubt, some stating that races were first run here as early as 1621 when Newmarket's regular meeting was prevented by an outbreak of the plague there. Others claim that it was founded here only in 1681, as the result of a visit by Charles II to Burford to see his mistress Nell Gwyn, during the time of his last Parliament's meeting at Oxford. There seems, however, to be little doubt that it was in the latter years of Charles II's reign that, with the patronage of the Duttons of nearby **Sherborne**, it really became a fashionable event. `Bibury Race Week' was still much in vogue in the days of George IV, when there was an impressive grandstand here complete with a cast-iron balcony. Despite this the course was closed in the mid-19th century, due largely to the ever increasing pressures of agricultural enclosure. The Bibury Race Club remains very much alive today, although it is now located at Salisbury.

The village was also the home of Robert Garne, the farmer who ran what was once the last surviving flock of the traditional Cotswold sheep, the animals that brought such prosperity to these hills and which were usually known as 'Cotswold Lions'. Happily this rare breed was just saved from extinction and may now be seen again in small numbers, notably at the **Cotswold Farm Park**, the owner's of which have done so much to preserve this and many other rare breeds of farm animal.

Thanks both to its racecourse and no doubt also to its sheep, Aldsworth has a solidly 18th- and early 19th-century flavour, with the church and manor house lying a little to the west, beyond a green crossed by a small stream. The Norman church has a short dumpy spire, and sits most comfortably in a rough, sloping churchyard with a fine collection of tombstones for company. The Perpendicular north aisle is a real beauty, being embellished with a splendid series of grotesque gargoyles outside, and with an elaborately carved niche within. Both porches are full of interest, but the north is particularly attractive, with rib vaulting and a niche thought to be for candles - possibly a 'poor man's chantry' (see **Bisley**).

ALKERTON (1 B14) *5 mi. W Banbury.* Looks across the deep valley of the little Sor Brook, to the larger village of Shenington. There are several attractive Hornton stone houses, all on steep slopes, with views westwards over the valley. Within the church, with its 13th-century tower, there is a real flavour of medieval times, with steps ascending from the nave to the chancel beneath the tower-crossing. Do not overlook the fascinating carvings around the outside cornice to the south aisle, with men and dogs, and a bear among the many figures. These are thought to be the work of a mid-14th-century mason, or group of masons, who also worked at **Adderbury, Bloxham** and Hanwell, just to the north of Banbury. The rectory was built by Thomas Lydyat, a 17th-century scholar and Fellow of New College, Oxford, who was tutor to Charles I's brother, Henry. While in Alkerton, be sure to visit the delightful 4-acre hillside gardens of Brook Cottage, with their wide variety of trees, shrubs and plants. Also walk south from here, down the valley of the Sor Brook, to Shutford, or northwards up the valley following the course of the **Macmillan Way**, to the scarp slopes above **Tysoe**.

ALSTONE (1 D7) *3½ mi. NW Winchcombe.* Like neighbouring **Alderton**, this is a 'transitional' village, with a pleasing blend of timber-framing and Cotswold stone. It is quietly situated below Woolstone Hill, an outlier of the true Cotswolds. Its little church was over-restored in 1880, when the walls were scraped and heavily re-pointed. However, there is a Norman doorway within the 17th-century porch, and the chancel-arch capitals are ornamented with interesting Norman detail.

Alstone Church

Alvescot Church

ALVESCOT (1-2 J12) *5 mi. SE Burford*. Straddling the B4020, this small village tries hard to ignore the noisy aircraft from the great runways of Brize Norton Airfield just to its north. It has two inns - the Plough, which lies rather inappropriately opposite a quaint little Strict Baptist chapel, and the Red Lion, a little further down the street. There is a small road between the two, leading to the church, which lies in a quiet setting to the north of the village. This is a pleasant cruciform building with a well proportioned Perpendicular tower and a good 14th-century south doorway. Inside there are lovely old roof timbers resting on carved corbels, some handsome 18th-century monuments, and brasses in the south aisle of Alice Malory (1579) and her husband and children.

AMBERLEY (1-2 K4) *1 mi. N Nailsworth*. A scattered village on the high, western edge of **Minchinhampton** Common, with splendid views over the deep valley of the little River Avon. Much of the novel *John Halifax Gentleman* was written here, when Mrs Craik, its authoress, lived for a short time at Amberley's Rose Cottage (see also **Tewkesbury**).

AMPNEY CRUCIS (1-2 K8) *2 mi. E Cirencester*. The largest of the three Ampneys, Crucis has a many-gabled inn, the Crown, on the main road, an old mill on the Ampney Brook and beyond it, a beautiful cruciform church tucked away beneath the wall of Ampney Park. In the churchyard is a remarkably well preserved 14th-century cross, the head of which was only rediscovered in 1854, having been previously built into the rood loft stair, probably to save it from destruction by the image destroyers who were so active both after Henry VIII's break with Rome, and also during

Tomb of George and Annie Lloyd

the Cromwellian period. See also the splendid 16th-century tomb of George and Annie Lloyd, with their five sons and seven daughters kneeling around them, the rare stone Perpendicular pulpit, and behind it a small door leading to the rood loft stair.

AMPNEY ST MARY (1-2 K9) *4 mi. E Cirencester.* This village was originally sited on the Ampney Brook, near the present main road, but it was moved almost a mile to the north-east, to the hamlet of Ashbrook, probably owing to a combination of the Black Death and repeated flooding of the brook. The village itself is unexceptional, but the modest little church with its central bell cote has remained on the original village site beside the brook and is well worth visiting. It is a small Norman building with an unusually complete series of Decorated windows, which were restored with a fortunately light hand in 1913. See especially the fascinating Norman lintel over the north doorway, the medieval south door, the stone chancel screen and the extensive series of medieval wall-paintings, including ones of *St Christopher* and *St George and the Dragon.*

Norman Lintel at Ampney St Mary

AMPNEY ST PETER (1-2 K9) *3½ mi. E Cirencester.* Situated to the immediate north of the A417, Ampney St Peter has several well restored houses and cottages and, like so many of today's Cotswold villages, is now almost too trim. The church, with its small saddleback tower, has a Saxon nave, but the restoration and rebuilding by Sir Giles Gilbert Scott in 1878 has left little feeling of antiquity here. However, do not miss the remains of a 14th-century cross in the churchyard, nor the small, possibly Saxon figure overlooking the font. There are pleasant walks southwards to **Harnhill** and **Driffield**, and on a low hill to the south-east are the extensive but not very exciting earthworks of the Iron Age settlement of Ranbury Rings *(no public access).*

ANDOVERSFORD (1-2 F8) *5 mi. E Cheltenham.* Now bypassed by the busy A40, this village has no special features. It is, however, the site of the lively, thrice-yearly horse sales, which were once held at **Stow-on-the-Wold.** These are held in May, July and October.

ARLINGTON (1-2 J9) *6 mi. NE Cirencester.* See **Bibury**, to which it is attached.

ARMSCOTE (1 A12) *3 mi. N Shipston-on-Stour.* Attractive, mellow-stone village situated no more than three miles from the northern bastion of the Cotswolds, Windmill Hill, above **Ilmington**. It has a fine Jacobean manor house, very Cotswold in flavour, and several no less pleasing houses of the same period. Armscote has no church, but there is an early 18th-century Friends' Meeting House, with a simple, unspoilt interior. Nearby there is a hospitable inn and on the road towards Halford, tucked away in a flower filled garden, a converted railway-carriage - a delightful remnant from the thirties, when many of these were to be seen in the countryside.

ASCOTT-UNDER-WYCHWOOD (1-2 F13) *5 mi. NE Burford.* A long, thin village in the lush Evenlode Valley, with a railway still making its mark on the landscape. This is Brunel's old Oxford, Worcester and Wolverhampton Railway, which keeps company with the Evenlode all the way from its confluence with the Glyme near Bladon, almost up to its source near Moreton-in-Marsh. The 16th- and 17th-century manor house stands on the north side of the village, within the earthworks of a medieval castle known as Ascott Doilly. In the village itself there is a beautifully converted mill house and a partly Norman church. The latter sits in a large churchyard with avenues of lime trees converging upon it, and is overlooked by a series of old stone houses on all four sides. The interior has been rather over-tidied (often the fate of churches restored by its Victorian architect G.E.

Street) but there is Norman arcading to the north aisle, and handsome triple sedilia may be seen beneath one of the chancel windows. Use the **Oxfordshire Way** to walk up the Evenlode Valley to **Shipton-under-Wychwood,** or down it to **Charlbury**. There is also a pleasant walk eastwards over the wolds and beside the edge of **Wychwood Forest** to **Leafield.**

ASHLEY (2 L6) *3 mi. NE Tetbury*. Minute village in fields not far from the course of the **Foss Way**, with a substantial 15th- and 17th-century manor house dominating the modest Norman church close by. There is a geometric design tympanum over its Norman south doorway and inside will be found a Norman chancel arch leading into an elaborate Victorian chancel. Do not miss the 17th-century wall monument with its poignant inscription, to Ann Hauers, who died at the age of twelve. There is also a charming 18th-century monument to Ferdinando Gorges, a descendant of an earlier Ferdinando who had established the North American colony of New Plymouth in 1628. There is a pleasant duckpond at the northern end of the village.

ASHTON KEYNES (2 L8) *5 mi. S Cirencester*. Described in 1826 by William Cobbett, in his classic description of the English countryside, *Rural Rides*, as 'a very curious place', Ashton Keynes still defies description today. The River Thames is here a small stream flowing through country much disturbed by gravel-workings, which are now mostly lakes occupied by various elements of the **Cotswold Water Park.** Flowing right through the village, the stream divides its houses and cottages from the main street, and it is accordingly crossed by a number of rather ordinary little bridges. It is only at Church Walk that the stream comes into its own, and it is well worth idling here before walking across fields to the church beyond. This has a splendid Norman chancel arch, an ornamented Norman font and a poignant wall monument (1800) by the noted sculptor, John Flaxman, showing Charlotte Nicholas on her death-bed.

ASTHALL (1-2 H12) *3 mi. E Burford.* This is one of the classic Windrush villages, complete with water-meadows, willow trees, and gabled Elizabethan manor

overlooking a small church and a tidy little inn. It was a great favourite of John Betjeman, who must often have come over here from Oxford when visiting the Mitford family in the thirties. They lived at the manor for six years, after moving from **Batsford,** and before their father, David, the 2nd Lord Redesdale, built Swinbrook House, north of neighbouring **Swinbrook**. Victorian restorers were not too kind to the interior of the partly Norman church, but the medieval glass in the Cornwall Chapel windows and the effigy of a lady with wimple and flowing robes are well worth inspecting. The latter is probably Lady Joan

A Tomb at Asthall

Cornwall, who held the manor in the 14th century. The charming 18th-century tombs in the churchyard should not be overlooked. Asthall lies on the course of the Roman **Akeman Street,** and the remains of a Roman settlement have been traced to the south-east of the village. It is possible to walk beyond the north bank of the Windrush, westwards to **Swinbrook** and on to **Widford**, where further evidence of Roman occupation is to be found.

ASTON MAGNA (1 C11) *3 mi. SE Chipping Campden*. Attractive stone village on hill slopes, looking over flat country that runs towards the valley of the Stour. It has a few pleasant houses and barns, and a little green, on which stand the base and lower part of a medieval cross. Overlooking the green is a church built in 1846 and now converted into a private dwelling. The circular earthworks to the south of the church are the remains of a medieval 'homestead moat', possibly connected with the Jordans, tenants of the bishop of Worcester, and recorded as occupiers in a document of 1182. Walk south-eastwards from Aston Magna, across fields and over the **Foss Way**, to the pleasant little hamlet of **Lower Lemington**.

ASTON SUBEDGE (1 B10) *4 mi. NE Broadway*. This quiet village is situated beneath the wooded Cotswold edge, with a small stream beside the road that leads up over the hill towards **Chipping Campden**. Houses, farms and a little church are situated amongst orchards, reminding us that we are on the very edge of the Vale of Evesham -

Converted church in Aston Magna

one of England's outstandingly prosperous fruit and market-gardening areas. The little church was built in 1797 and surprisingly there are signs of Greek influence about its bell turret and cornice. There is a delightful old clock, a small gallery and a canopied pulpit, all contemporary with the church itself. Opposite the church is the charming 17th-century manor house, once the home of Endymion Porter (1587-1649), who was an ambassador of Charles I, and well known at the courts of both James I and Charles I. It was here that he entertained Charles's nephew, Rupert, when the Prince came to the Cotswold Games organised by Porter's friend, Captain Robert Dover (see **Dover's Hill**).

17th century manor house Aston Subedge

AVENING (1-2 K5) *2 mi. SE Nailsworth*. This substantial village, with its pleasant old houses, shops and inns, was once prosperous from the manufacture of cloth. It is situated near the head of the valley of the little Gloucestershire Avon, the river that once powered its mills and provided vital water for the processing of its cloth. The great Longford Mill, north-westwards down the valley towards Nailsworth, no longer produces the fine West of England cloth, for which it was once noted. The handsome early-Norman church is well sited in a steep, sloping churchyard, and has an interesting interior including a small 'museum' in the south transept, the varied contents of which include models of the church at various stages of its construction, a Saxon skeleton and the tusks of a wild boar. Do not miss the effigy in the north transept of the pirate son of Lord Chandos of **Sudeley**, Henry Bridges, who in his youth *indulged in deeds of* *lawlessness and robbery almost unsurpassed.* Situated on a hillside about a quarter of a mile to the north of the church are three burial chambers, one with a rare 'porthole' entrance. All three were brought here from a long barrow near *Nag's Head,* excavated as long ago as 1806.

AYLWORTH (1-2 F9) *5½ mi. SW Stow-on-the-Wold* The site of a manor recorded in the Domesday Book, this is now only a quiet hamlet in an open valley, with a pleasant 17th- and 18th-century farmhouse. It is possible to walk eastwards down this valley to join the River Windrush below **Naunton** at **Harford Bridge.**

BADGEWORTH (1-2 F5) *3 mi. W Cheltenham.* A small village situated between heavily populated Cheltenham and Gloucester, with its church tucked away at the end of a short cul-de-sac. The large churchyard is approached through an attractively carved lychgate, and beyond lie the base of an old cross and several pleasant 18th- and 19th-century tombs (see especially those to Henry and William Bubb). The church has a well proportioned Perpendicular tower and a beautiful 14th-century north aisle chapel - regarded as the finest specimen of the Decorated period in Gloucestershire - with elaborate ballflower ornamentation to its doors and windows. Do not miss the splendid roof to the chapel, with its lovely angel-figure corbels.

BADMINTON (2 N3) *9 mi. SW Tetbury.* Great Badminton is a delightful estate village with houses and cottages of the 17th, 18th and 19th centuries, The church, built in 1785, is attached to the mansion and contains a splendid series of monuments to the Dukes of Beaufort. Badminton House dates from the

In Badgeworth Churchyard

latter half of the 17th century, when the Somerset family had to abandon Raglan Castle , which had been ruthlessly slighted in the Civil War. William Kent embellished the mansion in the 18th century and built the lovely Worcester Lodge at the northern end of the great park. This can be viewed from the A433, to the west of **Didmarton**. The game of badminton was invented here, its standard measurements being dictated by the dimensions of Badminton's large hall. However Badminton is now better known for the horse trials held in its magnificent park each spring.

Lodge at Badminton

BAGENDON (1-2 J7) *3 mi. N Cirencester*. Situated in a quiet wooded valley, this small village has a heavily restored church with Norman saddleback tower and Norman arcading. The chancel is considerably higher than the nave and was made so in medieval times, probably to avoid flooding. Features to note include the attractive triptych, incorporating a list of rectors, and the window in the north wall of the chancel by Christopher Whall.

The earthworks, Bagendon Dykes, situated to the south and west of the village, enclose an area of about 200 acres and are the remains of the Iron Age capital of the Dobunni, the Belgic tribe that flourished here immediately before the coming of the Romans. As part of their consistent policy of colonisation the conquerors soon 'civilised' the tribes they overcame by moving them into Roman-style provincial capitals - in this case Cirencester, or *Corinium Dobunnorum* as it was then called. Excavations of the Bagendon Dykes took place in the 1950s and were conducted by the formidable local archaeologist, Mrs Elsie Clifford, whose book A *Belgic Oppidum* provides a fascinating insight into the surprisingly high level of civilisation that the Dobunni had achieved well before the coming of the Romans, with a mint for their own coins, and the use of luxury goods imported from the Mediterranean world. Many of the fascinating finds from these excavations may be seen at Cirencester's Corinium Museum.

BAMPTON (1-2 J13) *4½ mi. SW Witney*. This little market town was once known as 'Bampton-in-the-Bush', as, in winter, there were no adequate roads linking it with the outside world; it still has the good fortune to be 'miles from anywhere'. It has many pleasant 17th- and 18th-century houses, a few inns and a minute early 19th-century Italianate Town Hall. Its church is of considerable interest, with a splendid 170-ft spire, at the base of which are four flying buttresses, each surmounted by a carved apostle. The contents of the interior include canopied sedilia in the chancel, a fine stone reredos, three brasses and an impressive 17th-century monument to George Tompson (1603) in the south transept. Do not miss the delightful Old Grammar School in Church Street, now used as a library, nor the gatehouse of Ham Court in Mill Street, a building once forming part of Bampton Castle, which had been built by the Earl of Pembroke in the 14th century.

There is a pleasant walk south-west from Bampton, via the hamlet of Weald, to Old Man's Bridge and Radcot Lock, both on the Upper Thames, thereby linking onto the **Thames Path**.

BANBURY (1 B16) A busy market town for many centuries, Banbury is now also an important industrial centre, and has grown very considerably in size in the last half of the twentieth-century. Despite much re-development it still has a few old alleys and quiet corners, which bring some relief to the super-efficient shopping areas which have sprung up. At least two of Banbury's famous old inns have disappeared, but the Reindeer in Parsons Street has survived. The large 17th-century Whateley Hall Hotel in the Horsefair, used to be called the Three Tuns, and the many well-known people who have once stayed here include Jonathan Swift, who is reputed to have taken the name *Gulliver* from a tombstone in the nearby churchyard.

Banbury Church

There is a fine sports centre, Spiceball Park, and by the old canal wharf nearby is Tooley's Boatyard, with its working forge, operational dry-dock and collection of antique equipment for repairing wooden narrow boats. This wharf is busy with colourful narrowboats throughout the summer months. Banbury Cross, situated at a cross-roads on the broad Horsefair, is a mid-19th century replacement of a medieval cross destroyed by the Puritans in the early-17th century. A well-known nursery rhyme refers to the cross:

Ride a cock-horse to Banbury Cross
To see a fine lady on a white horse;
With rings on her fingers and bells on her toes
She shall have music wherever she goes

This rhyme only appeared in print in the 18th century, but it is probably much older, and may possibly have referred to a visit here by Queen Elizabeth I. The cross stands in a wide street, which is overlooked by several pleasant old houses, amongst which is the interesting Banbury Museum and Tourist Information Centre. Not only did the citizens of Banbury destroy their old cross, but in 1792, they also blew up their medieval church with gunpowder, on the grounds that it was unsafe. The old church was replaced by an elegant building designed by S P Cockerell, the architect of **Sezincote**, and by his son C.R.Cockerell, who completed the tower and handsome portico in 1822. Unfortunately the interior was over-restored later in the 19th century and is not of great interest to visitors. Banbury Cakes, which are elliptical in shape, and made of light pastry lined with currants, have been made in Banbury for at least three hundred years, but they only became well known due to the efforts of local entrepreneur, Betty White, in the later years of the 18th century. They are of course still on sale in the town, and are delicious, especially when eaten fresh from a Banbury oven.

Banbury Cross

BARCHESTON (1 B12) ½ *mi. SE Shipston-on-Stour.* Minute hamlet just across the Stour from Shipston, with a manor house, rectory and church. The present manor house is largely 17th-century, but it was here in about 1560 that William Sheldon set up his tapestry-weaving enterprise, having first sent his man, Richard Hicks, to Flanders to learn the craft. The best known productions from the Barcheston looms were the Sheldon tapestry maps, fascinating examples not only of tapestry, but also of the early cartographer's art. Several of these have survived, and good examples are to be seen at the York Museum and in Oxford's Bodleian Library. Barcheston church has a 14th-century tower, and an interesting medieval interior, the contents of which include the tomb of William Willington and his wife, carved in alabaster, and a brass to Richard Humphray - both from the 16th century. There are pleasant walks beside the Stour, north to **Shipston-on-Stour**, and south to **Willington** and **Burmington**.

BARFORD ST JOHN (1 D16) *5 mi. S Banbury.* This faces **Barford St Michael** across the little Swere valley. Its small church lies behind a farmyard and although heavily restored, possesses a good Norman doorway and a tub font of the same period. Happily the monstrous array of radio aerials on a hill to the north do not intrude on this village unduly. Walk eastwards from here beside the Swere and then southwards to **Deddington**.

BARFORD ST MICHAEL (1 D15) *5 mi. S Banbury.* The church here has a squat Norman tower, and a Norman north doorway, which is one of Oxfordshire's outstanding art treasures. This has fantastic carvings of beak-heads and chevrons, and intertwining decoration on its capitals and tympanum. Do not miss the bench-ends nor the minute brass of William Fox and his wife, all placed in this delightful church in the 15th century. The long, low, thatched George Inn is also worth visiting.

Barford St. Michael

BARNSLEY (1-2 J9) *4 mi. NE Cirencester.* Traffic on the still-busy B4255 detracts from an otherwise very pleasing village of neat houses and trim gardens. Although topped by early 17th-century gables and finials, the largely Perpendicular church tower is thought to have been largely built by Sir Edmund Tame, the prosperous medieval wool merchant who lavished so much of his wealth on the splendid church at **Fairford**, and also on the much smaller one at **Rendcomb**. Sir Edmund frequently travelled between these two places and, probably for convenience, had a house at Barnsley, the half-way point on his journeys. Apart from its tower, the church is largely Norman in origin, and contains several interesting features. Do not miss the very early Norman window in the organ chamber, hewn out of a single piece of stone, which was moved here from **Daglingworth**.

Situated in the village and originally laid out in 1770, the delightful garden of Barnsley House, with its Gothic summerhouse and Classical temple, is regularly open to the public. The elegant Baroque-style early Georgian mansion of Barnsley Park is situated in an extensive park just to the north of the village, but is not open to the public. There is, however, a pleasant walk through the park and beyond to **Winson** and **Ablington** in the nearby Coln Valley.

BARROW WAKE (1-2 G6) *4 mi. S Cheltenham.* Situated down a cul-de-sac road off the A417 to the north of **Birdlip**, this is a fine viewpoint on the Cotswold edge, with a wide prospect over the Severn Valley to the Malverns and the Welsh hills. There are good parking facilities and an unusual stone indicator illustrating the geology of the surrounding area. It was near here, in the excavation of one of a series of Iron Age burial sites, that the famous Birdlip Mirror was unearthed. This outstanding example of Celtic (Iron Age) art, together with a variety of other treasures, is to be seen in Gloucester Museum.

Barrow Wake

BARTON (1-2 E9) *5½ mi. W Stow-on-the-Wold.* A modest hamlet, with a delightful 18th-century house overlooking a pool through which the infant River Windrush flows on its way southwards to **Naunton**. Records indicate that by 1185 there were two fulling mills here owned by the Knights Templar (see **Temple Guiting),** but the little river now drifts by, quite unconcerned with industry of any kind. There is a short but pleasant walk south-westwards, over the even smaller Castlett Stream to unspoilt **Guiting Power**, but do not be tempted to try parking a car at Barton.

The Green, Barton-on-the-Heath

BARTON-ON-THE-HEATH (1 D12) *3 mi. E Moreton-in-Marsh.* Quiet village on a small rise, with a tree-shaded green, on which stands a little 'well house', with an urn beneath a stone dome supported by three columns. This green is overlooked by handsome 17th-century Barton House, and beyond this lies a modest little Norman church, with small saddleback tower. Two sculptural details, one on the outside and one on the inside of a north chancel window, provide clues to the possible presence of an earlier Anglo-Danish building. These were common in the north and east of England, but it is unusual to find one so far to the south-west. Other features of interest include an amusing fragment of Norman sculpture (a little pig running up the chancel arch), a small brass to Edmund Bury (1559) in the chancel floor, a 15th-century font, and pieces of beautiful medieval stained glass in the chancel's north windows.

Lawyer Robert Dover, the founder of the *Cotswold Olympicks* (see **Dover's Hill**), and his wife Sibilla came here in 1650, to live with their son John, who had served as a Captain-of-Horse under Prince Rupert in the Civil War. Robert died in 1652 and was buried here, but his son continued to live at Barton until his own death in 1696. Walk south from here, either on field-path or road, to **Little Compton,** or south and east, up on to high country where the **Rollright Stones** lie.

BATSFORD (1 D11) *1½ mi. NW Moreton-in-Marsh.* A compact little estate-village at the gates of Batsford Park, a large 19th-century neo-Tudor mansion (1888-92), which can best be viewed from its arboretum (see below). Designed by Sir Ernest George, Batsford's building was supervised by the young architect Guy Dawber, who thereafter devoted his life to working in the Cotswolds, and who by so doing evolved his own 'Cotswold style' (see also **Eyford Park**). The church is slightly older than the house (1861-62), an ambitious neo-Norman building, with tall spire and apsidal chancel. It is worth visiting for the sake of the handsome wall monument to Thomas Edward Freeman (1808) by the sculptor Joseph Nollekins. Do not overlook the other monuments, to members of the Mitford family, the Lords Redesdale, the forebears of the fabled Mitford sisters, whose early years here, and at **Asthall** and **Swinbrook,** are so lovingly chronicled in Jessica Mitford's delightful book *Hons and Rebels*. However, for a full account of the Redesdales' life at Batsford and elsewhere, read Jonathan and Catherine Guinness's *The House of Mitford*.

Batsford Church

BATSFORD PARK ARBORETUM (1 D11) *Off A44, 1½ mi. W Moreton-in-Marsh.* Here are fifty acres of splendid woodlands, with scenic walks giving fine views eastwards over the broad Evenlode Valley towards the Oxfordshire Cotswolds. There are over a thousand different species of trees, bamboos and shrubs, many from China, Japan, Nepal and North America, together with bronze statues brought from Japan by the formidable traveller and diplomat, Bertie Mitford, the 1st Lord Redesdale, and creator in the 1880s of this fine arboretum. Read all about Bertie and his descendants in the fascinating biography, *The House of Mitford* (see **Batsford** above). Plants may be purchased from an adjoining Garden Centre and there is also a fascinating Falconry Centre with eagles, hawks owls and falcons being flown during each opening day. Tea shop open during the season.

BAUNTON (1-2 J8) *2 mi. N Cirencester.* Rather disturbed by traffic on Cirencester's north-eastern by-pass crossing a massive viaduct over the Churn valley here, this small village has a partly Norman church. This has a heavily restored interior, but should not be missed as it contains an outstanding 14th-century wall-painting of St Christopher wading a stream with the Child Jesus on his shoulder, and also a richly embroidered 15th-century altar frontal. There is an attractive walk northwards from the church, up beside the Churn to **North Cerney** and **Rendcomb**.

BECKBURY CAMP (1 D8) *3 mi. NE Winchcombe.* Large Iron Age promontory fort just to the north of **Farmcote,** with splendid views over **Hailes Abbey** towards Bredon Hill and the distant Malverns. The origins of the stone pillar at the north-west corner are obscure, but traditionally it is known as 'Cromwell's Seat' and is supposed to mark the spot where the much reviled Thomas Cromwell, Henry VIII's Commissioner, sat while watching the destruction of Hailes Abbey. There is a good circular walk up to these earthworks, first using part of the **Cotswold Way** from Hailes, and then northwards down to **Wood Stanway** before returning westwards to Hailes.

BELAS KNAP (1-2 E7) *2½ mi. S Winchcombe.* Neolithic (Stone Age) burial mound or long barrow dating from about 2500 BC. One of the finest examples in the country, it has been well restored by English Heritage. The restored false portal at the north end illustrates the great antiquity of the Cotswolds' dry-stone walling tradition. The four burial chambers within the mound are entered from the sides, and the long earth mound is surrounded by a dry stone revetting wall. The barrow is situated in high

Burial Chamber, Belas Knap   *False Portal, Belas Knap*

country, and may be reached by walking three-quarters-of-a-mile up from the minor road running south from **Winchcombe**. This path from the road forms part of the **Cotswold Way** and enthusiastic walkers can follow the Way from Winchcombe to Belas Knap, a distance of just under 3 miles, and then onwards across glorious open country to **Cleeve Hill**.

BERKELEY CASTLE (2 K1) *16 mi. SW Gloucester.* Although nearer to the Severn Estuary than the Cotswolds, the presence of this great feudal stronghold must have exerted considerable influence upon the latter in medieval times. Its origins date back to 1067

Berkeley Castle

when a castle was built here by Fitz Osborn, Earl of Hereford, but the present building is largely of the 12th century, with substantial alterations and improvements made two centuries later. In 1153 it was granted by Henry II to Robert Fizharding, from whom the Berkeley family are descended, and the Berkeleys still live here today. Described by Vita Sackville-West in her book, *English Country Houses*, as 'rose red and grey, the colour of old brocade', Berkeley Castle continues to impress all who come there with its mellow beauty and great strength. The formidable stone keep contains the Great Hall, the Morning Room (originally the Chapel of St Mary) with its beautifully painted medieval ceiling, and the dungeon where the unfortunate Edward II was so revoltingly murdered in 1327. The castle contains a fine collection of furniture, tapestries, silver, china and carved timberwork and there are attractive ornamental gardens and a Butterfly House.

While here, do not miss a visit to the Jenner Museum in the Chantry in Berkeley town's Church Lane. This commemorates Edward Jenner, the Berkeley doctor who pioneered vaccination against smallpox. The adjoining coach-house has been converted into a conference centre, thanks to the generosity of Japanese philanthropist, Mr Ryoichi Sasakawa.

BEVERSTON (2 L4) *2 mi. W Tetbury*. Small village on the A4135, with several cottages designed by Lewis Vulliamy for Robert Holford, who had purchased the Beverston Estate in 1842, and for whom Vulliamy also designed London's Dorchester House in Park Lane, and Beverston's neighbour, **Westonbirt**.

The church has an interesting Anglo-Saxon sculpture representing the Resurrection, on the south face of its tower. The pleasant white washed interior reveals several signs of Vulliamy's restoration of 1844 - the nave roof for instance - but the original parts of the 15th-century rood screen and the details in the south arcade capitals are well worth noting. Also do not miss a glimpse of the lovely 18th-century rectory on the opposite side of the roadway to the church.

Here is one of the few surviving Cotswold castles - a largely 13th-century building with 17th-century domestic additions and alterations. The original castle was held in the years before the Norman Conquest by Earl Godwin, father of King Harold, and was the family's base during their protracted grumbles on the subject of Edward the Confessor's leaning towards Norman, rather than Saxon advisers. After the Conquest, the castle was granted to Roger de Berkeley, whose descendants were eventually to base themselves at

Beverston Castle

Berkeley Castle, about twelve miles to the west. By the time of the Civil War it had been sold to a Sir Michael Hicks, and although held for a short time by the Royalists, its surrender was easily obtained. This was due, so his enemies maintained, to its garrison commander, the luckless but robust Colonel Oglethorpe, 'attending upon a young woman' at a neighbouring farm. The castle is not open to the public, but glimpses may be obtained from the A4135, and from the little roadway up to the church.

BIBURY (and ARLINGTON) (1-2 J9) *6 mi. NE Cirencester*. Bibury has perhaps never fully recovered from the day that William Morris described it, no doubt with some justice, as 'the most beautiful village in the Cotswolds'. But even without Morris's help it was inevitable that this enchanting village on the little River Coln, together with its immediate neighbour across the water, Arlington, should become so popular. Do not miss a visit here, but try to come during a weekday in early spring or late autumn. Park your car, if possible beyond the bridge just across from the pleasant creeper-covered Swan Hotel, and explore on foot.

First look at the Swan Hotel and the little windowless building nearby that once served as the village lock-up. Then call at the entertaining Bibury Trout Farm, where trout of all sizes may be observed and fed, and where 'catch-your-own' fishing is available. Trout may be purchased, and there is a gift shop.

Unless you wish first to walk up into the hamlet of Arlington, with its pleasant cottages around a small green, cross the B4425 from the mill and walk along the far side of Rack Isle. Now owned by the National Trust, this water-meadow was once used for drying cloth on racks after it had been worked by the weavers in the cottages beyond - the much photographed Arlington Row. Although owned by the National Trust, none of these most attractive early 17th-century cottages between wooded bank and reedy meadow are open to the public, and this adds to, rather than detracts from, their very special appeal. Now walk down Arlington Row and cross the River Coln by a little footbridge, inevitably stopping awhile to look into the clear, shallow water to see trout gliding by, apparently quite unconcerned by the noise and movement of ducks and moorhens, another feature of this delightful place.

Arlington Row, Bibury

Turn right onto the path alongside Bibury's greatest enemy, the ever-busy B4425, and after a short distance turn right into a mercifully quiet square, which is overlooked by a pleasant assortment of 17th- and 18th-century cottages, and beyond which is Bibury's very interesting church. Standing in a trim churchyard with cherub table tombs and fragrant rose-trees, this fine building dates back to Anglo-Saxon times, and features from this period include parts of the chancel arch and the fragments of a cross shaft. From 1130 until the Dissolution in 1539, this church belonged to Osney Abbey near Oxford, and there is no doubt that much monastic wealth was lavished upon it during these four centuries. See especially the Norman north and south doorways, the latter within a Norman porch. Also beyond the square, on the banks of the winding River Coln, lies Bibury Court, a fine, gabled Tudor and Stuart building, which has now been a hotel for some years.

It is possible to walk beyond Ablington, up the Coln Valley at least as far as **Winson** and **Coln Rogers,** or south-eastwards, down the valley to lovely **Coln St Aldwyns** and **Quenington**.

BIRDLIP (1-2 G6) *5 mi. S Cheltenham.* Small village marking the end of the Roman **Ermin Street's** steep climb up from the Severn Valley, it is happily now bypassed by the ever-busy A417. Great beech-woods clothe the steep Cotswold edge, and the atmosphere of a welcoming coaching stop still lingers here. There is a small church, built here as recently as 1957 to replace a Victorian one destroyed by fire. **The Cotswold Way** passes to the immediate west of Birdlip and this can be used to walk northwards to **Barrow Wake**, or southwards to **Cooper's Hill**.

BISLEY (1-2 J5) *4 mi. E Stroud.* Situated in a fold of the hills at the very head of the Toadsmoor Valley, and well to the north of the **Golden Valley**, this large village is quite delightful. Everywhere the eyes roam they are rewarded with good things. The clothiers of the nearby valleys brought their wealth with them, and spent it wisely - on splendid houses like Over Court with its charming gazebo overlooking the churchyard, on handsome Jaynes Court to the south-west of the church, and on the multitude of more modest but equally pleasant houses and cottages that are to be found throughout the village.

The church has a fine spire and a unique 13th-century 'Poor Souls' Light'. This 13th-century structure, England's only outdoor example, was used to hold candles for the saying of masses for those who could not afford candles of their own. The interior of the church is rather stark, having been over-zealously restored by the Victorians. However, do not overlook the effigy of a 13th-century knight, nor the font with its Norman bowl upon a 19th-century stem.

Close to the welcoming Bear Inn, with its stone pillars supporting an upper floor, is a pretty, early 19th-century ogee-gabled village lock-up. Some distance away, below the church, are Bisley Wells, which were restored, complete with Gothic detail, by Canon Thomas Keble, John Keble's younger brother, who was vicar here. It was he who revived the ceremony of Well Dressing, which still takes place here on Ascension Day - a custom practised much more widely in Derbyshire's Peak District. It was also largely due to Thomas Keble's enthusiasm that the church of neighbouring **Bussage** was built.

Gazebo at Bisley

Local legend tells of how the future Queen Elizabeth I, when about ten years old, was living at Over Court, and that when she died here, her guardians were too frightened to tell Henry VIII. These frightened but resourceful men therefore substituted a local boy, and it was he, the famous 'Bisley Boy', who eventually became 'Queen' - hence 'her' virginity. This whole story appears to have been invented in a light-hearted vein by Canon Keble and his friends, following the discovery of the skeleton of a young girl in the garden of Over Court. There is a good walk north-eastward from Bisley crossing the heads of two valleys to **Miserden**.

BLACK BOURTON (1-2 J13) *5 mi. SW Witney.* On a road cut off at its northern end by Brize Norton Airfield, this small village is subjected to the noise of monstrous jet aircraft taking off and landing nearby. All signs of the great manor house of the Hungerford family, Bourton Place, have vanished but the church is well worth visiting. This has a pretty little Norman priest's doorway and a large porch leading into a pleasingly plastered interior, which is redolent of the past. The outstanding treasure here is the

Tympanum at Black Bourton

series of splendid 13th-century wall-paintings - very vigorous and the very essence of medieval faith and art. However, do not overlook the attractive stone corbel figures, nor the handsome monument to Lady Hungerford (1592) - all in pale stone.

BLADON (1 G16) *1 mi. SE Woodstock.* Scattered along the A4095, this village lies just to the south of the great woodlands that make up the far boundary of Blenheim Park. Born at **Blenheim Palace** in 1874, Sir Winston Churchill chose to be buried at Bladon. His simple grave is situated in the churchyard beside that of his father, Lord Randolph, and will for many years to come be a place of pilgrimage for those who remember him as Britain's greatest statesman. The church was almost entirely rebuilt in 1891 to the design of that prolific Victorian architect, Sir Arthur Blomfield, but it is not of great interest to visitors.

BLEDINGTON (1-2 F12) *4 mi. SE Stow-on-the-Wold.* This large, partly modern village in the broad valley of the River Evenlode is centred upon a wide rough green complete with the very attractive King's Head Inn and a little stream with noisy ducks. The ducks are apparently all known by their individual names and are greatly cherished, so please drive with special care here! The church is situated on the southern edge of the green with a row of pleasant cottages overlooking the churchyard. Although it has earlier origins most of the good things to be found in the church are from the 15th century, with fine roofs to nave and chancel, a lovely old doorway with its original door, and above all, a splendid series of Perpendicular windows, several of which contain outstandingly beautiful stained glass. These are believed to be the work of John Prudde, the Westminster craftsman who also produced the glass for Warwick's Beauchamp Chapel. The money for all these improvements came from the prosperous Winchcombe Abbey, which held the living, and which probably had a grange here.

Bledington lies on the **Oxfordshire Way,** and this can be used to walk westwards up on to the wolds at Wyck Beacon and down again to **Bourton-on-the-Water,** or south-eastwards down the valley, through the woodlands of **Bruern Abbey** and on to **Shipton-under-Wychwood.**

BLENHEIM PALACE (1 G15) *To immediate SW of Woodstock.* This, the greatest of the English palaces, was the state's reward to its triumphant general, John Churchill, Duke of Marlborough. Built between 1705 and 1730, it was designed by John Vanbrugh in a heroic, Baroque style. Vanbrugh resigned in 1717 after prolonged disputes with the notoriously difficult Duchess, Sarah, but fortunately the main elements of the palace had by then been almost completed. Vanbrugh's design is magnificent, if perhaps a little overwhelming, but the fantastic 2500-acre park, improved by Capability Brown some fifty years later, has absorbed it effortlessly.

Approached by car- and coach-borne visitors from the A44, at the Oxford end of **Woodstock,** Blenheim is best seen first by pedestrians, entering through Nicholas Hawksmoor's massive Woodstock Gate, the gateway at the quiet western end of the town (see **Woodstock**). Here is a prospect of palace, bridge and great lake, with sweeping banks clad here and there with noble woodlands - the work of Vanbrugh and Capability Brown brought to glorious perfection.

Built more as a national monument than a home, the palace offers its visitors a series of magnificent spectacles at every turn. First there is the massive east gate, and then the drama of the Great Court, with its colonnaded wings and its great portico looking northwards, beyond Vanbrugh's bridge and Brown's lakes, to the wide avenue of trees punctuated by the tall 'Column of Victory'.

Blenheim Palace

The Great Hall, with its ceiling painted by Sir James Thornhill, provides an appropriate introduction to the further splendours within. The superb Baroque rooms are richly furnished, their contents including the famous Brussels

Blenheim Palace

tapestries, depicting scenes from Marlborough's campaigns, doorways by Nicholas Hawksmoor, paintings by Louis Laguerre, carvings by Grinling Gibbons, and a wealth of paintings added in the centuries that followed. Amongst all this grandeur there is a small room off the west corridor where Winston Churchill was born in 1874, and which now contains an interesting exhibition devoted to his memory. The Long Library contains no fewer than 10,000 volumes in a room 183 feet long.

On the west side of the Great Court is the chapel, which was completed only in 1731, and which is largely the work of Nicholas Hawksmoor. Here will be found the splendid monument to the 1st Duke and his Duchess, designed by William Kent and executed by Rysbrack - a poignant but fitting climax to any visit to this noble building.

Delightful formal gardens on the south side of the palace complement the great park. There are also restaurants, gift shops, and a Miniature Railway.

BLOCKLEY (1 C10) *3 mi. NW Moreton-in-Marsh.* A delightful village, owned in medieval times by the bishops of Worcester, and built on the steep slopes of a hollow beneath the high wolds, near the head of a small but prolific stream. It was this stream that provided the power required for no fewer than six silk mills, when Blockley was at the height of its prosperity in the early years of the 19th century. These mills provided much of the silk required by the ribbon manufacturers of Coventry, and at one time well over 500 people were employed here. See the old mill (now a private house) beyond the pool below the church.

Still unspoilt by tourism, Blockley's steep little streets and terraces are full of character, with 17th- and 18th-century houses accompanied by dignified 19th-century buildings. Despite the prosperity of the village, the limitations of geography prevented the railway coming any closer than **Paxford**, but Blockley was not to be put off entirely, for there remains to this day an inn of character, still proudly entitled *The Great Western Arms*. The church has a large airy interior, with plenty of plain glass and a flat ceiling. There is a Norman chancel, which was probably once vaulted, and a tower built as late as 1725, by local mason and quarry-owner Thomas Woodward, who appears to have copied certain features from the fine tower of his own parish church at **Chipping Campden.** Do not overlook the series of handsome monuments inside the church to various owners of nearby **Northwick Park,** at least two of which are by the celebrated 18th-century sculptor, J.M.Rysbrack, nor the two monumental brasses, both of priests - one in the chancel floor, and one (unusually) in the centre of the sedilia.

The site of the medieval village of Upton is up on the wolds well to the west of the village. Its presence was recorded in the Domesday Book and it has been excavated by archaeologists, but no trace of it now remains above ground. It was almost certainly depopulated in the 14th century on the orders of one of the bishops of Worcester, who would have no doubt required the land for profitable sheep grazing. The bishops were probably also responsible for the depopulation of three other medieval villages in the area - Dorn, Upper Ditchford and Lower Ditchford.

Also explore the delights of Blockley on foot, and if possible walk to its south-western end, and up a track into Dovedale Woods. Use the Ordnance Survey's Outdoor Leisure Map 45 to walk up the wooded valley known as The Warren and return to Blockley via Norcombe Wood. There are also attractive walks south-eastwards to **Batsford** and **Bourton-on-the-Hill**.

BLOXHAM (1 C15) *3 mi SW Banbury*. A large ironstone village strung out along the undulating A361 with sufficient strength of character to overcome the disadvantages of over-busy traffic. It has well built houses, cottages and inns, no two of which are at the same level. The little Bloxham Village Museum is housed in the Old Court House in Church Street and its collection reflects past life in the village. At the Banbury end of the village stands Bloxham School, most of which was designed by one of our favourite Victorian architects, G E Street. Street also had a hand in the restoration of the fine parish church at the other end of the village, a building of considerable scale, with a magnificent 14th-century spire and an austere but dignified interior, which was not spoilt by Street's

Thorneycroft Monument, Bloxham

very restrained restoration work. Here will be found a fascinating series of 14th-century carved figures, probably the work of the same mason, or group of masons, who worked at **Adderbury,** and also possibly at **Alkerton** and Hanwell, just to the north of Banbury. See also the very grand 18th-century tomb of Sir John Thorneycroft, and the east window of 1869, which was the work of William Morris and his friends, Edward Burne-Jones and Philip Webb. Walk north-west from here across the fields to **Broughton,** or eastwards, partly along a disused railway line (the old Banbury and Cheltenham Direct Railway) to **Adderbury.**

BOURNES GREEN (1-2 J5) *4 mi. E Stroud*. Pretty hillside hamlet between **Bisley, Oakridge** and **France Lynch**, with steep narrow roads and pleasant views down a small valley where there was once a Roman villa (nothing now visible).

BOURTON-ON-THE-HILL (1 D10) *2 mi. W Moreton-in-Marsh.* If only this village could be bypassed, all would be perfection. Even so, traffic rumbling up Bourton's steep and none too wide street does not entirely spoil this charming village. At the top of the hill stands an 18th-century stone built inn, the Horse and Groom; then the road goes down past pretty little terraces of 17th- and 18th-century cottages, past the warm stone church, to the bottom of the village, which is here enriched by the elegant early 18th-century Bourton House, in the grounds of which stands a fine 16th-century barn (dated 1570). The delightful gardens here are regularly open to the public. In 1598, an earlier Bourton House was purchased by the parents of the unfortunate Sir Thomas Overbury, who was poisoned while a prisoner in the Tower of London, at the age of only thirty-two.

Bourton-on-the-Hill Church

Bourton-on-the-Hill was once owned by the abbots of Westminster, who had great sheep runs on nearby Bourton Downs, and no doubt it was wealth from their wool sales that paid for the handsome 15th-century clerestory of the church. This feature together with the church's fine three-stage tower gives it a totally Perpendicular look. However, within the pleasant cream-washed interior the massive arcade columns reveal its Norman origins - the pointed arches were probably a 12th- or 13th-century alteration. There are old stone floors and a minute 18th-century gallery near the north door. The beautiful bell-metal Winchester Bushel and Peck, dated 1816, are a rare survival of these once commonly used English standard measures. A law dated 1587 specified that each parish had to have such measures, and they were used by local magistrates in the settlement of disputes (usually those relating to the payment of the hated tithes). Do not overlook the 15th-century octagonal font, nor the colourful 18th-century wall tablets.

BOURTON-ON-THE-WATER (1-2 F10) *3 mi. SW Stow-on-the-Wold.* This large village is probably the most visited tourist attraction of the whole Cotswolds, with a wealth of attractions to be visited. It is an unashamedly pretty place, with a series of ornamental bridges (the earliest of which dates back to 1756) spanning the clear waters of the River Windrush, which here runs beside broad, tree-shaded greens. Immediately to the east of the village are the earthworks of Salmonsbury Camp, an Iron Age settlement, and evidence of Roman occupation has been uncovered near the point where the **Foss Way** crosses the River Windrush.

If arriving by car use the car park at the south-eastern end of the village (there is another car park in Station Road) and explore on foot. Immediately to the left, on the road back into the village, is the fascinating Dragonfly Maze, which has over a quarter of a mile of pathways, with an ornate pavilion at its centre. Just beyond the maze is Birdland, a delightful bird-sanctuary, which was established by the late, much loved Len Hill. This is now situated in stream-side gardens, and also includes a lively display of penguins, a reminder of the fact that Len Hill purchased two small islands in the Falklands some years ago, both of them rich in penguins and other birds. Not far beyond this, on the right of the road, beside the Old New Inn, is the Model Village, a beautifully made one-ninth scale replica of the village in Cotswold stone, which inevitably includes a model of the model.

Walk over the bridge opposite the Old New Inn, to look at the Pottery in little Clapton Row, and then turn right into Victoria Road to visit the Perfume Exhibition. Not far beyond this will be found the Cotswold Motor Museum, which are housed in the attractive water-mill. Almost opposite, on the High Street, is the Model Railway. However before doing so it might be preferable to first visit the Parish Church, which is well to the north. This is in an odd mixture of styles but its combination of medieval chancel, Georgian tower and Victorian nave has resulted in a pleasant and certainly interesting building. Apart from this there is a wealth of lovely buildings in Bourton-on-the-Water, and many stream-side walks.

Before returning to the car park, walk down Cemetery Lane, which is the best approach to Bourton's expanding 'Pools' or 'Quarry Lakes', flooded gravel workings on which nature reserves are now established. It is possible to spot swans, moorhens, mallard and other wildfowl here. These pools can be included in a pleasant circular walk, first making use of the opening stages of the **Oxfordshire Way** to **Wyck Rissington,** then turning south to **Little Rissington,** and finally returning to Bourton via the pools. Other walks from Bourton include one northwards to **Lower Slaughter**, and a long and pleasant one, largely beside the Windrush, north-westwards to **Harford Bridge** and **Naunton.**

Bourton-on-the-Water

BOX (1-2 K4) *¹/₂ mi. NE Nailsworth.* Small village on a steep hillside below Minchinhampton Common, with a little church built as recently as 1953, and some pleasant views down into the Avon Valley.

BOXWELL (2 L3) *4 mi. E Wotton-under-Edge.* Here in a quiet and beautiful valley well to the west of the A46 is a small 13th-century church which is full of character, and which is complete with a most unusual stone bellcote topped with a miniature spire. This church lies beside Boxwell Court, which looks Victorian at first sight, but which in fact dates from the 15th century. It may be possible to drive as far as Boxwell Farm, but from here onwards it is necessary to walk.

BRAILES (1 C13) *3 mi. W Shipston-on-Stour.* Upper and Lower Brailes make up a village of considerable size, strung out along the winding B4035, Shipston-Banbury road. In medieval times it was an important market town, with the protection of a castle, the earthworks of which are clearly visible from the road, and which may be visited on foot. It was once the third largest town in Warwickshire, after Warwick and Coventry, and slight signs of many roads and buildings are visible from the air, in fields adjoining the present main road. There are many pleasant old houses in the village and also two attractive inns, the 16th-century *George* in Lower Brailes and *The Gate* in Upper Brailes. However Brailes is best noted for the splendid Perpendicular tower of its large church, known locally as the 'Cathedral of the Feldon', the Feldon being the rich pastoral area of southern Warwickshire in which the village lies. The walls of its lofty interior were unfortunately scraped in 1879, and it has a rather cold feeling. However its sheer size reminds the visitor of the long vanished importance of Brailes. The village lies in some delightful countryside beneath the shelter of Brailes Hill, itself topped by a small clump of trees, a landmark which is visible from many parts of the north-eastern Cotswolds. There are many fine walks across the fields, northwards to **Winderton** and **Compton Wynyates** and south-westwards alongside a brook to **Sutton-under-Brailes** and **Stourton.**

BRIMPSFIELD (1-2 H6) *6 mi. S Cheltenham*. Small village in quiet hill country not far from the Cotswold edge at Birdlip. The manor of Brimpsfield was given by William the Conqueror to the Giffard family, who established two castles here, a wooden one on a mound over towards the **Ermin Way**, and later on a large stone building close to the church. However in 1322 John Giffard was foolish enough to cross Edward II's path, and he was consequently hanged at Gloucester and his castle demolished. This was never rebuilt, but its substantial earthworks are still visible in trees to the right of the path to the church. This is situated on the edge of the village in a large churchyard with many 18th-century tombstones. It has a 15th-century tower which descends into the centre of the building, providing enthusiasts with a fascinating architectural puzzle. Do not overlook the scanty remains, in the walls of a barn over to the left of the churchyard, of a 12th-century priory, which once belonged to the abbey of Fontenay in distant Burgundy. There is a fine circular walk starting from a point just to the north of Brimpsfield and takes in **Syde** and **Caudle Green**. For details refer to the Ordnance Survey's Landranger Map 163.

BRIMSCOMBE (1-2 K4) *1 mi. N Minchinhampton*. Situated in the deep **Golden Valley**, this is a rather scrappy village with a Victorian church on the hillside above. Brimscombe 'port' was the headquarters of the ill-fated **Thames and Severn Canal,** and it was here that cargoes were trans-shipped from the broad Severn trows coming up the **Stroudwater Canal**, to the narrow-boats heading eastwards on its narrower counterpart. Several pleasant old buildings beside the canal still bear witness to the architectural harmony of the early Industrial Revolution. Weeping willows and mellow brick enhance this atmosphere despite the presence of a number of small 'industrial units'.

BRIZE NORTON (1-2 J13) *3 mi. W Witney*. The great airfield on its doorstep overshadows this once quiet village, but the church still stands in its neat churchyard, and there is a satisfactory Norman south doorway within its medieval porch. Do not overlook the Norman font with its arcade decoration, nor the 14th-century effigy of a knight.

BROAD CAMPDEN (1 C10) *1 mi. S Chipping Campden*. Quieter and much smaller than nearby **Chipping Campden**, Broad Campden is tucked away in a small valley, with woods never far away - a delicious little village, well removed from the dangers of mass tourism, with a warm little inn, the Baker's Arms, and an outstandingly good guest house, the Malt House. It also has a series of delightful old houses, a small Victorian chapel and an 18th-century Friends' Meeting House with many of its original furnishings intact. Charles Ashbee (see **Chipping Campden**) converted a derelict Norman chapel into a house for himself soon after his arrival in the area in 1905.

BROADWAY (1 C9) *5 mi. SE Evesham*. Situated below the steep scarp face of the Cotswolds, here topped by the stone-built folly of **Broadway Tower,** Broadway has a fine wide street bordered by trim greens and a bewilderingly beautiful series of old stone houses dating largely from the 17th and 18th centuries. Although it must have benefited from Cotswold wool in medieval times, its real prosperity dates from the coaching era, when, in about 1736, the old turnpike road southwards up to **Snowshill** was replaced by a new road up **Fish Hill**. From this time onwards the increasingly large volume of coach traffic made use of Broadway as a staging halt on the journey between London, Worcester and beyond, and at one time no fewer than seven coaches were passing through the village each day. The opening of the London and Worcester railway line in 1856 soon brought this era to a close, but Broadway did not have to wait long for its own recovery.

The very railways that had killed the coach trade soon brought enquiring visitors to the area, many bringing their bicycles with them. William Morris, staying with friends at **Broadway Tower,** appears to have been one of the 'discoverers' of Broadway's charms, and he was soon followed by many friends and acquaintances from the artistic world, including Henry James, Sir John Sargent, Mary Anderson, and Frank Millet (who eventually settled in the village). And so, in a few years, most of Broadway's old houses were restored to new heights of perfection, and its reputation as a show village has continued to grow ever since. A fair proportion of these fine houses are now devoted to the needs of its visitors, with hotels and antique shops much in evidence, but despite this, its character remains largely intact.

If arriving by car, try to park at the main car park, which is approached from the road towards Snowshill just short of the New Church, or from the other car park, which is just off the B4632 road to Willersey. If parking at the latter it is suggested that you walk through to the High Street and first walk up this, looking at the fine old houses between here and the top end of the village, which is blocked off from the by-pass near the bottom of **Fish Hill.** Then turn about and walk right down the wide and always busy High Street. Then on downwards, passing a number of shops, hotels and restaurants on the way including, well down on the right, the Lygon Arms, one of England's most pleasant country hotels, and not far beyond, on the opposite side of the road, there is a bright little shopping precinct, Cotswold Court. It is possible to walk through here to the main car park. Just beyond the War Memorial on its wide triangular green, turn left and walk at least as far as the handsomely towered Victorian 'New Church' on the left.

If possible walk well beyond this, past the old houses of Bury End and Pye Corner, to the 'Old Church' of St Eadburgha. This lies on the road up to **Snowshill,** in a quiet valley leading into the hills about a mile to the south of the village, and looking over a small stream at the bottom of the churchyard. It is a cruciform building with Norman origins and has a delightfully unspoilt interior, which is full of atmosphere. It is possible to walk back from here over the fields to join the High Street not far from the turn to the car park.

Broadway lies astride the **Cotswold Way**, and the village's Willersey Road Car Park is the starting point of a walk up the hill to **Broadway Tower,** making use of this long-distance path. There are also several other walks that can be taken from Broadway, all of which are shown on the Ordnance Survey's Outdoor Leisure Map 45.

BROADWAY TOWER AND BROADWAY TOWER COUNTRY PARK (1 C9) *1½ mi. SE Broadway.* At 1024 feet above sea level, this is the Cotswolds' second highest point (**Cleeve Hill** just beats it at 1083 feet). The 65-foot Gothick folly was completed in the year 1798 to the design of James Wyatt, for the 6th Earl of Coventry, of Croome Court, his country seat about fifteen miles to the north-west. Many divergent theories have been advanced regarding its original purpose, but it now appears likely that it was to celebrate the first centenary of the Coventry earldom - a creation of 1697. This was sufficient justification in an age of follies, and would anyway have provided kudos for its owner and employment for the needy.

The tower is an outstanding landmark to those who live in the Severn and Avon valleys, and it is one of England's finest viewpoints. On a clear day a dozen counties may be seen from its windy castellated roof, with the massive outline of the Black Mountains in the far west, and the long line of the Berkshire Downs to the south. In the rooms below the roof there are interesting exhibitions - one devoted to William Morris, who spent holidays here with his friends Burne-Jones and Rossetti, one to the history of the tower itself, which was once used by bibliophile Sir Thomas Phillips to house his private printing press.

Broadway Tower

The highly eccentric Sir Thomas, who lived at the handsome 18th-century mansion of Middle Hill House, not far to the south of the Tower, once (with no small ambition) wrote to a friend, 'I wish to have one copy of every Book in the world.' But this feverish amassing of books was in some ways only secondary to his passion for the collection and preservation of manuscripts, and for this service present-day scholars are much in his debt. For a more detailed account of Sir Thomas's passion for collecting and its effect upon his unfortunate family, read Jocelin Finberg's *The Cotswolds.*

Other facilities provided within the Broadway Tower Country Park include a car park, picnic area, and restaurant. There are also a small number of red deer to be seen in fields close by. Broadway Tower, like Broadway itself, lies astride the **Cotswold Way,** and it is possible to use this to walk either to **Broadway** or to **Chipping Campden.**

BROADWELL, near Stow-on-the-Wold. (1-2 E11) *1½ mi. NE Stow-on-the-Wold.* Pleasant village spread around a wide green and sheltering beneath a hillside rising up towards **Stow-on-the-Wold.** The green is overlooked by the hospitable Fox Inn, and there is a small ford at its lower end. Beyond the green is a handsome Georgian manor house, and there are several 17th-century farmhouses not far away. The church stands in a tree-shaded churchyard, with many beautiful 17th-century table tombs. It has an elegant Perpendicular tower, complete with reset Norman tympanum over its outer turret stair entrance. Do not miss the 17th-century monument showing Herbert Weston and his wife both kneeling at a prayer desk.

BROADWELL, near Lechlade. (1-2 J12) *3½ mi. NE Lechlade.* Small village not far to the north of the flat Thames gravel country, with two stone gate pillars the only surviving evidence of a long-vanished manor house. However, there are several pleasant stone houses and an inn of character called the Five Bells. The cruciform, largely Norman church has a fine 13th-century spire which appears to have a slight twist, and by the churchyard gate the extensive remains of a medieval cross. The Norman south doorway has been over-restored, the interior has been ruthlessly scraped, and there are shiny tiles and pitch-pine pews much in evidence, but do not overlook the dramatic Victorian glass depicting the Three Kings, nor the wall monuments to John Huband (1668) and Sophia Colston (1802).

BROCKHAMPTON (1-2 F8) *4 mi. S Winchcombe.* Hamlet with a large, mainly 19th-century mansion now converted into flats and, neatly tucked away, an inn called the Craven Arms . This is watershed country, for the lovely River Coln rises near here and flows south to join the Thames, while at nearby **Charlton Abbots,** the little River Isbourne starts its northward journey to join the Avon at **Evesham.** There are good walks west from here up on to **Cleeve Common,** or south down the Coln Valley.

BROOKTHORPE (1-2 H4) *5 mi N Stroud.* Minute village sandwiched between the Cotswold edge and the noisy M5 motorway. The 13th-century church has a saddleback tower and on one of the north arcade pillars are carved the names of the parishioners who died in the First World War - an unusual and rather pleasing way of recording their sacrifice. Beside the church stands Brookthorpe Court, a partly 17th-century building in timber and stone, emphasising this village's position between hill and valley country.

BROUGHTON AND BROUGHTON CASTLE (1 C15) *3 mi. SW Banbury.* The small village on the B 4035 is itself unexceptional, but the nearby castle and church are of great interest. A fortified manor house was built here in the early 14th century, and in 1377 it came into the ownership of William of Wykeham, Bishop of Winchester and founder of New College, Oxford and Winchester College. In 1405 Thomas Wykeham turned the manor house into a true castle, and also built the gatehouse.

His granddaughter married Sir William Fiennes, Lord Saye and Sele, in 1451, and Broughton has remained in the hands of the Fiennes family until the present day. The castle was modified in the 16th century, being turned into a house by removal of most of the battlements, the alteration of the roof lines and the heightening of the great hall.

Broughton has remained largely unchanged since that time. It is surrounded by a wide moat, and is one of the most romantically situated castles in the country. The interior is full of interest and a visitor here will learn much of England's history from the part that various members of the Fiennes family have played in it, especially in the period leading up to, and during, the Civil War. Celia Fiennes, whose diary gives such a fascinating insight into travel in England in the late-17th century, was a member of the family, and although she was the daughter of a second son, she was a frequent visitor

Church and Castle, Broughton

here. Writing in 1687 she refers to Broughton thus: *its an old house moted round and a parke and gardens, but were much left to decay and ruine, when my brother came to it.*

The adjoining church has a fine chancel screen and a splendid series of monuments, largely of members of the Fiennes family, but also of several earlier owners of Broughton Castle. Despite restoration work carried out by Sir Gilbert Scott and his son G.G.Scott in the 19th century, this church is still full of atmosphere and well worth visiting.

Effigies in Broughton Church

BROUGHTON POGGS (1-2 J12) (*See Filkins & Broughton Poggs.*)

BRUERN ABBEY (1-2 F12) *5 mi. N Burford*. A Cistercian abbey was founded here in the reign of King Stephen, but the dignified 18th-century mansion glimpsed from the road lies a little to the north of the original monastic site beside the River Evenlode. The abbey was sold to Sir Thomas Brydges soon after the Dissolution (1539) and the last abbot had to end his days as rector of **Wigginton**, near Banbury. There is very little to see at Bruern, but the roads leading to it from the south and east pass pleasant woodlands, and there is a charming mill house on the Evenlode, close to the mansion. The **Oxfordshire Way** passes through woodlands close to Bruern Abbey on its way between **Bledington** and **Shipton-under-Wychwood**, and it is also possible to walk westwards to **Idbury** or **Fifield**.

BUCKLAND (1 C9) *1½ mi. SW Broadway*. This is delightfully situated at the end of a road leading up into a combe in the hills, and overlooked by the not very obvious earthworks of an Iron Age settlement known as Burhill. Buckland is a small village, but it has several pleasant houses and cottages and a fine manor house, which was much restored in the 19th century and which is now a luxurious hotel. The nearby church has an interesting interior, with some 15th-century glass (restored by William Morris at his own expense), an exquisitely carved and painted panel said to have come from **Hailes Abbey**, splendid Jacobean canopied seating and a pulpit of the same period. Do not miss the rare 16th-century bowl in maple wood, with a minute silver disc in its base depicting St Margaret (or possibly St Michael). The lovely rectory dates from the 15th century and although now in private hands, it was, for many years, the oldest medieval parsonage in Gloucestershire still in use, and one of the oldest in the country. It is not open to the public, but it has a fine Great Hall with open timber roof and some interesting medieval stained glass.

There is a pleasant walk north-eastwards over the hill to **Broadway**, or south-westwards over the fields to **Laverton** and on to **Stanton. The Cotswold Way** runs just to the east, along the hills above the village, and it is easy to link on to it from here.

BUCKLE STREET (1 D10 etc) (Not shown on map.) This pre-Roman trackway was called *Buggildway* in Anglo-Saxon times, but has been known as Buckle Street since the 17th century. It ran southwards from the **Jurassic Way** on the Cotswold edge, near **Broadway Tower**, in a gently curving line over high wold country to end at **Bourton-on-the-Water.** Its name was probably derived from an Anglo-Saxon lady called Burghild, and she would possibly gain some satisfaction from

Buckland Church

knowing that the course of her road, unlike that of the Romans' **Ryknild Street** nearby, is still followed by a minor road today. Its name is not shown on the Ordnance Survey's Landranger maps, but it is on Outdoor Leisure Map 45.

BURFORD (1-2 H12) *9 mi. SE Stow-on-the-Wold*. This lovely old town has an impressive main street lined with a series of fine old houses, and dropping down from the wolds to the valley of the Windrush. The river is crossed by a stout medieval bridge which has resisted the pressures of highway improvers for many years. In coaching days this carried much traffic between the Midlands and the south coast (as it unfortunately still does). However, the main route from London and Oxford to Cheltenham and much of the West Country also originally ran through the town, with a crossing of routes by the old Tolsey House, and it was only in 1812 that the east-west traffic was diverted onto the wolds above.

However, prosperity came to Burford much earlier than this - through trade in wool and cloth, work in the great stone quarries nearby (at the hamlet of Upton just to the west of the town, and at the nearby villages of **Taynton, Little Barrington and Windrush**), and also the manufacture of fine saddlery, specimens of which were presented to both Charles II and William III. The quarries in the Burford district were worked from early medieval times. In the 17th century their master-mason owners, the Strongs of Great Barrington and Taynton and the Kempsters of Upton and Burford, were noted for their fine craftsmanship, especially in the years following London's Great Fire when members of both families were employed by Sir Christopher Wren in the building of St Paul's Cathedral. Stone from these quarries was also used in the construction of **Blenheim Palace** and many buildings in Oxford including the Sheldonian Theatre. Saddlery continued to prosper for many years, partly because of the proximity of the Bibury Races which were held regularly for over 200 years on a course near **Aldsworth,** about three miles to the south-west. To add to the jollity Charles II and his mistress Nell Gwyn used to stay in the town during Bibury Race Week and perhaps for good reason her son by the king was eventually given the title, Earl of Burford.

As with other towns and cities astride the country's major routes, Burford's great coaching days date from the time when the much improved turnpike roads made journeys speedy beyond previous belief. Providing for the feeding and bedding-down of both travellers and their horses, and for the supply of fresh horses, was a considerable trade in itself, and by 1801 Burford's population had reached 1500. 'Burford Bait', the inns' gargantuan meals often incorporating venison 'obtained' (most likely poached) from Wychwood Forest, was a byword amongst travellers throughout southern England. Coaches coming through here had such splendid names as *Nimrod and Tantivy, Defiance, Retaliator and Mazeppa*. These were heroic days for Burford and they are brilliantly described in Edith Brill's book, *Old Cotswold*.

Burford

It is sad to relate that the coming of the railways brought this colourful era to an abrupt end. Burford's decline had already set in with the diversion of the Oxford to Cheltenham road onto the wolds, and to make matters worse no railway line came its way. The Bibury Races also ceased, owing partly to enclosure of the land on which they had been run. So for a time Burford slumbered, kept alive by the owners of the various fine houses who continued to treasure its qualities, and by agricultural trade from the surrounding countryside. It was also not too long before the first holiday visitors started to arrive, and since the coming of the first motor cars and charabancs to its then dusty streets, their numbers have continued to grow. Today, however, despite its over-busy roads and the demands of its visitors, Burford still remains a delight to all who come here.

Explore this charming little town from the Main Car Park to the east of the High Street. First walk back over the River Windrush and turn right into Church Lane. Soon pass the attractive Great Almshouses, which were founded by the Earl of Warwick in 1457, and which were partly rebuilt in 1828. Almost opposite these are some of the old buildings of Burford Grammar School, which was founded by prosperous cloth merchant, Simon Wisdom, in 1577.

Just beyond the almshouses, in a churchyard around two sides of which the Windrush flows, is the very interesting Parish Church. This has a Norman tower capped by a slender 15th-century spire, and dates largely from the 15th century - a time when Burford's prosperity from wool was at its peak. See especially the handsome two-storeyed south porch with its fan vaulted ceiling, and the elaborate tomb of Lord Chief Justice Sir Lawrence Tanfield in the North Chapel. Also buried in the church is William

Lenthall, noted for his defiance of Charles I when, as Speaker of the Long Parliament, he was recorded as declaring that, 'I have neither eyes to see nor tongue to speak in this place, but as this house is pleased to direct me'. At his own request his last resting place was only marked with an anonymous inscription, but even this was swept away during 19th-century restoration work. Christopher Kempster (or Kit, as he was usually known locally), master-mason of nearby Upton hamlet, has fared better - his monument remains in the south transept complete with weeping cherub carved by his son, William.

On the rim of the church's font will be found the crudely carved inscription *Anthony Sedley Prisner 1649*. Sedley was one of a party of Roundhead mutineers who were imprisoned in the church, and then forced to watch the execution of three of their comrades before eventually receiving Cromwell's pardon. Lengthy restoration of the church in the 1870s brought much criticism from the increasingly concerned William Morris, but the vicar at that time, the Rev. Cass, was not to be turned from his purpose. He is believed to have responded to Morris's comments thus: 'The church Sir is mine, and if I choose to I shall stand on my head in it'. While there is no record of his ever having performed this gymnastic threat, the final results of his restoration were certainly not to Morris's liking, and do not compare favourably with Morris's own work at **Inglesham.**

Now walk into the High Street, first turning right to go down to the fine medieval bridge over the Windrush, with the creeper-covered Weavers' Cottages on the right, just before it. These were also built by Simon Wisdom as part of his endowment of the Grammar School (see above). Turn around at the bridge and start to walk back up the High Street, first passing on the right the little shopping precinct of Bear Court, once the

Burford

yard of the Bear Inn. Turn right by the Tudor Falkland Hall into Priory Lane, soon passing on the right the fine Elizabethan Priory, which was once owned by Speaker Lenthall (see above). This is now an Anglican convent.

Continue up Priory Lane and turn left into Sheep Street, first passing the 15th-century Lamb Inn on the left, with the Old Brewery next door. Immediately beyond this is the 17th-century Bay Tree Hotel, which once belonged to Sir Lawrence Tanfield.

Now turn right, back into the High Street by the little Tolsey, a market house of Tudor origin, where Burford's prosperous wool merchants once held their meetings, and which now houses a small but very interesting local museum. Walk up the High Street far enough to admire the fine view down the hill, here bordered by grassy banks and lined with tall lime-trees. Then cross over to the other side and start to walk downhill. Nearly opposite the Tolsey, pass the handsome 18th-century Bull Hotel, the High Street's only brick-faced building. Turn right into Witney Street, to look at the fine 17th-century Great House, thought to have been built by Christopher Kempster, and then return to the High Street. Before turning right down High Street, note on the opposite side the archway of the former George Hotel, where Charles II once stayed with Nell Gwyn during Bibury Race Week. Being opposite to Witney Street, this archway was well placed to receive the arriving London coaches, which could then depart in the direction of Gloucester from the rear of the hotel yard. Walk down High Street, passing the handsome classical-fronted Methodist Chapel, which was converted from a private house in 1849. To complete your walk round Burford, turn right into Church Lane to return to the Main Car Park.

BURMINGTON (1 C12) *2 mi S Shipston-on-Stour.* Small village above the Stour valley, with a modest, largely Victorian church in a well mown churchyard, backed by the manor house. The only items of real interest inside the church are the Norman corbels, which have been built into the Victorian chancel arch. The pleasant little Victorian school now serves as a village hall, and there is an attractive brick and timber granary on staddle stones, a short distance away - a reminder that here we are only on the outer confines of Cotswold country. There is a good walk, north from here, over the fields to Willington, **Barcheston and Shipston-on-Stour,** mostly along the banks of the Stour.

Barn at Burmington

BUSCOT (1-2 K11) 2 mi. SE Lechlade. Minute village owned by the National Trust, with a small church which can be reached down a separate lane leading from the A417. This building has an east window by Edward Burne-Jones (the home of his friend William Morris was at **Kelmscot,** under two miles away), a pulpit made from a re-used Flemish triptych, a fine 17th-century Spanish lectern and delightful monuments to Margaret and Elizabeth Loveden. Beside it is the handsome early 18th-century 'Old Parsonage', visits to which can be made on Wednesdays in summer only, by written appointment with the National Trust's tenant.

The village lies a short distance to the east, mostly to the immediate north of the A417. Very much an estate village of **Buscot Park**, many of its modest buildings were rebuilt or restored in the 1930s. There is an inn on the main road called the Apple Tree, and two National Trust car parks from either of which it is possible to walk to Buscot Weir, a lock on the River Thames. Two footbridges cross the river here and beyond them there is a path along its north bank, either westwards to St John's Lock and **Lechlade** or eastwards to **Kelmscot.** This is now part of the **Thames Path.**

There is also a small but attractive National Trust car park called the Malthouses, situated on the A417 a short distance to the west of the road down to Buscot Church. Here were once busy warehouses and quays, where goods were trans-shipped from small craft coming from further upstream, largely along the Thames and Severn Canal, to larger barges bound downstream, mostly for London.

BUSCOT PARK (1-2 K12) *3 mi. SE Lechlade.* Owned by the National Trust, this pleasant Adam-style house, dating from 1780, is set in a 55-acre park, with beautiful water gardens running down to a tree-bordered lake, and an attractive walled kitchen-garden. The elegant interior of the house is enhanced by a fine collection of furniture and paintings, and the parlour is decorated with the noted series of paintings of The Sleeping Beauty by Sir Edward Burne-Jones.

BUSSAGE (1-2 J5) *2 mi. SE Stroud.* Small village on steep slopes above the wooded Toadsmoor Valley, with a prettily sited little Victorian church. This was almost entirely paid for by the donations of Oxford undergraduates organised by Thomas Keble, younger brother of John Keble, and vicar of nearby **Bisley.** The south aisle and the porch were the work of the imaginative architect George Bodley, who also designed the churches at **France Lynch** and **Selsley.**

CALCOT (1-2 H9) *2½ mi. NW Bibury.* A quiet hamlet on the gentle eastern slopes of the Coln Valley with several pleasant cottages lining its single street.

CALMSDEN (1-2 H8) *5 mi. NE Cirencester.* This pleasant little hamlet has a row of attractively glazed early 19th-century estate cottages and a rare 14th-century wayside cross. Come this way in springtime to see water bubbling up amongst daffodils at the nearby spring.

Cam Churchyard

Calmsden Cross

CAM (2 K2) *1 mi. N Dursley.* Large village in the industrialised valley of the little River Cam. One cloth mill remains here, producing high quality West of England cloth, used largely for tennis balls, billiard tables and cloth for guardsmen's uniforms. Upper Cam Church is a large building, believed to have been paid for by Lord Berkeley in the hope of saving his eternal soul following his involvement in the murder of Edward II at **Berkeley Castle.** The church's interior was partially scraped by the Victorians, but its contents include a Jacobean pulpit on a slender base, a pleasant assortment of 18th-century wall monuments, and an unusual tablet to the Rev. W.C. Holder, featuring a model of his vicarage.

CAMPDEN LANE (1 C10 etc.) (Not shown on map.) This medieval trackway must once have been in regular use by pack-horse trains carrying wool from the warehouses of the Chipping Campden merchants to the port of Bristol, and also probably salt from Droitwich. It follows the approximate course of the **Jurassic Way** for some of its route, although further south it may have followed the course of the Romans' **White Way**.

CAMPDEN RAILWAY TUNNEL (1 B10) (Not shown on map.) *1½ mi. NE Chipping Campden.* The most attractive road between **Chipping Campden** and **Hidcote Manor Garden** passes a wooded embankment which was formed by spoil from the tunnel excavated for the Oxford, Worcester and Wolverhampton Railway, built between 1845 and 1853. This tunnel was the site of the so-called `Battle of Mickleton', when the great railway builder and engineer, Isambard Kingdom Brunel, led a gang of no fewer than two thousand navvies armed with picks, shovels and even pistols, in an ultimately successful attempt to oust the navvies of the original contractor, who had refused to leave the site. Read the full story of the battle, and of Brunel's fascinating career, in L.T.C. Rolt's outstanding biography.

CARTERTON (1-2 J12) *4 mi. SE Burford.* Quite alien in character to the surrounding countryside, this is a garrison town for the great airfield of Brize Norton.

CASSEY COMPTON (1-2 G8) *4 mi. W Northleach.* Here, in the beautifully wooded Coln Valley, is a delightful, partly demolished 17th-century mansion looking south to the point where the Romans' White Way crosses the road coming up the valley from **Fossebridge.** 18th-century engravings depict an ambitious house surrounded by formal gardens, but the estate was split up in the 19th century. In the 1920s John Buchan, amongst several others, tried without success to buy the house, and it is easy to see why it would have appealed to a writer with such a strong

Cassey Compton

appreciation of mystery and landscape. Read more about this fascinating house in James Lees-Milne's *Some Cotswold Country Houses.* Unfenced roads and wooded verges appear to offer picnic opportunities in plenty, but please observe any requests not to park that may be displayed. Walk south-west from here down the **White Way,** before heading south-east through Chedworth Woods towards **Chedworth Roman Villa.**

CASTLE COMBE (2 P4) *9 mi. SW Malmesbury.* Well to the south of the classic Cotswolds, much visited Castle Combe lies snugly in the wooded valley of the little By Brook, with several fine old buildings around its beautiful Market Cross. This reminds us of wealth once created here by cloth weavers and merchants. The substantial tower of the largely Perpendicular church was built in 1434 at the expense of clothiers of the district, and the church's interior, although much restored in the 19th century, is well worth visiting. The Market Cross is overlooked by two pleasant hotels, the Castle and the White Hart. Walk down from here, passing many attractive stone cottages, to the lovely old bridge over the By Brook. It was here in 1966 that the streamside below was temporarily transformed by the producers of the film *Dr Doolittle* into a tiny 'harbour' complete with boats and jetty - a move not universally popular at the time. There is a good walk southwards from here to Ford and Slaughterford.

Castle Combe

CAUDLE GREEN (1-2 H6) *7 mi. NW Cirencester.* Quiet hamlet looking north-eastwards across a deep valley to Syde, with a small rough green overlooked by a handsome 18th-century farmhouse. There is a pleasant walk northwards up a wooded valley to **Brimpsfield**.

Farmhouse at Caudle Green

CERNEY WICK (2 L9) *5 mi. SE Cirencester.* Small village in flat Thames gravel country, with large flooded pits to the west (now part of the **Cotswold Water Park**) and the line of the old **Thames and Severn Canal** to the east. There is a small Victorian church here and a 'round house' with 18th-century Gothic windows, one of a series built for the canal's maintenance men. The little River Churn flows just to the east of the village, on its way to join the Thames at neighbouring **Cricklade**. Walk from Cerney Wick following the course of the old canal, either south-eastwards to **Cricklade** or north-westwards to **Siddington** and **Cirencester.**

CHADLINGTON (1-2 F13) *3 mi. S Chipping Norton.* A long village looking south over the Evenlode Valley towards **Wychwood Forest,** with much modern development and a

Chadlington Manor

pub and restaurant called the Tite Inn. There is a pleasant 17th- and 18th-century manor house with a substantial church close by. The church's exterior is enriched with a multitude of fascinating gargoyles, while within will be found a clerestory and a series of richly carved corbel figures. There are fine walks northwards over the farmlands of Chadlington Downs, one of which goes past the hamlet of **Dean** before passing the Hawk Stone, an isolated eight-foot-high sarsen stone - possibly the sole surviving stone of a long-vanished burial chamber.

CHALFORD (1-2 J5) *3 mi. SE Stroud.* A large and highly attractive village of the early Industrial Revolution, built on ascending terraces on the south-facing slopes of the **Golden Valley.** Approached by a bemusing series of narrow and often very steep lanes and alleyways, are a multitude of late 18th- and early 19th-century houses, most of which once belonged to prosperous clothiers. These are in company with many delightful cottages once inhabited by the more humble weavers. The lanes here are so steep that until recent times panniered donkeys were used to deliver milk, bread and coal. In the valley below there are old mills on the banks of the now derelict **Thames and Severn Canal,** and on the main A419 road there is a rather severe 18th-century church, much altered in Victorian times. This does, however, contain several items of more recent Cotswold craftsmanship including panelling and a font cover by Norman Jewson, and a lectern by Peter Waals, Gimson's foreman cabinet-maker at **Daneway,** and a close colleague of Jewson's.

CHARINGWORTH (1 B11) *3 mi. E Chipping Campden.* A modest hamlet on hill slopes looking southwards over orchard country, with a fine early-Tudor manor house which is now a luxury hotel. There is a pleasant open road northwards from here, around the Cotswolds' far northern edge below Windmill Hill and then dropping steeply down to **Ilmington.**

CHARLBURY (1-2 F14) *6 mi. N Witney.* This small town is snugly situated in the Evenlode Valley well away from busy main roads. It looks across the valley to the fine 600-acre **Cornbury Park,** which is itself almost surrounded by the great woodlands of **Wychwood Forest**. For many centuries Charlbury was noted for its gloves, and at the height of its prosperity, in 1852, the town's glovers employed over a thousand people. This trade has now almost ceased, but the coming of the railway, which still survives here, has contributed to Charlbury's special charm. Despite the presence of many retired people and commuting Oxonians, the town has kept much of its rural flavour, and it has a

Charlbury

mouth-watering selection of country inns.

The largely Perpendicular church was heavily restored by the Victorians, but blends in well with the stone-fronted shops and inns nearby. The small green, known as Playing Close, has a series of attractive cottages looking across to a little neo-Jacobean drinking fountain.

It is possible to walk eastwards from Charlbury, along bridleways running not far from the fine mansion of **Ditchley Park,** and the meandering **Oxfordshire Way** also passes through the town. There is also a fine circular walk taking in **Finstock,** part of **Cornbury Park,** Chilson and **Shorthampton.**

CHARLTON ABBOTS (1-2 E8) *2½ mi. S Winchcombe.* A hamlet with fine views over the Isbourne valley from its lofty churchyard. The church was virtually rebuilt in the 19th century but in its simple interior will be found a late Norman tub font and an attractive modern oak pulpit. The beautifully gabled manor house close by dates from the Elizabethan and Jacobean periods. This is all on high watershed country, for in the valley below is the source of the little River Isbourne which flows northwards from here to join the Avon, while less than a mile to the south the River Coln starts its journey southwards to the Thames. Walk westwards from Charlton Abbots over hill country to Cleeve Hill, or northwards, down the Isbourne valley, to **Sudeley Castle** and **Winchcombe.**

Charlton Abbots Manor

CHARTERVILLE ALLOTMENTS (1-2 H13) *3 mi. W Witney, to immediate S of Minster Lovell.* It was here, in 1847, that 300 acres lying each side of the road were purchased by one of the Chartists (forerunners of the Socialists), and in a typically 19th-century exercise in rural paternalism, this was split up into a number of smallholdings. These were then ploughed up and handed over to poor families from the industrial towns, each being endowed with thirty pounds and a pig. But sadly, like so many idealistic enterprises, it soon foundered. A handful of the little dwellings remain largely unaltered, but most have been smartened up beyond easy recognition, and now appear to be the homes of independent folk whose views might not easily be reconciled with the liberal ideals that led to their construction.

CHASTLETON (1 D12) *3 mi. SE Moreton-in-Marsh.* A modest stone village, situated on the lower slopes of the Cotswolds, and whose high point is the splendid Stuart manor of Chastleton House, now owned by the National Trust. It was built by Walter Jones, a prosperous Witney wool merchant who had purchased the estate from Robert Catesby in 1602. Probably designed by Robert Smythson, the architect perhaps best known for Hardwick Hall in Derbyshire, it has a fine five-gabled south front and a fascinating and highly atmospheric interior largely undisturbed by 18th- or 19th-century alteration. Its structure has recently been completely restored by the National Trust, but such care has been taken with this work that its patina of age has been successfully retained. The most outstanding feature is the Long Gallery at the top of the house which has a beautifully ornamented, tunnel-vaulted ceiling. There is a topiary garden at the side of the house, an attractive 18th-century arched dovecot across the road and medieval barns close by, where there is an exhibition telling the story of Chastleton's restoration by the Trust.

Dovecot at Chastleton

While visiting here, ask to be told the story of Arthur Jones's plight after the Battle of Worcester, and how he was hidden from Roundhead troops by his enterprising wife Sarah, who spiked their wine flagons with laudanum, thus allowing the now desperate Arthur to escape. Although Chastleton can be reached on foot (perhaps using part of the **Macmillan Way**), most visitors will follow signs to a car park to it south-east, and from here it is only a short walk across one field to the house. Do not try to drive through the village of Chastleton.

The nearby church dates from the 12th century, although it was considerably enlarged about 200 years later. See especially the medieval floor tiles, the two interesting brasses and the wall tablets to two members of the Jones family. Walk southwards to Adlestrop and Oddington following the course of the **Macmillan Way,** or south-eastwards to **Cornwell**, passing through **Chastleton Barrow.**

Chastleton House

CHASTLETON BARROW (1 D12) *1 mi. SE Chastleton*. A well preserved, but thickly wooded, circular Iron Age settlement. Unusually, its builders faced the encircling banks with large blocks of stone and some of these have survived. This may be approached by a bridleway from the road above **Chastleton.**

CHAVENAGE HOUSE (2 L4) *1½ mi. NW Tetbury.* This delightful Elizabethan manor house is visible from the road and is also sometimes open to the public. Oliver Cromwell made a special visit here to persuade the owner, Colonel Nathaniel Stephens,

Chavenage House

to agree to the execution of Charles I. The unfortunate colonel soon deeply regretted giving his agreement and died, full of remorse, less than three months after the King's execution. Cromwell is believed to have slept in the handsome Tapestry Room, which is shown to visitors. It is possible to walk behind the manor to the little family chapel nearby. This was virtually rebuilt in the 19th century and is not of great interest apart from some 17th-century tomb figures which have been reset in the porch. Walk south-westwards from here following the course of the **Macmillan Way,** along a bridleway to **Beverston.**

CHEDWORTH (1-2 H8) *4 mi. SW Northleach.* A large village spread out along a quiet valley, through which a railway branch-line once ran. The best part of the village is centred upon the Seven Tuns Inn, with a spring bubbling out of a wall opposite and an interesting church with late Norman origins a short distance beyond. A pleasant cobbled path leads past old tombstones to the south door of this building, which was considerably enriched in the prosperous Perpendicular period. Light floods in through tall windows on the south side, onto a stout Norman tub font and onto the contrastingly elegant 15th-century stone pulpit. Do not overlook the lovely modern sculpture of the Virgin and Child carved by Helen Rock in 1911. If possible climb up the path beyond the church for good views over the village. It is possible to walk down the valley to **Fossebridge** passing through the delectable hamlet of Pancakehill, but to visit the great Chedworth Woods and the **Chedworth Roman Villa,** follow the course of the **Macmillan Way,** which runs through the village.

CHEDWORTH ROMAN VILLA (1-2 G8) *3½ mi. W Northleach.* Situated in a beautifully wooded stretch of the Coln Valley, this is undoubtedly Britain's most attractively sited Roman villa. (The Romans often appear to have been as adept in their choice of villa sites as the Cistercians were in siting their great abbeys.) Discovered in 1864, it proved on excavation to be one of the finest examples of a Roman villa in Britain and dates from about AD 120 - 400. It has been in the care of the National Trust since 1924 and the beautifully preserved remains include bath suites, a hypocaust and mosaic pavements, with one in the west wing depicting the four seasons. There is also a museum complete with a very interesting video film telling the story

Hypocaust at Chedworth Roman Villa

of life in Roman Britain, and a well stocked shop. The villa may be approached on foot from either **Yanworth** or **Chedworth** by following the course of the **Macmillan Way.**

CHELTENHAM SPA (1-2 F6) *7 mi. E Gloucester.* This large and elegant spa town is situated on the very edge of the Severn Plain, just below the sometimes craggy scarp face of the Cotswolds, and not far from their highest point, **Cleeve Hill.** Once a small market town, its humble beginning as a spa was occasioned by the discovery in 1716 of salt crystals at a small spring. This was soon enclosed and incorporated into Cheltenham's first pump-room, but it was some years later that the original owner's son-in-law, one Henry Skillicorne, erected a more permanent building and employed the term 'spa'. The fame of Cheltenham's waters soon began to spread and the arrival of George III in 1788 for a five-week 'taking of the waters' finally established Cheltenham as a major spa town.

Pittville Pump Room, Cheltenham

Passing through here in 1826, William Cobbett noted *'a new row of the most gaudy and fantastical dwelling places'* and described the area in general as *'a nasty, flat, stupid spot, without anything pleasant near it.'* However, these were only the views of a rather jaundiced and often prickly traveller, and there were many others who lavished their praises upon a spa town that continued to thrive throughout the 19th century. It was then that a large number of army officers and administrators and their families, many suffering from tropical liver complaints, retired here to benefit from its health-giving waters, thus altering Cheltenham from a town chiefly for spa visitors to a largely residential one.

It continues to thrive today, although now more as a holiday and shopping town, with considerable light industry being kept well at bay on its fringes. It has been further enhanced by the establishment of three major public schools, two for boys and one for girls. It has some of the finest Regency buildings in the country, these being grouped along terraces, around squares, crescents, parks and gardens, and on either side of Cheltenham's jewel, the handsome tree-lined Promenade, with its fine shops and elegant buildings. There is an annual Festival of Music and also a Festival of Literature, and the famous Cheltenham Gold Cup meeting is held on the fine racecourse just to the north of the town on the A435 Evesham Road well beyond Pittville Park.

Most visitors to Cheltenham will first head for the Promenade, which is today complemented by the Regent Arcade, a fine two-storey shopping arcade running parallel, just to its west, and linking in to the busy High Street, where many of the major multiple stores will be found.

Other elegant shopping areas include Montpellier Street, with its attendant Courtyard development, both best approached by a short walk through Imperial Gardens and possibly

Fountain at Cheltenham

Montpellier Gardens. The Cheltenham Art Gallery and Museum, with various items including its nationally important Arts and Crafts Collection, is in Clarence Street.

On the north side of the town will be found the extensive Pittville Park with its Nature and Fitness Trails and the Pittville Pump Room. On the south-east side of the town is Sandford Park, which has an open-air swimming pool.

CHERINGTON, Warwickshire (1 C13) *3 mi SE Shipston-on-Stour.* This modest stone village is situated in the upper Stour valley between **Brailes** and Stourton Hill. It has a handsome 17th-century manor house, further enriched by a charming 18th-century Gothick porch. The largely 13th-century church is full of interest. It has a well proportioned tower, fine Perpendicular windows, some with interesting medieval glass, a Jacobean altar table and rail, and a delightful series of carved corbel figures beneath the roof beams. However Cherington's greatest treasure is the lovely 14th-century canopied tomb chest, topped with an effigy of a `civilian', whose name is unfortunately not known. There is a pleasant, partly open road leading south from here across Weston Park, towards **Long Compton.** This park once contained a fine early 19th-century mansion, but it was pulled down in 1934. It's site is still shown on Ordnance Survey maps, but almost no trace remains above ground. Read the fascinating story of Weston in *A Prospect of Weston in Warwickshire,* by Michael Warriner, published by The Roundwood Press, but now out of print. Walk on this road, or use the bridle-path running roughly parallel with it, up to Margett's Hill, and then partly along the **Macmillan Way,** to **Long Compton.**

CHERINGTON, Gloucestershire (1-2 K5) *3½ mi. E Nailsworth.* Several pleasant 18th- and early 19th-century cottages look across a large green, on which is a Victorian drinking fountain inscribed *Let Him that is athirst, come.* The largely 13th-century church has a Norman south doorway with tympanum and an Early English chancel which has unfortunately been scraped and heavily repointed. The elegant pulpit incorporates carved medieval panels (possibly Flemish) and there is a handsome Renaissance candle-holder beside it. It is possible to walk eastwards from here to **Hazelton** and **Tarlton** using part of the **Macmillan Way.**

The Green at Cherington, Gloucestershire

CHIPPING CAMPDEN (1 C10) *5 mi. NW Moreton-in-Marsh.* Chipping was an Old English

Chipping Campden Market Hall

word meaning 'market', and Campden had a weekly market and no fewer than three annual fairs as early as the mid-13th century. In the 14th and 15th centuries it was without doubt the most important trading centre for wool in the northern Cotswolds, and its name would have been familiar to wool merchants on the quays of Bruges and Antwerp, and most other cloth-trading ports of western Europe. William Grevel, described as 'the flower of the wool merchants of all England' on his memorial brass in the Parish Church, built Grevel's House in about 1380. With its splendid

Perpendicular style gabled, two-storeyed window, this was to become one of the first of a very beautiful series of buildings in the honey-coloured local stone which were erected in the centuries which followed. The nearby Woolstaplers' Hall was built at about the same time as Grevel's House, by another prosperous wool merchant, Robert Calf.

The lovely Market Hall was built in 1627 by Sir Baptist Hicks *for the sale of cheese, butter and poultry.* He had made his money in the cloth trade, not in Chipping Campden, but in the southern Cotswolds and in London; for by this time Campden's wool trading prosperity had almost ceased, due to the fact that since Edward III's time Flemish weavers had been encouraged to come to England, and wool was handled directly by the clothiers in the Stroud valley and elsewhere, rather than by exporting merchants. Sir Baptist built himself the fine Campden House not far to the south of the church, but sadly this was later burnt down by Royalists during the Civil War. It was claimed that this was to prevent it falling into the hands of Cromwell's forces, but it appears more likely to have been set alight in a drunken spree by disgruntled soldiers before they were forced to flee. The only significant survivals are the lodges and gatehouse, two ruined pavilions and an almonry. One of these pavilions has been restored by the Landmark Trust, but is not open to the public.

However, just below the church is Sir Baptist's most enduring legacy, a row of delightful almshouses built by him in 1612. Sir Baptist became Baron Hicks and Viscount Campden in 1628 (appointments no doubt arising from the substantial loans that he had recently made to his sovereign) but sadly he died only a year later. He and his wife are buried beneath a splendid marble monument in Campden Church. This is one of the great Cotswold wool churches, a fine Perpendicular building with a handsome 15th-century pinnacled tower. Its interior is perhaps a little cold in feeling, but it contains a number of

Chipping Campden Market Hall

interesting monumental brasses, a series of monuments in the Noel Chapel, and an outstanding collection of medieval English embroidery, including copes and altar hangings.

Chipping Campden's prosperity declined greatly in the 18th and 19th centuries, although local mason and quarry-owner, Thomas Woodward, left an enduring mark on the High Street, with the building of the elegantly classical Bedfont House in about 1745. From this time Chipping Campden appears to have slept largely undisturbed by intrusions until the early years of the 20th century. Then in 1902 Charles Ashbee, a disciple of William Morris and Ruskin, moved his Guild and School of Handicraft from London's East End to Chipping Campden. This migration of fifty craftsmen and their families was a brave endeavour and full of idealism, but the Guild did not survive the rigours of economic depression, the First World War, and above all, the mutual suspicion that appears to have soon arisen between the incoming Cockney craftsmen and the natives of Chipping Campden. However, Ashbee's ideals have in part survived, thanks largely to the artist and architect F.L.Griggs, who established the Campden Trust in 1929, and who did so much to preserve the Chipping Campden that we see today; thanks also to George Hart, his son and grandson, craftsmen in precious metals, who have kept the tradition of the Guild very much alive; and also, more recently, to Robert Welch, the talented industrial designer, whose work may be seen at his studio shop in the High Street.

Chipping Campden's present-day character still owes much to F.L.Griggs and his friends, and remains largely unspoilt. There are now more tourist shops, restaurants and hotels than there were in Griggs's day, but there are still a few genuine country-town shops and small inns left. It therefore remains a pleasure to walk the length of the High Street, and up past the almshouses, to the splendidly towered church, and on to the open land beyond, The Coneygree, which belongs to the National Trust. Before leaving this most attractive of Cotswold towns do not overlook the Ernest Wilson Memorial Garden, opened in memory of the great plant collector, who was born at Chipping Campden in 1876, and who made a series of expeditions to the Far East in the first thirty years of this century. This delightful garden is situated in the lower half of the old Vicarage garden, and fronts on to Leysbourne, which runs northwards beyond the High Street. Chipping Campden is the northern terminus of the **Cotswold Way,** the long-distance footpath which runs from here, following the approximate line of the Cotswold scarp, down to Bath, a distance of about a hundred miles. Why not walk the first few miles at least, up over the fields as far as **Dover's Hill.** Start by walking west, down the High Street, and turning right into Back Ends and Hoo Lane, and then following the sign to the left marked 'Cotswold Way'.

CHIPPING NORTON (1-2 E13) *14 mi. SW Banbury.* Lively little market town where the everyday lives of those who live and work there have so far not been overshadowed by tourism. It stands on west facing slopes, with the large Victorian Bliss's Valley Tweed Mill in the valley still looking less at home here than it would in some darker, deeper valley in West Yorkshire. It was in fact designed by George Woodhouse, an architect from Yorkshire's neighbour, Lancashire. Built in 1872, it closed only in 1980 and is now converted into flats.

The long Market Square, or Chepynge, as it was called in medieval times (hence Chipping) is dominated by a handsome 19th-century Town Hall designed by George Repton, son of the better known Humphry Repton, the landscape designer. Opposite the Town Hall, in the Victorian 'Co-op Hall', is the Chipping Norton Local History Museum, with exhibits of agricultural equipment, the Bliss Tweed Mill and Hitchman's Brewery. There is also a 'thirties' kitchen. The Square, which in the 19th century must have resounded to the horns of the twenty two coaches that were then passing through Chipping Norton daily, is also overlooked by pleasant 17th-, 18th- and 19th-century hotels, inns and shops.

The row of quaint, gabled almshouses was built in 1640 on Church Street, the cul-de-sac leading down to the Parish Church, which lies in the valley bottom. This fine, largely

Perpendicular building, which was no doubt mainly funded with money amassed in the wool trade, has an unusual hexagonal porch with a vaulted ceiling. The church tower was rebuilt in 1825, but it is sad to recall that from its tall predecessor was hanged a brave but unfortunate cleric who, in the times following Henry VIII's break with the Church of Rome, obstinately refused to make use of Cranmer's English Prayer Book. The church's handsome interior was over-restored by the Victorians, but the tombs of Richard Croft and Thomas Rickardes, and the interesting series of brasses, make a

Almshouses, Chipping Norton

visit here well worth while. To the immediate north of the church are the extensive motte and bailey earthworks of a 12th-century castle.

There is a good walk eastwards from Chipping Norton, down the Glyme Valley, through Old Chalford and **Lidstone** to **Enstone**, and returning along the western fringes of **Heythrop Park.**

CHIPPING SODBURY (2 N2) *8 mi. NW Bristol.* A small market town having, like Chipping Norton, a long Market Square, or Chepynge, as it was called in medieval times (hence Chipping). Known as Broad Street, this is bordered with a wonderful assortment of houses from every period, but largely 17th-century Cotswold stone buildings or Georgian ones of mellow brick. Most of these are occupied by bright and cheerful shops and despite its proximity to Bristol, Chipping Sodbury has retained a lively country flavour. A weekly cattle market was held in Broad Street until 1954, when it was stopped due to health regulations.

Before exploring the town be sure to call at the helpful Tourist Information Centre at the Clock Tower in Broad Street. The buildings in Broad Street include the Town Hall, which although re-fronted by the Victorians, dates back to Tudor times as a Guild Hall. One of the earliest buildings in the town is Tudor House, in Hatter's Lane, to the west of Broad Street, but see also the adjoining Horse Street which has a similar assortment of buildings.

The Parish Church of St John, which is in Wick Road, has a tall, slender tower and dates back to the 13th century. It was however restored in the 19th century by G E Street, best known as the architect of London's Law Courts. Beyond the church runs the little River Frome, which can be followed on foot from the **Cotswold Way** at Old Sodbury to Frenchay, near Bristol, on the 14-mile long Frome Valley Walkway.

CHURCHILL (1-2 E12) *2½ mi. SW Chipping Norton.* Much of this village is strung out along the B4450, but its early 19th-century church is of some interest, being modelled on at least two Oxford buildings. The elegant west tower is a replica of Magdalen College's tower, and the hammerbeam roof within was inspired by the hall of Christ Church. The nearby Memorial Fountain, a rather bizarre exercise in Victorian Gothic, was built in

1870 in memory of James Langston, whose money had paid for the new church. There is also a memorial stone to William Smith, a pioneer of the science of geology, who spent his childhood years at Churchill.

Only the chancel of the old church remains, and this is used as a mortuary chapel. It looks across a broad valley towards **Daylesford House,** reminding us that the great Warren Hastings was born at Churchill in 1732, in an early Georgian cottage which lies on the road between the new and old churches. It was always Hastings' ambition to buy back the family estate at Daylesford, and this aim was eventually achieved on his return from India.

, Churchyard Gate Churchill

CHURCH HANBOROUGH (1 H15) *3 mi. SW Woodstock.* Small village in wooded country to the west of the River Evenlode, with a pretty Victorian school house and a wonderfully 'atmospheric' church. This has a tall, slender spire and there are yew trees lining the path to a large north porch, which shelters a fine Norman doorway complete with a tympanum depicting *The Lion of St Mark, St Peter* and the *Agnus Dei.* The monumental brasses include the shrouded figure of Dr Alexander Belsyre, the first president of St John's College, Oxford. The largely Perpendicular interior, with its old stone floors, is full of character and there is an interesting 15th-century rood screen and a roof of the same period supported on attractive corbel figures.

CIRENCESTER (1-2 K8) *15 mi. SE Cheltenham.* This busy market town stands on the site of Corinium Dubunnorum, for a time Roman Britain's second largest city, and meeting point of three major Roman roads - the **Ermin Way**, the **Foss Way** and **Akeman Street**. Evidence of much of the ancient forum and basilica, and also of many houses, has been uncovered over the years, but little now shows above ground apart from a stretch of the

Roman town wall on the far side of the Abbey Grounds, and an impressively large, turf-covered amphitheatre to the south of the ring road. This is in the care of English Heritage, and is open at any reasonable time. Although Cirencester was largely neglected by the Anglo-Saxons, it regained its importance in early medieval times. It soon grew rich on the wool trade, owing in the first place to the enterprise of the great Cirencester Abbey, and latterly to the activities of the towns prosperous wool and cloth merchants. It remains today the undisputed centre of life and work in the southern Cotswolds - a lively market town and attractive tourist centre.

Parish Church, Cirencester

The pressures of modern tourism have been responsible for some change, but many of the cheerfully coloured shops in the Market Place have retained their country flavour, and over all preside the magnificent 162-ft Perpendicular tower and three-storeyed south porch of the Parish Church. The porch, one of England's finest, was built by the abbey at the end of the 15th century. After the Dissolution it was known as the Town Hall and was only handed back to the vicar in the 18th century. Endowed with the wealth of the town's wool merchants, the splendid interior of this largely 15th-century church has a fine roof illuminated by clerestory windows, medieval stained glass in the east and west windows, a painted 'wine-glass' pulpit, and many interesting brasses.

There is the Corn Hall which is on the south side of the Market Place, almost opposite the Parish Church. Not far away, in Park Street, is the most interesting Corinium Museum, which houses one of Britain's best collections of Romano-British material, together with displays illustrating the medieval Cotswolds and the wool trade. See also the series of lovely old houses in nearby Coxwell Street, the surviving arcade of St John's Hospital in Spitalgate Street, the delightful Abbey Grounds, with swans and wildfowl on a large pool and, to their immediate east, a stretch of the Roman Town Wall and a Norman gatehouse known as The Spital Gate, the only surviving building of Cirencester Abbey.

Before leaving the town, do not miss a visit to Brewery Arts in Brewery Court off Cricklade Street, which houses a number of independent craft businesses, with a craft shop, gallery and coffee shop. See below for **Cirencester Park,** the town entrance to which is at the end of Cecily Hill on the west side of the town.

CIRENCESTER PARK (1-2 K8) *To the immediate west of Cirencester.* (Not shown on map.) The mansion which lies at the town end of the park was built by the 1st Earl Bathurst in 1714-18, almost certainly to his own design. The house cannot be visited by the public, but most of its great park is open. Notices clearly proclaim that, 'You are welcome on foot and on horseback by permission of the Earl Bathurst. Dogs, cars, cycles or unaccompanied children are not allowed. Take your litter home.'

The writer Alexander Pope gave his advice on the layout of this great park and there is a small rusticated shelter known as Pope's Seat near the polo ground. The 1st Earl Bathurst lived until the age of ninety-one, dying only in 1775, and for most of the long years following the building of the house, he was constantly adding features to his great park. Apart from Pope's Seat, these include a tall Doric column topped by a statue of Queen Anne, the Hexagon, to the north of the Broad Ride, and a large Gothic folly, known as Alfred's Hall. His Broad Ride, or Broad Avenue, stretches westwards from the town entrance at Cecily Hill almost to **Sapperton,** a distance of nearly five miles.

Wander almost at will in these great woods and open parklands, but always remember that you are a privileged guest, and not there by right.

Cirencester Park Gate

No vehicles are allowed and entrance is normally free, apart from the polo grounds where matches are usually held on each Sunday from May to September, and where an entry fee is charged (entry for polo spectators is from the A419, Stroud road, to the west of the town).

CLANFIELD (1-2 K12) *4 mi. N Faringdon.* This long straggling village, with its two attractive inns, is less than two miles north of the Thames, but is still predominantly Cotswold in flavour. The interior of the church has been over-restored, but the exterior is well proportioned and is enlivened, high up on the 14th-century tower, by a carving of St Stephen complete with four stones - the symbols of his martyrdom.

CLAPTON-ON-THE-HILL (1-2 G10) *2 mi. S Bourton-on-the-Water.* Small village on a hill looking across the Windrush Valley to the ridge where the great hangars of a long-closed airfield remain. The little church has simple Norman features, including a south doorway with a plain tympanum, and a tub font, but the pointed chancel arch is Early English. There is a walk down across the fields to **Bourton-on-the-Water**, and a quiet road leads to **Great Rissington,** crossing the Windrush at New Bridge.

Clanfield

CLEEVE HILL and CLEEVE COMMON (1-2 E7) *2½ mi. W Winchcombe.* This broad expanse of open common land slopes gently upwards from the Winchcombe side to West Down, the Cotswolds' highest point (1082 ft). It is grand country to walk or ride over, and there is a wealth of wildlife to be observed in addition to the grazing sheep and cattle, and homo-sapiens in the form of the golfers on the northern fringes. From the steep, Cheltenham side, there are splendid views over the Severn Valley to the Malverns, to May Hill, and the distant mountains of Wales in the haze beyond. The best access points are from Cleeve Hill village, astride the B4632 Winhcombe to Cheltenham road, from **Postlip** and Corndean Lane, both near Winchcombe and from the vicinity of the radio masts three miles north of **Whittington.**

Cleeve Hill Topograph

COALEY (2 K3) *2½ mi. NE Dursley.* Small village lying below the Cotswold edge. Flowering cherries line the churchyard path, which is overlooked by a finely pinnacled Perpendicular tower. The rest of the church was built in the 1850s and contains little of interest apart from an attractive 17th-century brass depicting Daniel Stayno, complete with his wife and their three children.

COALEY PEAK PICNIC SITE (2 K3) *4 mi. SW Stroud.* (Not shown on map.) A lovely open space above steep scarp slopes near the top of **Frocester Hill,** from whence there are splendid views (with topograph to help with identification) over the winding Severn Estuary to the Forest of Dean and the distant Welsh hills . There are also a number of display boards depicting the wildlife of the area.

COATES (1-2 K7) *3 mi. W Cirencester.* Small village on the high wolds with a neat Perpendicular-towered church in company with a rectory and farmhouse - two most attractive buildings. Beyond the tidy churchyard and through a Norman doorway, the church itself will be found to have a simple but most pleasing interior. Walk south-westwards from here to the **Tunnel House Inn,** and then south and east along the course of the old **Thames and Severn Canal** to **Thames Head,** the source of the River Thames.

COBERLEY (1-2 G6) *4 mi. S Cheltenham Spa.* This small village is delightfully situated near the head of the Churn Valley, less than a mile from the Churn's source at **Seven Springs.** The church lies a little way to the east of the village and is approached by a path beneath an archway in a farm building (visitors may feel that they are intruding, but there is no alternative). The church was largely rebuilt in the 19th century, but the Perpendicular tower and the 14th-century south chapel have survived. This chapel contains the effigies of Sir Thomas Berkeley, who fought at Crecy, and of his wife Joan, who remarried after Sir Thomas's death and became the mother of Sir Richard (Dick) Whittington. There is a monument in the sanctuary of a knight holding a heart, commemorating the burial here in 1295 of Sir

Canal Round House near Coates

Giles Berkeley's heart, the rest of his body having been buried at Little Malvern. The high walls by the churchyard and the large flat area beyond are the only surviving evidence of a mansion that stood here until the 18th century. It is possible to take a pleasant circular walk from here, down the Churn Valley to **Cowley, Cockleford** and **Colesbourne,** returning via Pinswell Plantation and **Upper Coberley.**

COCKLEFORD (1-2 G6) *5 mi. S Cheltenham.* Hamlet on the edge of woodland in the Churn Valley with an attractive pool and an excellent inn called the Green Dragon, which would make an ideal halting point on a walk around here (see Coberley, above).

COLD ASTON (1-2 F10) *4 mi. N Northleach.* This village was once widely known as Aston Blank. Documents indicate that it first became known as 'Cold' in 1287, and then as 'Blank' in 1554, and until recent years both names were in common use. Now the

arbiters have finally settled on 'Cold' - and with some justification, for this is a high wold village set in typically rolling Cotswold country, with dry-stone walls providing the only shelter from the strong winds that often blow across here. A large sycamore tree provides welcome shelter on its green, which is itself overlooked on one side by the handsome Georgian Sycamore House, and on the other by the low-built Plough Inn. The largely Norman church has a very plain exterior, but once inside the Norman south door the visitor will find pleasant stone vaulting beneath the tower, a colourful 17th-century monument complete

Sycamore House, Cold Aston

with cherubs, and the remnants of a 14th-century stone reredos in the east wall. Walk south-westwards from here partly along the course of the **Macmillan Way,** down a track known as Bangup Lane to **Turkdean,** and then possibly on to **Hazleton,** before returning via **Notgrove** - a fine upland journey of almost ten miles.

COLESBOURNE (1-2 H7) *6 mi. SE Cheltenham.* Small, scattered village in the wooded Churn Valley. Its church has a Perpendicular tower, and inside will be found a fine, vase-shaped 15th-century stone pulpit on a slender octagonal stem. The large number of exotic trees to be found in the surrounding park is due to the activities of Squire Henry Elwes (1846-1922), soldier, big-game hunter, botanist, and above all forester. Elwes roamed the world in search of exotic tree specimens and brought many of these back to be planted in his park here at Colesbourne. Timber for the new bowsprit and masts of the restored SS Great Britain at Bristol have all come from the great woodlands of this estate. Walk north-westwards from here to **Upper Coberley** passing below the earthworks of the Iron Age Norbury Camp, and on to Seven Springs to link with the **Cotswold Way,** or return via **Coberley** and **Cowley.**

COLN ROGERS (1-2 H9) *2½ mi. NW Bibury.* The lovely Coln Valley broadens out here and there are woods above the stream, looking back to the Saxon church, which is tucked well away from the road. Much of the original Saxon nave and chancel remains - see especially the chancel arch, and one of the windows in the north side made out of a single piece of stone. Note also the beautifully simple 15th-century stone pulpit. Walk up the valley to **Calcot** and **Coln St Dennis,** or down it to **Winson** and **Ablington.**

Colesbourne Church

Pulpit, Coln Rogers

COLN ST ALDWYNS (1-2 J10) *2½ mi. N Fairford.* This delightful village has a much restored church and an Elizabethan manor house looking over the clear waters of the Coln to beech-woods beyond. The interior of the church was heavily restored in the mid-19th century and is rather dull, but there are a number of beautifully sculptured tombstones beneath trees in the churchyard. John Keble, father of the famous John Keble, was vicar here from 1782 to 1835, and young John was his curate during the last ten of these years. Memorial windows in the church recall these connections. Do not miss a visit to the charming New Inn where fan-tail doves are usually to be found in its yard, and a friendly welcome within. The course of the Roman **Akeman Street** passes just to the north of the village, but there is no right-of-way along it here. However, it is possible to walk beside the little River Coln, upstream to **Bibury,** or downstream to **Quenington.**

COLN ST DENNIS (1-2 H9) *3 mi. NW Bibury.* Prettily sited village, with a tall-towered Norman church looking out across water-meadows bordering the clear-watered Coln. Apart from its very top, even the central tower is Norman, and the west tower arch, although under great stress, still survives intact (the east tower arch had to be rebuilt when the tower's top was added in the 15th century). Do not miss the weird collection of Norman corbel

Beside the Coln at Coln St Aldwyns

figures supporting the nave roof, nor the very attractive 18th-century wall-monuments.

COMBE (1 G15) *2 mi. W Woodstock.* Attractive village to the west of **Blenheim Park**, with the pretty Cockerel Inn looking across a wide, tree-shaded green towards the church. This is a delightful little building with a vaulted north porch and a Perpendicular doorway opening onto old stone-flagged floors. Inside are a medieval stone pulpit built into a wall, a beautifully carved 15th-century font, triple sedilia and a richly coloured 'Doom' wall-painting.

Coln St Dennis Church

Enthusiasts have lovingly restored an original mid-19th century sawmill with beam engine at Combe Mill on the nearby River Evenlode, and this is put in steam for visitors on several weekends in the summer. There is also a working blacksmith's forge and a patternmaker's shop.

COMPTON ABDALE (1-2 G8) *3 mi. W Northleach.* Small village in a deep valley, with a church built into a steep bank overlooking its crossroads. This has a finely pinnacled and gargoyled Perpendicular tower, but the rest, including its interior, was over-restored in the late 19th and early 20th centuries. Below the churchyard there is a little stone 'crocodile' from where a spring gushes out, to flow down beside the road on its way to join the Coln at **Cassey Compton.** There is a good walk south-eastwards from here, over the hills to **Yanworth,** then along the wooded Coln Valley to **Cassey Compton,** before returning to Compton Abdale.

COMPTON WYNYATES (1 B13) *4 mi. E Shipston-on-Stour.* A beautiful Tudor mansion of mellow brick in a lovely setting amongst wooded hillsides. The unusual occurrence of brick in this predominantly stone countryside is probably accounted for by King Henry's gift to William Compton, of the ruined castle of Fulbroke, near Warwick, and Sir William's subsequent use of the salvaged materials at Compton Wynyates. Royal visitors included not only Henry VIII, but also Elizabeth I, James I and Charles I.

Compton Abdale

Most of the moat was filled in at the end of the Civil War, and the once famous clipped Yews have gone long ago. The house is no longer open to the public, and there are only distant glimpses of it from the neighbouring countryside. On the skyline behind the house there is a stone tower-windmill complete with sails, and this can be reached by a path that starts from a tree-lined track off a minor road well to the north-east of the house. It is possible to walk down the other side of the hill on which it stands, into Upper Tysoe. Compton Pike, well to the south-west of the house, looks like the top of a spire peering over the edge of the hillside until it is encountered close by. Only then is it revealed as a short, sharp, pyramid-like structure. Was it built to confuse and amuse, or was it the base of a beacon? Opinions on this remain divided.

CONDICOTE (1 D10) *3 mi. NW Stow-on-the-Wold.* A quiet upland village lying just to the east of the Romans' **Ryknild Street,** the section south of here being known as Condicote Lane. The village is centred upon a large rough green encircled by young trees and which in spring is bright with daffodils. It is overlooked by a 14th-century

wayside cross, four handsome farmhouses and a little Norman church. Unfortunately this was heavily 'restored' in 1888 when the walls were ruthlessly scraped and repointed. However, the Norman south doorway with its patterned tympanum was left largely undisturbed, and there is an interesting little figure beneath the 13th-century piscina. The small earthworks on the east side of the village, marked 'henge' on the Ordnance Survey's Landranger map, are thought to be the remains of a Bronze Age ceremonial site. It

Wayside Cross, Condicote

is possible to walk south from here along the course of the **Ryknild Street,** now mostly a grass-grown track, almost to **Upper Slaughter.** There is a pleasant return route from the latter through part of **Eyford Park,** making use of minor roads in the final stage back to Condicote.

COOPER'S HILL (1-2 G5) *5 mi. SE Gloucester.* This great spur jutting out from the Cotswold edge is now within a 137-acre nature reserve. There is an interesting 2-mile nature trail starting from the now much restricted Fiddler's Elbow Car Park on the A46, up through beech-woods and over open grassland, and leading finally to a maypole at the top. There are fine views from here over the Severn Valley, and the maypole marks the point where the famous cheese-rolling races start. These are held on Spring Bank Holiday Mondays and consist of dangerous chases after seven-pound wooden discs, representing cheeses, down a 200-yard, 1-in-1 slope, each winner being rewarded with a real cheese. There are many other quaint side-events including dancing, wrestling and such bucolic fun as face-pulling through a horse-collar!

CORNBURY PARK (1-2 G14) *1 mi. SW Charlbury.* Splendid 600-acre deer park occupying the north-eastern sector of **Wychwood Forest,** with great avenues of trees and a chain of lakes. Cornbury House, originally a medieval hunting lodge, is a fine 17th-century mansion, built initially by the great master-mason Nicholas Stone, and completed by Hugh May, Controller of the Royal Works at Windsor Castle. The quarry-owning Timothy Strong of **Taynton**, near Burford, was the contractor. Charles II's Lord Chancellor, the Earl of Clarendon, for whom the house was built, started work on his history of the Great Rebellion here, although he was exiled to France long before its completion. Tantalising glimpses of the 'sweete parke' described by diarist John Evelyn are obtainable from the gates to the immediate south-west of **Charlbury**, and from a footpath starting from the gates and going southwards to Finstock along its eastern fringes. From Finstock it is possible to walk north-westwards across the park on a right-of-way, returning to Charlbury via the hamlets of Chilson and **Shorthampton.**

CORNWELL (1-2 E12) *3 mi. W Chipping Norton.* This delightful little village and its fine manor house were 'discovered' by a wealthy American lady in 1938 when they were both in a very run-down state. Realising the possibilities, she bought the whole estate and at once engaged the outstanding Welsh architect Clough Williams-Ellis to restore it for her. Williams-Ellis added several very personal touches which will remind visitors of his better-known work, the colourful, Italianate village of Portmeirion in North Wales.

There is a small green with a village hall nearby, and a stream overlooked by cottages on slopes beyond. A short distance along the road to Chipping Norton, there is a glimpse through wrought-iron gates of the enchanting manor house, with its handsome 18th-century front concealing an earlier core. Between house and gates are beautiful terraced gardens which were also laid out by Clough Williams-Ellis when he restored the manor. Sadly the American lady's English husband was killed while serving in the Royal Air Force during the War, and neither of them ever lived in the lovely house that they had so imaginatively brought back to life. The small church lies in parkland beyond the village and may be approached by a

Cornwell

signposted path leading off a small road to the north of the village. This low building has a central bell-turret, and a pleasant but heavily restored interior. Do not overlook the font with its base made up of four carved lions. It is possible to walk south-westwards from here, to Daylesford Hill Farm and on to **Oddington,** or north-westwards to **Chastleton.**

COTSWOLD FARM PARK (1-2 E9) *5 mi. W Stow-on-the-Wold.* A unique collection of rare breeds of British farm livestock displayed in a beautiful farm setting in high wold country, with pets and baby animals on show for the benefit of younger children. This is the creation of Cotswold farmer, Joe Henson, an outstanding pioneer in the preservation of rare breeds, and someone to whom we all owe a great deal. There is an adventure playground, farm trail, restaurant, gift shop and education centre.

THE COTSWOLD VILLAGE TRAIL (Not shown on map). A 90 mile trail created by Nigel Bailey from **Mickleton** in the North to **Westonbirt** in the South.

COTSWOLD WATER PARK (2 L8) *Approximately 5 mi. S Cirencester.* (Not shown on map.) This very extensive leisure facility already consists of about a hundred lakes in two distinct areas - the first between Kemble and Cricklade, and the second between Fairford and Lechlade. Now described in a colourful leaflet as '30 Square Miles of Adventure', they are the result of about sixty years of gravel extraction in this part of the Upper Thames Valley, a process which is still continuing.

Details of the varied leisure facilities that the park has to offer, summarised in the invaluable leaflet with map, are available at the Keynes Country Park Information Centre, to the east of **Somerford Keynes.** In addition to bird-watching these facilities include game and coarse fishing, board sailing, lakeside walking, picnics, rowing boat,

Moorhen

pedalo and canoe hire, motor boat racing, water skiing, caravanning and camping, and horse riding. It is, of course, the number of lakes and the distance between most of them that allow these very varied activities to take place without seriously impinging upon each other. For this reason many of these lakes now provide a significant wetland habitat, and in winter offer splendid opportunities for birdwatchers who come to spot the great quantities of wildfowl which migrate here. There are also three Nature Reserves within the park.

THE COTSWOLD WAY (Not shown on map.) This long-distance footpath follows the Cotswold edge country for about 100 miles between Bath and Chipping Campden. It provides a strenuous walk taking between seven and nine days, although many people will wish to tackle portions of the route on separate days, especially if they have young families. Most of the route runs through the area covered by this guide. Both Mark Richard's guide to the *Cotswold Way* and *the Cotswold Way* Movie, along with a *Cotswold Way* maps are invaluable companions on this challenging and most interesting walk, with its splendid views over the valleys of the Avon and Severn, and the hill country beyond. If you are interested in the Cotswold Way then please contact *Reardon Publishing the Cotswold Publisher at PO Box 919, Cheltenham GL50 9AN* for a full list of products covering the Cotswold Way including guides, maps, movies, prints and post cards or visit the website *www.reardon.co.uk*

COTSWOLD WILDLIFE PARK (1-2 J12) *3 mi. S Burford.* This is situated in 200 acres of gardens and parkland surrounding Bradwell Grove, an early 19th-century mansion in the Tudor style. It is attractively laid out, and contains a wide variety of animals, the larger of which are to be found in open areas in the wooded park. Smaller animals are displayed in an imaginatively converted walled garden, and there are picnic areas, a narrow-gauge railway, an adventure playground and a licensed restaurant.

COWLEY (1-2 G6) *4½ mi. S Cheltenham.* Small estate village pleasantly sited in the wooded upper reaches of the Coln Valley. Cowley Manor is a 19th-century Italianate

Cowley Manor Gardens

mansion in beautifully maintained grounds, complete with a lake and ornamental ponds. The church, which stands beside the manor, was much restored in the years following the building of its neighbour, and is not of outstanding interest. However, its white-painted interior contains a simple bowl-shaped Norman font, a primitive Perpendicular stone pulpit and the effigy of a 14th-century priest. Several quiet roads radiate from Cowley and there are also walks north-west to **Crickley Hill,** and northwards to **Seven Springs via Coberley**.

CRANHAM (1-2 H5) *6 mi. NE Stroud.* This widespread village lies near the head of a valley running north-eastwards from **Painswick**, and has an extensive common to the south and great beech woodlands to the north and east *(see Cranham Woods).*
Here will be found a friendly little inn, the Black Horse, but also rather too many 'between the wars' bungalows. The largely 15th-century church stands high up, well to the south-east of the village, with fine views over the valley. Interesting features include two pairs of sheep shears carved on the second stage of the tower (a reminder once again of the importance of Cotswold wool in times gone by), and within, an early 16th-century rood screen, a lovely triptych reredos and a handsome monument to Obadiah Done (1758) - *Rector of this parish 57 years.*

CRANHAM WOODS (1-2 H5) *6 mi. NE Stroud.* (Not shown on map.) These splendid woodlands are situated between **Birdlip** and **Prinknash**, and are largely of beech. They include Cranham Wood itself, and also Buckle Wood, Buckholt Wood (much of which is a National Nature Reserve), Witcombe Wood and Brockworth Wood. To explore these woods, it is perhaps best to park at the Fiddler's Elbow Car Park on the A46, Cheltenham to Painswick road, although this has now been much restricted.

CRAWLEY (1-2 H14) *1½ mi. NW Witney.* This hamlet has an inn, a few farms and cottages looking down on its small stream, and an old blanket mill on the Windrush a short distance to its south.

CRICKLADE (2 L9) *7 mi. SE Cirencester.* Small town on the upper reaches of the Thames (not navigable at this point) and just to the west of the Romans' great road, the **Ermin Way.** Its centre stands within the remains of town walls said to have originated in the time of Alfred the Great, although Romano-British pottery has, not surprisingly, been discovered in their foundations. The largely 17th- and 18th-century buildings in the High Street are dominated by the proud tower of St Samson's Church, which was built by the Duke of Northumberland in 1553. This has massive arcading, and impressive vaulting beneath the duke's tower, but the smaller and simpler interior of nearby St Mary's Church is possibly of greater interest. This has an excellent Norman chancel arch and an attractive timbered roof with traceried bordering. The Cricklade Museum in Calcutt Street includes material of social history, Roman and Saxon occupation, and an interesting archive with over 2,000 photographs.

St Samson's Church, Cricklade

It is possible to walk northwards from Cricklade, first beside the infant Thames, then following the course of the old **Thames and Severn Canal to Cerney Wick,** before going westwards to the **Cotswold Water Park.**

CRICKLEY HILL COUNTRY PARK (1-2 G6) *4 mi. S Cheltenham.* 114 acres of grassland and woodland on the Cotswold edge, owned jointly by the Gloucestershire County Council and the National Trust. There are fine views over the Severn Valley, the earthworks of a settlement occupied in both Neolithic and Iron Age times, and nearby, the Devil's Table, an attractive rocky outcrop, which should not be confused with the nearby and more dramatic **Devil's Chimney.** This country park is on the course of the **Cotswold Way** and there are car parks, toilets, picnic areas, walks and information boards.

CUTSDEAN (1 D9) *4½ mi. S Broadway.* Tidy little upland village centred on a wide green on slopes above the infant Windrush, less than a mile below its source at Field Barn, **Taddington.** Its church lies beyond a large farmyard, and is a long narrow Victorian building, with a medieval tower providing the only item of any real interest. Was there an Anglo-Saxon chief called Cod? Did this village take his name, becoming 'Cod's dene'? And did the hill country in which it lies become known as 'Cod's Wold' or Cotswold?. This is a very likely theory, but it will probably always remain unproved. There is no doubt, however, that Cutsdean's setting amongst the high wolds is the very essence of Cotswold country. From here it is possible to walk up the valley to the source of the Windrush at Field Barn, or down it to **Ford** and **Temple Guiting.**

Cutsdean

DAGLINGWORTH (1-2 J7) *3 mi. NW Cirencester.* Modest village strung out along the valley of the little Dunt stream. The manor house is sited at Lower End on its southern side, and has in its garden a fine medieval circular dovecot complete with a revolving ladder giving access to all 500 nesting places. The church and rectory stand well above the rest of the village, to the north. The church, largely rebuilt in the 1840s, has a Saxon doorway, and part of a Roman altar, made into a window by the Saxons. The three carvings set into the walls were rediscovered in 1850 and form a unique and highly satisfying group of primitive Saxon sculpture. See also the interesting Saxon sundial over the doorway, and the fine 15th-century door below. It is possible to walk southwards from here along a track to **Cirencester Park,** or north-westwards up the valley to the lovely little church at **Duntisbourne Rouse.**

Saxon Carving, Daglingworth

DANEWAY (1-2 J6) *5 mi. W Cirencester.* Here, deep in the Frome Valley, was the western end of the **Thames and Severn Canal's** two-mile-long tunnel from **Coates.** The Daneway Inn, like the **Tunnel House Inn** at the Coates end, must have provided

Canal Tunnel Portal, Daneway

countless thousands of pints for the thirsty leggers during the canal's working life between 1789 and 1911. Leggers were the men who had to propel the heavily laden barges through the tunnel by lying along the sides of their decks and pushing with their feet on the tunnel walls. The inn's car park is built on the site of the last of forty-four locks that had to be built between here and Stroud.

Nearby Daneway House, a delightful manor house dating from the 14th century, was used as workshops and showrooms in the early 20th century by the Arts and Crafts furniture makers and disciples of William Morris, Ernest and Sidney Barnsley, and Ernest Gimson. It was let to them by the Earl Bathurst, together with rent-free cottages in **Sapperton,** when he required Pinbury Park (see **Edgeworth**) for his own family. They gathered further artists and craftsmen about them, including Norman Jewson, the architect, and Peter Waals, the Dutch foreman cabinet maker. Read more about this richly productive venture in Norman Jewson's autobiography, *By Chance I did Rove.*

It is possible to walk down beside the still partly water-filled **Thames and Severn Canal** to **Chalford** or eastwards to the sadly decayed western portal of the canal tunnel, and then steeply upwards to **Sapperton.** Ask the landlord of the Daneway Inn if you wish to use his car park - but only if you are eating or drinking here. The park is sometimes too crowded, but permission may usually be obtained.

DARLINGSCOTT (1 B11) *2 mi. NW Shipston-on-Stour.* Minute village, less than two miles to the east of the Cotswold edge, with a pleasant series of Cotswold stone farmhouses and cottages emphasising this proximity. The small church of St George was built as late as 1874, but it has richly carved chancel arch capitals, and other signs of Victorian enthusiasm for carved detail. In 1836, a branch of the **Stratford and Moreton Tramway** was opened, to run between Darlingscott and **Shipston-on-Stour.** Much of its course may still be traced to the south of the village.

Walk west from Darlingscott, across the fields past Southfield, up near Windmill Hill, and down the drive passing **Foxcote House**, towards **Ebrington**, to sample the unique flavour of the Cotswolds' north-eastern fringes.

DAYLESFORD (1-2 E12) *4 mi. E Stow-on-the-Wold.* Small estate village at the gates of Daylesford House, money from which must have paid for the building of the small but splendidly elaborate Victorian church. This was designed by J.L.Pearson, best known as the architect of Truro Cathedral. See especially Pearson's pretty tub-shaped pulpit, the brass to William Gardiner (1632) and the elegant monument outside the east window, simply inscribed 'Warren Hastings 1818'.

Born at nearby Churchill in 1732, Hastings had always hoped to buy back the family estate at Daylesford, and in 1787, four years after retiring from his controversial career as Governor of the East India Company's Bengal, he was able to do so. So, not anticipating the eventually crippling expense of defending himself during his seven-year-long trial in the House of Lords, he soon set about building a fine mansion to the design of Samuel Pepys Cockerell, architect to the East India Company, and later the architect of better-known Sezincote. Unlike Sezincote, Daylesford is almost entirely classical, and only has a central dome in the Muslim style. It is surrounded by dense woodland, but in winter it is just visible from the public road a few yards south-east of Daylesford village. It is possible to walk around the outer boundaries of the estate, either from **Oddington, Adlestrop** or **Cornwell,** but in summer there are no views of the house even from the paths followed.

DEAN (1-2 F13) *3 mi. SE Chipping Norton.* Unspoilt hamlet on the upper slopes of a small valley running south to the Evenlode. There is a fine manor house amongst trees above the road and a bridleway running north-north-east across high downland country to **Lidstone.**

Dean Hamlet

DEDDINGTON (1 D16) *6 mi. S Banbury.* A trim ironstone village, much of which is astride the busy A4260, Banbury to Oxford road. The grassy ramparts are all that remain of a large medieval motte and bailey castle. It was here, on June 10th 1312, that Edward II's favourite, Piers Gaveston, already a prisoner of the Earl of Pembroke, was seized by the Earl of Warwick, who Gaveston had rather unwisely nicknamed `the black cur of Arden'. The prisoner was then taken on mule-back to Warwick Castle and on July 1st was beheaded on nearby Blacklow Hill.

The fine Decorated and Perpendicular style church lies between the castle mound and the main road. It has a well proportioned interior, with clerestory windows and a window over the chancel arch, all 15th-century work. The contents of the interior is not of outstanding interest, but do not miss the Jacobean pulpit, nor the small 14th century brass.

Sir Thomas Pope, founder of Trinity College, Oxford, friend of Sir Thomas More, and one time guardian of the young queen-to-be, Elizabeth, was born at Deddington in 1508. He is buried in Trinity College chapel. Other pleasant old buildings in Deddington include the little Town Hall (for this was a market town until the 18th century), the Jacobean Kings Arms, and the 18th century Three Tuns.

DEERHURST (1 D5) *4½ mi. SW Tewkesbury.* This small village, with its orchards and timber-framed cottages, and its setting in fields just beyond the high banks of the River Severn, is rather far removed from the Cotswolds. However, its church, one of the oldest in England, is one of the few largely Anglo-Saxon buildings to have survived and is well worth visiting. It was part of a monastery founded in the 8th or 9th century, and there are fragmentary clues to the existence of a cloister. There are no fewer than thirty Anglo-Saxon doorways and windows to be seen, together with a late 9th-century font, interesting 15th- and 16th-century brasses, and a fine early 17th-century communion rail.

Standing 200 yards to the south-west of the church is a half-timbered farmhouse, at the west end of which is the small Anglo-Saxon Odda's Chapel (in the care of English Heritage). Thanks to the discovery of an inscribed stone, we know that this was built by Earl Odda and was dedicated on 12th April 1065 - an exact dating, which is unique in

Delly End

pre-Conquest building. The nave has survived almost to its full height and is divided from the chancel by an arch.

It is possible to walk from the village over a meadow to the banks of the Severn, and then northwards beside the river to **Tewkesbury,** or south to Apperley and Wainlode Hill.

DELLY END (1-2 H14) *2mi. N Witney*. Pretty hamlet grouped around a well mown green, complete with a domed war memorial on four slender pillars, and overlooked by a series of delectable stone houses including a handsome early Georgian manor house.

DEVIL'S CHIMNEY (1-2 G6) *2 mi. S Cheltenham*. Dramatic limestone pinnacle detached from the Cotswold edge, with splendid views over it to Cheltenham and beyond to the Malvern Hills. It was formed by quarrymen who left it intact when working the large

surrounding quarries, stone from which was used for the building of much of 18th- and 19th-century Cheltenham. It was once a popular challenge for local climbers, who used to leave a coin on the cap for the Devil, and no less than thirteen people once stood on its top. Although now strictly forbidden, this practice combined with natural erosion, has taken its toll to such an extent that nearly £25,000 has had to be spent on repairs in recent years. To reach the Chimney drive south from Cheltenham on the B4070 for about two miles, and fork left on Leckhampton Hill up a steep road. Park on the left after about half a mile and follow the sign to the Devil's Chimney. Because of the extensive quarrying great care should be taken. Some of the path forms part of the **Cotswold Way** and from here it is possible to walk eastwards along Charlton Kings Common, and then south to **Seven Springs.** There is also a small car park at the foot of the hill, reached by a short road to the east of the B4070. This park is just beyond Tramway Cottage, reminding visitors that it is close to the

Devil's Chimney

course of the gravity-worked tramway which once carried stone from the great quarries above. Opened in 1798, this was the very first railway on the Cotswolds.

Didbrook Church

DIDBROOK (1 D8) *3 mi. NE Winchcombe*. Small village below the Cotswold edge with a pleasant mixture of timber and stone in its buildings - see especially several examples of 'cruck' construction in various cottage ends, these possibly dating back to the 15th century. The church was rebuilt about 1475 by William Whitchurch, the abbot of nearby **Hailes,** and is wholly Perpendicular in style. Note the lovely old roof, and the various wood furnishings, including benches, family pew, lectern, pulpit and communion rail. The descent of the tower into the nave, with its three open arches, is most unusual. It is possible to walk south from Didbrook, over the fields to **Hailes Abbey,** then up a track and left to **Beckbury Camp,** and return via Stumps Cross and **Wood Stanway** - a fine circular walk using the Ordnance Survey's Landranger Map 150.

DIDMARTON (2 M4) *6 Mi. SW Tetbury.* Handsome stone village astride the busy A433, with a Victorian church which has a few interesting monuments and a fascinating medieval one, which has a completely unspoilt 18th-century interior. Here will be found a fine three-decker pulpit, high-backed pews and a number of wall monuments of the same period. There are two reredos here, both incorporating the Ten Commandments, the Lord's Prayer, and the Creed, one behind the altar and a spare one at the west end. There is an attractive minor road leading southwards through part of Badminton's parklands to **Little and Great Badminton.**

DITCHLEY PARK (1 F15) *4¹/₂ Mi. NW Woodstock.* A splendid mansion in a 300-acre park, complete with pleasant gardens, a lake, temples and woodlands. The house, which by coincidence lies on the exact course of the Iron Age **Grim's Ditch**, was designed in the 1770s by James Gibbs, the architect of St Martin-in-the-Fields, with interior decorations by William Kent. Ditchley was the weekend headquarters of Winston Churchill during the Second World War, and it is now an international conference centre. There is an attractive approach road running from the A3400 at Over Kiddington, but the more usual approach is from the north-eastern end of **Charlbury.**

Ditchley Park

DIXTON (1 D7) *2¹/₂ mi. NW Winchcombe.* Hamlet below the Cotswold edge with a fine 16th-century gabled manor house and, above it, the earthworks of a probable Iron Age settlement on Dixton Hill. Walk south from here, up over Nottingham Hill (the site of another Iron Age settlement) to **Cleeve Hill**.

DONNINGTON (1 D11) *1¹/₂ mi. N Stow-on-the-Wold.* There are fine views over the Evenlode Valley from this modest hamlet in the hills. It was here that Lord Astley, with 3000 Royalist troops, surrendered to the Parliamentarians on 21 March 1646, in the final defeat of the long and bitter Civil War. Sitting dejected amongst his captors at the end of the battle the weary Lord Astley was heard to say, *'Gentlemen, yee may now sit downe and play, for you have done all your worke, if you do not fall out among yourselves.'*

Donnington Brewery

Over a mile to the west, beyond the A424, lies Donnington Brewery. Although not open to visitors this must surely be Britain's most delectable brewery. The accompanying lake, or mill pond, is the source of the little River Dikler, and its waters still turn a great mill-wheel. Donnington Brewery owns a fair number of inns, all in and around the Cotswolds, and was brewing real ale long after the large breweries ceased to do so, and long before the Campaign for Real Ale forced many of them to resume. It is a truly Cotswold undertaking, with these inns always appearing to add to, rather than detract from, the charm of the towns and villages in which they are situated. If you appreciate real ale, keep an eye open for Donnington's well painted inn signs. Not far to the west of the brewery, on the road towards Condicote, the Donnington Fish Farm is largely concerned with the rearing of rainbow trout. Visitors may see trout at various stages of development, feed the larger fish, purchase fresh or smoked trout, and fly-fish in a small lake.

THE DONNINGTON WAY (Not shown on map.) This long-distance footpath links all the Donnington Inns giving the walker an 82 mile route around the Cotswolds.

DOUGHTON (2 L5) *2 mi. SW Tetbury.* A hamlet astride the busy A433 with a number of 17th- and 18th-century stone houses having a feel of Wiltshire about them; Doughton is in Gloucestershire, but the Wiltshire border is only about two miles to the south. Handsome 18th-century Highgrove House, standing in a modest park to the immediate west of the hamlet and not visible from the road, was built for the Paul family, wealthy clothiers of Huguenot descent, one of whom, Sir George Onesiphorus Paul, became a noted prison reformer (see also **Northleach, Rodborough** and **Woodchester**). Highgrove House is the country home of the Prince of Wales.

DOVER'S HILL (1 B10) *1 mi. NW Chipping Campden.* This is a delightful crescent-shaped field-walk poised on the very edge of the Cotswold scarp, and was acquired by the National Trust in 1928, thanks to the efforts of Chipping Campden's F.L.Griggs, and to the generosity of that great historian, G.M.Trevelyan. There is a small car park here, and one can walk along the hillside, down into the edge of dense woodland below, or even back down to **Chipping Campden** on a footpath, which is part of the **Cotswold Way.** On a clear day views over the Avon Valley and the Midland Plain extend to Bredon, the Malverns, and the distant outlines of the Black Mountains and Shropshire's Long Mynd. Identification of these distant hills is made easier and more interesting by a well engraved viewing topograph not far beyond the car park.

Dover's Hill was the site of the famous 'Cotswold Olympicks'. They were founded in 1612 by local lawyer Robert Dover with the approval of James I, the monarch having been approached through Dover's friend at Court, Endymion Porter, who lived at nearby **Aston Subedge.** These games, then held on the Thursday and Friday after Whit Sunday, included the usual horse racing, hare coursing, dancing and wrestling, but there were also two essentially local contests of a more violent nature: single-stick fighting, in which the contestants fought with one arm tied behind their backs, sometimes for hours at a time, with the sole intention of 'breaking the other's head'; and shin-kicking, the purpose of which was to reduce one's opponent to such agonies that he was forced to concede defeat. The more enthusiastic shin-kickers used to 'harden up' by beating their own shins with planks, or even in extreme cases with hammers, in the weeks prior to the games.

Although temporarily suppressed during the Cromwellian period, the games were otherwise held regularly each year until the mid-19th century. By this time they had become the scene of considerable violence and drunkenness, a situation greatly worsened by the presence of Irish navvies, who were then building the nearby **Campden Railway Tunnel,** and they were discontinued in 1853, following an Act of Parliament enclosing the land. In 1951 the games were again revived, and since then they have been held each year on the Friday following the Spring Bank Holiday, followed on the Saturday by the Scuttlebrook Wake, a colourful fair which culminates in a torch-light procession from Dover's Hill back down into Chipping Campden.

DOWDESWELL (1-2 F7) *3 mi. E Cheltenham.* This small village is pleasantly situated on a hillside, happily just far enough away from the busy A40 to avoid its noise. The cruciform church, with its small stone spire, is situated below the road, beside a Tudor farmhouse. It has two mid-19th-century galleries within, one for the use of the manor and one for the rectory. Do not miss the 16th-century brass of a priest, nor the handsome monument on the chancel wall, to William Rogers (1734).

Dowdeswell Church

The A40 road beside Dowdeswell Reservoir is one of the few places in Britain where the writer has seen a notice declaring 'Drivers beware - toads crossing road'. This road-crossing apparently forms part of a regular migratory route and efforts are being made to save as many as possible of this increasingly threatened species. **The Cotswold Way** crosses the A40 just below the reservoir dam on its way between **Cleeve Hill** and the **Devil's Chimney.**

DOWN AMPNEY *(2 L9) 5 mi. SE Cirencester.* A long straggling village in flat countryside about two miles north of the Thames, with only two buildings of any real interest, both of which lie quietly amongst trees at its southern end - the cruciform church and nearby Down Ampney House. The church has a fine 14th-century spire and a large porch about a hundred years younger. The interior was richly restored, perhaps over-restored, at the start of the 20th century, but it contains a number of items which should not be missed. Amongst these are the effigies of a knight (in black marble) and a lady (in stone) in the south transept, a 17th-century monument to two knights of the Hungerford family, Sir John and Sir Anthony, acting as a reredos in the north transept, and the excellent copy of Giorgione's *Madonna of Castel Franco.* There is a stained-glass window in memory of the many young airmen who flew from the nearby airfield, and who sadly did not return. Standing beside the church is Down Ampney House, the fine 15th-century manor house of the Hungerford family, which was embellished by Sir John Soane in 1799.

Monument at Down Ampney

The composer Ralph Vaughan Williams was born in the village in 1872, the son of its vicar, and he spent the first three years of his life at what is now the old vicarage. He named his best-known hymn *Down Ampney*, in memory of his childhood years here.

DRAYCOTT *(1 C10) 3 mi. SE Chipping Campden.* An expanding hamlet lying in a broad valley overlooked by low wooded hills, with an attractive row of cottages leading to a small 18th-century farmhouse. Walk southwards from here, up the fields to the road above **Batsford Park,** and then down again to **Blockley.**

DRIFFIELD *(1-2 K9) 3 mi. E Cirencester.* Small village with pleasantly noisy duckpond, and a church which was rebuilt in 1734 and heavily restored in 1836, almost certainly by the redoubtable Victorian architect, William Butterfield, perhaps best known for his design for Keble College, Oxford. Do not miss the inscription to George Hanger, Lord Coleraine, whose gambling debts almost certainly explain the odd high-walled garden nearby: this was part of a mansion sold to pay his debts and subsequently demolished. The inscription reads: *He lived and died a firm believer in one God and in one God only. He was also a practical Christian as far as his frail nature did allow him to be so.* But this statement appears to have been over-charitable to a rake whose eccentric manner, according to another source, became *too free and coarse even for the Prince Regent.* In fear of the Devil, he asked to be 'buried' above ground, but he was eventually interred beneath the organ.

DUNS TEW *(1 D16) 7 mi. N Woodstock.* A tidy stone and thatch village with a character inn called the White Horse and a delicious circular dovecot, which was covered with climbing roses when we last passed this way. The church, with its large squat tower, stands beside a fine manor house in a rose-decked churchyard with two pretty, early-19th-century tombstones near the south door. However, the interior has been over-restored and is not of great interest apart from some sculptured figures on corbels and arcade capitals. Walk south-westwards from here, to **Middle Barton** and loop round northwards via **Sandford St Martin, Ledwell** and **Over Worton.**

DUNTISBOURNE ABBOTS (1-2 J6) *5 mi. NW Cirencester.* Situated in the valley of the little Dunt stream, this small but very trim village once belonged to the abbots of Gloucester - hence its name. Dating back to Norman times, the church has a low saddleback-roofed tower. The chancel has been restored since the Second World War - white painted and very pleasant - but the rest is still scraped and rather severe, a legacy of its earlier 'restoration' in 1872. There is a Youth Hostel nearby. The Hoar Stone Long

Duntisbourne Abbots

Barrow, with the Hoar Stone itself at its eastern end, is situated close to a road about a mile to the south of the village.

DUNTISBOURNE LEER (1-2 J6) *4½ mi. NW Cirencester.* The unusual name of this hamlet in the Dunt Valley is derived from the abbey of Lire in far off Normandy, to which it belonged until 1416, when it was given to Cirencester Abbey. There are two farmhouses and attendant buildings, all attractively grouped around a ford.

DUNTISBOURNE ROUSE (1-2 J7) 4 mi. NW Cirencester. Here is a delightful, largely Norman church, still displaying evidence of its Saxon origins, and standing in a sloping churchyard overlooking the Dunt stream, with a fine 14th-century cross for company. Like Duntisbourne Abbots it has a saddleback roof to its tower, and it has a charming interior complete with box pews, octagonal Norman font, stalls in the chancel (with misericords which probably came from Cirencester Abbey), and medieval paintings upon its north chancel wall. It is built upon such a steep slope that there is a crypt at its eastern end - a most unusual feature in so small a church.

Duntisbourne Rouse lies on the **Macmillan Way** and this can be followed eastwards and then south to **Sapperton** There is also a pleasant walk above woodlands on the east side of the Dunt valley down to **Daglingworth.**

DURSLEY (2 K2) *8 mi. SW Stroud.* Busy market town beneath the Cotswold edge, with extensive industry which has replaced its long-vanished cloth trade. It is centred upon a delightful 18th-century market house, which also acts as the Town Hall, and which displays an elegant statue of Queen Anne in a niche well above its arcading. The nearby church has a beautifully vaulted Perpendicular porch, but its interior was over-restored in the 19th century. However, it has a most impressive tower, which was rebuilt in the Gothic style in the early years of the 18th century after most of the earlier tower and spire had collapsed in 1698. Part of Stinchcombe Hill, about a mile to the west of the town, is used as a golf course, but there is parking space for cars, with good

Town Hall, Dursley

walking opportunities and fine views over the Berkeley Vale, especially from Drakestone Point. This is on the course of the **Cotswold Way,** which may be followed south from here to **North Nibley** and **Wootton-under-Edge.**

DYRHAM (2 P2) *4 mi. S Chipping Sodbury.* In the care of the National Trust, this fine early 18th-century mansion nestles beneath the Cotswold edge overlooking the Severn Valley. It is approached by a long drive winding down through a great park in which fallow deer roam. This highly romantic setting introduces the visitor to a house that contains furniture and pictures, the majority of which have been there since it was built for William Blaythwayt, Secretary at War and Secretary of State to William III between 1691 and 1710. The east front looks up to the deer park while the west front looks over a garden with lawns, flower borders and a pool, all of which is also overlooked by an interesting little medieval

Dyrham

church. Almost joined on to the north wing of the house, this has much plain glass and light woodwork, a fine Jacobean pulpit, brasses of a knight and his lady and an impressive late 16th-century monument to George Wynter and his wife. Dyrham's fine park may be visited all through the year while the mansion (together with restaurant and shop) is open during spring, summer and autumn.

EASTINGTON, near Northleach (1-2 H10) *1 mi. SE Northleach.* Hamlet in a bowl-like setting in the wolds, with the little River Leach flowing beside the road. There are fine barns and a small mid-Victorian chapel on a slope overlooking the valley. At Upper End, half a mile to the north-east, are a lovely 15th-century manor house and a circular dovecot, both of which belonged to Gloucester Abbey before the Dissolution. There is a pleasant road running south-eastwards from Eastington, beside the beech-woods of **Lodge Park** and on over open country to **Aldsworth.** It is possible to walk up the valley of the little River Leach to **Northleach** and onwards to this river's source at Hampnett, which lies astride the **Macmillan Way.**

Eastington Church

EASTINGTON, near Stonehouse (2 J3) *2 mi. W Stonehouse.* A rather scrappy village nearer the M5 motorway than the Cotswold edge. However the church lies well away to the north-east, in a large churchyard bordering on the River Frome, with flowering cherries on its banks. It has a 14th-century tower but is otherwise almost entirely Perpendicular, with a handsome south aisle added by the Duke of Buckingham of Thornbury Castle shortly before his execution in 1521. This is a building full of interest, further enriched by the work of three of our favourite 20th-century restorers: Sir Ninian Comper, S.E. Dykes-Bower and F.C.Eden.

*Kings Head,
Eastington Church*

EASTLEACH MARTIN and **EASTLEACH TURVILLE** (1-2 J11) *4 mi. N Lechlade.* Here are two parish churches looking at each other across the clear waters of the little River Leach. Today Turville is by far the larger of the two settlements, but Martin has the larger church. Founded by one of William the Conqueror's knights, Richard Fitzpons, this still has a few of its original Norman features, including the south doorway and the supporting piers of the chancel arch. However, one of its best features is the 14th-century north transept with its three beautiful Decorated-style windows. Turville's church, although smaller than Martin's, is even more interesting, with an early 14th-century saddleback tower and a Norman tympanum over the south doorway. Inside the largely 13th-century interior will be found a fine canopied tomb and a pleasing pulpit, reading desk and lectern.

Footbridge at Eastleach

Be sure to spend time wandering up the slopes of Turville, past the war memorial, as far as the friendly little Victoria Inn, and back down again to cross the stone footbridge to return to Martin. This is known as Keble Bridge, probably due to the lordship of the manor of Turville being held by the Kebles in the 16th and 17th centuries, and not because the better-known John Keble held the curacy of the two parishes as a mere non-resident in the 19th century.

Come here in early spring to find the banks of the Leach scattered with daffodils, but avoid Sundays if possible, as this spot then tends to be much visited by local motorists. The road southwards from Martin to **Southrop** is open to the Leach in places, but to enjoy this delightful valley to the full take the footpath southwards from Turville, also to **Southrop.** However, the finest walk from Turville is that up the valley of the Leach to the point where it is crossed by the **Akeman Street,** and over Macaroni Downs to Ladbarrow Farm and beyond to **Windrush.** See Ordnance Survey Landranger Sheet 163 for details.

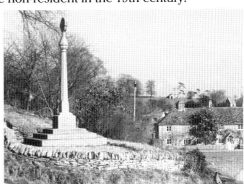
War Memorial at Eastleach

EBRINGTON (1 B11) *2 mi. E Chipping Campden.* A beautiful village overlooking a valley, through which the little Knee Brook flows on its way to join the Stour above **Shipston-on-Stour.** 'Yubberton', as many of the locals still call it, has many attractively thatched stone cottages lining its little sunken roads leading to the centre, which is overlooked by a war memorial and the handsomely signed Ebrington Arms. The church stands on a small ridge above the rest of the village close to the largely 17th-century manor house. It has a good solid tower and a Norman south doorway with a geometric design upon its tympanum, rather similar in style to the one at **Great Rollright.** Inside the church there are a few medieval bench-ends, a large, heavily restored pulpit dated 1679, and a charming little medieval glass roundel illustrating the month of October - probably one of a series of twelve - with a jaunty peasant sowing grain. The whole interior has been over-restored, but there are several fine monuments to members of the Keyte and Fortescue families. See especially the monument to Sir John Fortescue, who was Lord Chief Justice of England during some of the most troubled years of the Wars of the Roses. Despite a reversal of his fortunes following the defeat of the Lancastrians at Tewkesbury in 1471, he was allowed a gentle retirement at

Ebrington

Ebrington until his death some years later, at the age of ninety. This was most unusual in an age when defeated enemies were usually dispatched with the utmost brutality. The two 17th-century Keyte monuments are equally interesting and we particularly like the notice reading, *William Keyte Esq., A.D. 1632, left by will the milk of ten good and sufficient kine to the poor of Ebrington from May 10th - November 1st for ever.* It is sad to read a note below which indicates that *This charge was redeemed 1952;* no doubt a practical step, but how dull! William Keyte's son, Sir John Keyte, must also have been a man of substance, as it is known that he raised a troop of horse 'at his own expense' in support of his sovereign, during the Civil War.

The best walk from Ebrington leads north-eastwards, past **Foxcote House** to **Ilmington,** returning via Nebsworth and Ebrington Hill. Links may also be made to the road northwards over **Lark Stoke,** or across to **Hidcote.** All these walks are over windy, often open wold country, with fine views over the Midland plain, the Northamptonshire uplands and the hills on the borders of Oxfordshire on the distant skyline.

EDGE (1-2 H4) *3 mi. N Stroud.* Small village with views westwards over the Severn Valley, and eastwards to **Painswick.** Its modest Victorian church has a neat little stone spire, but is otherwise unexceptional. There was at least one cloth mill here until the early 19th century. Beatrix Potter used to visit friends at Harescombe Grange, just to the north of the village, and it was while staying here that she was inspired to write her delightful story, *The Tailor of Gloucester* (see **Gloucester** for the House of the Tailor of Gloucester). Walk south-west from Edge and then west, along the Cotswold edge to **Haresfield Beacon,** following part of the **Cotswold Way.**

EDGEHILL (1 A14) *7 mi. NW Banbury.* Small village just behind the scarp face from which it takes its name. There are two buildings of interest, a thatched cottage, and a 'castle'. Both are the work of Sanderson Miller, 18th-century gentleman architect, and squire of neighbouring **Radway** and are, like many of his buildings, in the Gothic style. The 'castle', which is now a lively inn, was built on the point where Charles I's standard was raised on Sunday morning, 23rd October in the year 1642, at the start of the first major battle of the Civil War. The Parliamentary forces under the Earl of Essex, had come from the north and west, and the Royalists from the south and east, and on that fateful Sunday morning they were facing each other across the broad country that lies between Kineton and Edgehill, with the Parliamentarians based on Kineton and the Royalists on Edgehill. Initially it appeared that the Royalist cavalry, under the command of the King's nephew, Prince Rupert, had triumphed, but much impetus was lost

Castle Inn, Edgehill

while Rupert's undisciplined horsemen plundered the baggage train of the Parliamentarian commanders in Kineton. Edgehill's results were therefore not as decisive as they might have been, and although there were heavy casualties on both sides, the two armies withdrew at the end of the day, both remaining as effective fighting forces. The actual site of the battle is now largely in the hands of the Ministry of Defence, but there is a small modern monument beside the road to Kineton. Good views over the country where the battle must have raged may be had from the garden of the Castle Inn, or from the bottom of the woods that clothe part of Edgehill's slopes. These woods were planted by Sanderson Miller, along the upper edge of his park at **Radway.**

There are two paths down through these woods to **Radway,** and together they make a delightful circular walk. It is also possible to follow part of the **Macmillan Way** along the top of the woods to Sun Rising Hill, where there is a convenient layby on the A422, Banbury to Stratford road.

The 17th-century diarist Celia Fiennes, coming to see Edgehill in about 1690, wrote *where was the famous Battle fought in Cromwell's tyme, the ridge of hills runns a great length and so high that the land beneath it appears vastly distant ... tho formidable to look down on it and turnes ones head round, the wind allwayes blows with great volience there*. It happily remains very much the same to this day.

Tombstones at Edgeworth

EDGEWORTH (1-2 J6) *5 mi. NW Cirencester*. Here are a church and a manor house looking down over wooded slopes into the deep valley of the little River Frome. The church has retained certain evidence of its Saxon origins, and its Norman features include a south doorway and much of the chancel. The interior has been over-restored, but there are a few 15th-century bench-ends with poppy heads, and the medieval stained glass featuring a bishop should not be missed. There is a medieval cross in the churchyard, which overlooks the valley. The nearby Jacobean manor house was much restored and enlarged in the 19th century, but remains an enviably beautiful building. The stables are topped by a pretty little bellcote which overlooks the adjoining churchyard.

Pinbury Park, an idyllic manor house on the eastern slopes of the valley between here and **Daneway,** was once the home of the noted Gloucestershire county historian, Sir Robert Atkyns, who is buried at **Sapperton.** In the early years of the 20th century it was let by the Earl Bathurst to the Arts and Crafts Movement's Ernest Gimson and the Barnsley brothers, who had workshops in the adjoining buildings. On Pinbury being required by Lord Bathurst for his family, he let **Daneway** to them for their workshops and showrooms, and allowed them to build cottages for themselves at **Sapperton.** The Ordnance Survey's Landranger Sheet 163 will reveal a wealth of walks in this outstandingly beautiful area with its deep valleys and great beech-woods.

ELKSTONE (1-2 H6) *6 mi. S Cheltenham*. This small, rather undistinguished village is relieved by both its handsome 18th-century rectory and its exceptionally interesting church. Standing in a churchyard with pleasant table tombs, this has a fine Perpendicular west tower, but it is the fascinating corbel figures around the outside of the nave, and the splendid tympanum over the south doorway, that provide an introduction to what must be the best-preserved Norman church in the Cotswolds. Inside will be found a beautiful little vaulted Norman chancel with a wealth of fine

Chest Tomb, Elkstone

architectural detail. There are also box pews and good 17th-century furnishings including pulpit, reading desk and communion rails. Do not miss this remarkable little church.

ENSTONE (1-2 E14) *4 mi. SE Chipping Norton.* Church Enstone and Neat Enstone face each other across the valley of the little River Glyme. The old Litchfield Arms in Neat Enstone, one a prosperous coaching inn on the busy Oxford road, is now no more, having been replaced by a housing estate. Fashionable visitors once came to Enstone to visit 'Queen Henrietta's Waterworks', a grotto with springs, waterfall, a banquet hall and the inevitable hired 'hermit'. This was established here in 1636 and survived with varying fortunes until the close of the 18th century. Sadly there is now no trace of *the famous wells* - etc. described by the diarist John Evelyn in 1664. Despite partial relief by the M40, traffic continues to thunder through Neat Enstone, but fortunately Church Enstone lies well away from the busy A44. It is prettily sited on slopes above the Glyme, with an attractive inn, the Crown by a little road lined with cottages leading up to the church. This has retained its character well and is full of interest. See especially the fine Norman south doorway, the 15th-century porch and the touching monument to Stevens Wisdom in the south aisle.

To the south of Neat Enstone, set in bushes behind a cross-roads where a minor road to Ditchley crosses the B4022, is the Hoar Stone. This is a burial chamber dating from about 2000BC and consisting of three great stones, the largest being nine feet high. At one time this must all have been covered by a large mound to form a round barrow, but no trace of the mound remains.

ERMIN WAY (1-2 J7 etc.) (Not shown on map.) A Roman road which extended from Silchester, near Reading, through **Cricklade** and **Cirencester,** to the legionary fortress at **Gloucester.** Modern dual-carriageway roads still follow its straight course across the Cotswolds, now bypassing almost every town and village.

EUBURY CAMP (1 D10) *To NE of Condicote.* (Not shown on map.) Crescent-shaped earthworks in pleasant wold country just beyond **Condicote**. The Camp is possibly the remains of an Iron Age settlement, although its origins are far from clear.

EVENLODE (1 D11) *2 mi. SE Moreton-in-Marsh.* Lying in the broad valley of the River Evenlode, this scattered village has a Georgian rectory and several substantial farmhouses, one with pretty Gothic windows. The attractive church lies on the western edge of the village in a churchyard containing several interesting 18th- and 19th-century tombs. It has a fine late Norman chancel arch with a mason's mark on its south side, a pleasing rood loft stair and a carved 15th-century pulpit. There are pleasant field paths eastwards to **Chastleton.**

Farmhouse at Evenlode

EVESHAM (1 B8) *16 mi. NE Cheltenham.* Busy market town and centre of the 'Vale of Evesham', noted as one of England's most important market gardening and fruit growing areas. Evesham grew up in early medieval times within the protection of a great loop of the River Avon and owes much of its early prosperity to a swineherd called Eof, who saw a vision of the Virgin Mary, and to Egwin, Bishop of Worcester, who visited the site of the miracle. This event lead to the founding of a Benedictine Abbey in AD714 and from this time onwards pilgrims came in ever increasing numbers to worship at the shrine of St Egwin. Following the defeat of Simon de Montfort and the Barons at the Battle of Evesham in 1265, they also came to pay homage to someone who they came to regard as a martyr for the people. The great abbey, the church of which was as large as Gloucester Cathedral, continued to prosper until the Dissolution in 1539, but the only significant remains are the fine Bell Tower built by the last abbot, Clement Lichfield and the Almonry.

A walk round Evesham should definitely start at the timbered Almonry for not only is it a fine building, but it contains an outstanding museum, which provides an excellent introduction to the town, and it also houses a most helpful Tourist Information Centre, which can supply a number of booklets and leaflets. Having made sure to look at the model of the Abbey as it must have been before the Dissolution, head for the nearby churchyard to look at the Bell Tower and consider how completely it must have been overshadowed by the great abbey church. Now, perhaps go beneath the Bell Tower and walk down to the banks of the Avon where it is possible to take a boat trip on the Avon, before returning to look at St Lawrence's Church. This has been 'redundant' for many years, but is still open to visitors. This largely Perpendicular building is especially noted for its beautifully vaulted chantry chapel of Abbot Lichfield. The adjacent Parish Church of All Saints is also largely Perpendicular in style, but it was

Bell Tower, Evesham

severely 'restored' in the 19th century. It does however contain a beautifully vaulted Lady Chapel, which was built by Abbot Lichfield. From here go through the narrow Abbot Reginald's Gateway into the small Market Place, to look at the beautifully restored Round House - a 15th-century timber-framed merchant's house. From here turn right into bustling Bridge Street and then first left into Cowl Street, where many of the old cottages have been converted into shops. There are many options, but wherever you

The Round House, Evesham

wander in Evesham you will come across bright and cheerful shops, old buildings of character and the pleasant atmosphere of a typical English market town.

EWEN (1-2 K7) *3 mi. S Cirencester.* This quiet residential hamlet lies in flat countryside with the infant Thames flowing only a few yards to its south. The attractive Wild Duck Inn provides excellent restaurant and bar meals. Walk southwards from here, partly beside the Thames, to **Somerford Keynes** and the western fringes of the **Cotswold Water Park.**

EYFORD PARK (1-2 E10) *2½ mi. W Stow-on-the-Wold.* An elegant 'Queen Anne' mansion built by Sir Guy Dawber in 1910 in a fine park with a lake, near the source of the River Eye - the small stream later to enrich **Upper and Lower Slaughter.** This house stands on the site of a mansion built in 1870, which was contemporary with the surviving lodge on the B4068. The Victorian mansion also stood near the site of an earlier house, where the Duke of Shrewsbury, Charles Talbot, once entertained William III. Apparently there is a tablet on a well in the park claiming that Milton wrote part of *Paradise Lost* while seated beside it. Neither the well nor the house are visible from the B4068, but there is a pleasant walk northwards from this road, passing close behind the house before heading across country to a minor road near Chalk Hill. There is an attractive row of late 18th-century cottages close to the point where the walk leaves the B4068.

FAIRFORD (1-2 K10) *4 mi. W Lechlade.* In the 19th century an Anglo-Saxon cemetery was excavated just to the west of Fairford, so the history of this warm little town on the River Coln stretches far back into the past. However, the great antiquary John Leland, Henry VIII's librarian, claimed that *Faireforde never flourished afore ye Tames* *came to it,* and there is no doubt that its prosperity in late medieval times was almost entirely due to the wealth of the Tames, one of the Cotswolds' greatest wool-merchant families. It was the most illustrious member of this family, John Tame, and his son Edmund who built the magnificent late Perpendicular Fairford Church.

This wonderfully proportioned building stands at the north end of the High Street, beyond the Market Place. It has a massive central tower, the rich sculptural details of which include the arms of John Tame. The interior has a fine oak-beamed roof supported on interesting stone corbels, great piers supporting the central tower, and a fascinating series of carved misericords beneath the choir stalls. But the greatest glory of Fairford is its remarkably complete series of stained-glass windows. Most of these are almost certainly the work of the Fleming, Barnard Flower, who was employed by Henry VIII to glaze the windows of both his new Lady Chapel at Westminster Abbey and King's College Chapel, Cambridge (the latter not being completed until after Flower's death).

Mill and Church, Fairford

It is thought that, although all the glass came from the same workshops, a number of English and possibly French craftsmen must also have contributed their skills. Before leaving this most beautiful church, pause for a while at John Tame's fine altar tomb between the choir and the Lady Chapel, to remember the debt that we owe both to him and to the craftsmen he employed. Another well-known Cotswold craftsman is buried in the churchyard beneath a fine table tomb - master-mason Valentine Strong, one of the quarry-owning Strongs of **Taynton,** who died while he was building the mansion of Park House (see below). Read all about the Strong family in Edith Brill's interesting book, *Life and Tradition in the Cotswolds.*

The buildings in the High Street and the Market Place, although not as impressive as the church, are a pleasant mixture, largely of the 17th and 18th centuries, the number of hotels and inns reminding us that Fairford was once an important posting stage on the London to Gloucester coaching run. See especially the charming old Bull Hotel. John Keble was born in 1792 at Keble House on the north side of London Road, for although his father was the vicar of nearby **Coln St Aldwyns** he preferred to live in Fairford. The church overlooks the water-meadows of the River Coln, which flows to the west of the town, and there is a pleasant mill house and an old bridge from where one can look upstream across the parkland of Park House - itself demolished in 1955. Milton End lies on the west side of the river, and is separated by it from the rest of the town. For further details of Fairford's story read June Lewis's brief but excellent *History of Fairford.*

FARMCOTE (1 D8) *2 mi. E Winchcombe.* This hamlet is perched on the very edge of the Cotswold scarp and has wonderful views over valley country to Bredon Hill and the Malverns. It has a delightful little church, or to be ecclesiastically correct 'a chapel of ease'. Its exterior appears to have been heavily restored, but once inside, the visitor will be pleasantly surprised to find it a simple and unspoilt Norman building. See especially the Jacobean two-decker pulpit and altar rail, the 16th-century benches and the handsomely canopied tomb of Henry and Mary Stratford in pale, unpainted stone. It is possible to join the **Cotswold Way** by going northwards down a bridleway to **Hailes Abbey.** The Iron Age promontory fort of **Beckbury Camp** is about half a mile to the north of the hamlet, and this can also be reached by using part of the **Cotswold Way.**

FARMINGTON (1-2 G10) *1½ mi. NE Northleach.* Small village on high ground between the valleys of the Leach and the Sherborne Brook and centred upon an extensive green on which stands a little octagonal pumphouse. Farmington Lodge is partly 18th- and partly 19th-century in origin, and has four massive Doric columns gracing its front - all rather swish for little Farmington. The church which lies across the road from the Lodge is a largely Norman building, complete with Norman south doorway, chancel arch and north aisle arcade. The well proportioned tower was added in the 15th century and is a good example of late Perpendicular work. Lying just to the west of the village is Norbury Camp, an

The Green at Farmington

Iron Age settlement with the remains of a Stone Age long barrow within the north-west corner of its earthworks.It is possible to make a circular walk from here, taking in **Eastington,** the head of the Leach Valley, and **Northleach** using the Ordnance Survey's Landranger Map 163. There is also a pleasant minor road eastwards down the Sherborne and Windrush Valleys to **Sherborne, Windrush, Little Barrington** and **Burford.**

FIFIELD (1-2 G12) *4 mi. N Burford.* Modest village looking over the Evenlode Valley to **Bruern Abbey** around which are extensive woodlands. These were once the major source of timber for the hurdle makers of Fifield, who until the 1950s had worked here for centuries. The church stands in a wide, open churchyard and has a small octagonal 14th-century tower topped by a minute spire. Although much restored, it is worth visiting, if only to look at the charming 17th-century brass of Mary Palmer, complete with her eight children and a baby in christening robes. While here, do not overlook the interesting fragments of medieval glass. Take a circular walk by first dropping north-eastwards into the valley, and returning through woods to Bould and neighbouring **Idbury,** using the Ordnance Survey's Landranger Map 163.

FILKINS and BROUGHTON POGGS (1-2 J12) *3½ mi. NE Lechlade.* Situated in low country only about four miles north of the Thames, these two are now virtually one village and are happily bypassed by the busy A361. Broughton Poggs Church is a small Norman building with a squat saddleback tower, and is tucked away behind farm buildings. It has several Norman features including two small doorways, a narrow chancel arch and a tub-shaped font. Not far to the north is the cheerful Five Alls Inn and then, beyond it, is Filkins Church. This was designed in the French Gothic style by G.E. Street, a Victorian architect best known for his work on London's Law Courts. Not far away is another inn, the Lamb and many nearby cottage gardens are edged by large stone slabs or slates. This unusual work was carried out many years ago by Sir Stafford Cripps's estate foreman, and ex-quarryman, George Swinford. Set up by George in the 1920's, the minute Swinford Museum, has a fine collection of domestic, agricultural, trade and craft tools, but it is only open infrequently. At the nearby Cotswold Woollen Weavers visitors may watch traditional weaving machinery at work, but they should read the rather sad notice displayed in the mill, which states: - *No one in the world makes replacements for our looms and when this machinery finally grinds to a halt full scale cloth production will disappear.* It is to be hoped that this situation will not arise for a very long time. There is also a small but most interesting exhibition, tracing the history of sheep and wool-weaving in the Cotswolds, a woollen shop, an art gallery and a coffee shop.

FINSTOCK (1-2 G14) *2 mi. S Charlbury.* This was described by John Wesley, who visited it no less than three times in the 1770s, as *this delightful solitude, its inhabitants being a plain and artless people,* which was no doubt a compliment coming from Wesley ! Finstock today is a fragmented village, with a fine gabled manor house and a plain Victorian church. Its lies in wooded country above the Cherwell valley and there is a fine walk westwards through **Cornbury Park,** or northwards to **Charlbury.**

FISH HILL (1 C9) *½ mi. E Broadway.* (Not shown on map.) Long winding hill out of Broadway up onto the Cotswold edge. There is some doubt as to the date when this replaced the old road to London which ran up Conigree Lane, now the private drive to Middle Hill, but Fish Hill is certainly shown on Ogilvy's *Britannia,* first published in 1675. In 1736 Fish Hill was engineered into 'a well-formed serpentine road', and this construction probably coincided with the building near its top of what was the Fish Inn, an interesting little 18th-century stone building, originally intended as a gazebo by its builder, Sir John Coterill. Nearby will be found the Fish Hill Car Park and Picnic Area, which is complete with toilets, useful information boards showing woodland walks starting from here and a viewing topograph. **The Cotswold Way** passes through this area on its route between **Chipping Campden** and **Broadway. The Broadway Tower Country Park** is about half a mile to the south-west.

FORD (1 D9) *4 mi. E Winchcombe.* Pleasant hamlet on the slopes of the upper Windrush, less than two miles below its source above **Taddington.** There is a hospitable inn, the Plough, which has an oft-quoted verse on a board above its door exhorting *ye weary travellers that pass by ... to step in and quaff my nut brown ale ... twill make your lagging trotters dance.* Please read it all if you pass this way. It is possible to walk from here, up the Windrush Valley to **Cutsdean** and **Taddington,** or down it to **Temple Guiting.** There is also a good walk eastwards along tracks, and then along a wooded valley to **Hinchwick.**

FOSSEBRIDGE (1-2 H9) *3 mi. SW Northleach.* This small hamlet marks the point where the **Foss Way** drops into a steep-sided valley to cross the River Coln. There is a hotel beside the bridge, and it is possible to walk from here up the Coln Valley to **Yanworth** and **Chedworth Roman Villa,** or up the valley of a small tributary stream to the village of **Chedworth.**

FOSS WAY (Not shown on map.) This Roman road runs diagonally across the Cotswolds through the towns of **Moreton-in-Marsh, Stow-on-the-Wold** and **Cirencester,** on its way between Lincoln and Exeter, a total distance of 182 miles. Its course between the Stour Valley near Shipston-on-Stour and Cirencester is followed by the A429, and for a few miles beyond Cirencester by the A433. Beyond this it is now, apart from an early interruption at Kemble Airfield, little more than a track, and in practice it is not always easy to follow, even on foot.

The permanent Roman occupation of Britain commenced in 43 AD, almost a hundred years after Julius Caesar's brief invasions in 55 and 54 B.C., and within only four years the new Governor, Ostorius, had concluded its first stage by establishing a civil boundary along a line that was soon to become the fine road now known as the Foss Way. This then became a temporary frontier between the subjugated Iron Age tribes of the south and east, and their wilder, still un-conquered counterparts in the more mountainous and less easily controlled north and west.

In the years that followed its construction, its purpose must have been largely military, with forts and marching camps established upon it at regular intervals (of which there is little visible evidence in the area covered by this guide), and with roads leading off it to north and west carrying the legions towards the more troubled areas that lay beyond. It is one of the most direct of all Roman roads, and it is claimed that its course never diverges more than six miles from a theoretical straight line between Lincoln and Axminster in Devon. The best accounts of the Foss Way, and the other Roman roads in the area, the **Ermin Way,** the **Ryknild Street** and the **White Way,** are to be found in I.D.Margary's classic work, *Roman Roads in Britain.*

THE FOUR SHIRE STONE (1 D12) *1½ mi. E Moreton-in-Marsh.* A handsome 18th-century monument topped by a sundial and ball, marking the original meeting point of four counties: Oxfordshire, Gloucestershire, Warwickshire and Worcestershire. This still applies to the first three, but the isolated 'island' of Worcestershire, which owed its presence here to the once wide-ranging domains of the Bishops of Worcester, was swallowed up in Gloucestershire many years ago.

FOXCOTE, near Andoversford (1-2 F7) *4 mi. SE Cheltenham.* Small hamlet about a mile to the south-west of **Andoversford,** with a fine 17th-century manor house just to its south. There is a pleasant path southwards from here to **Withington.**

FOXCOTE, near Ilmington (1 B11) *1 mi. SW Ilmington.* This fine early 18th-century mansion, possibly built by Edward Woodward of Chipping Campden, is not open to visitors, but there is a public right of way for walkers down its long curving drive, and beyond it on a rougher track, to the village of **Ebrington.** Starting from the road between Ilmington and the hamlet of **Charingworth,** this is an attractive walk, and a return journey may be made via Ebrington Hill and Nebsworth using the Ordnance Survey's Landranger Sheet 151.

FRAMPTON MANSELL (1-2 K6) *6½ mi. W Cirencester.* This small village stands on the steep southern slopes of the **Golden Valley,** with a handsome neo-Norman church and a delightful little inn called the Crown. The sound of steam engines coming up the old GWR line in the valley below is no longer to be heard, but diesel-hauled trains may still be seen crossing the tall viaduct below the village, and there are pretty stretches of the old **Thames and Severn Canal** in the depths of the valley, beside the little River Frome.

FRANCE LYNCH (1-2 J5) *3½ mi. E Stroud.* This steep hillside village is today almost part of **Chalford,** and shares with it the same delightful flavour. It has a small inn and an unusually effective Victorian church, which was the work of the architect George Bodley, perhaps best known as the designer of far-off Washington Cathedral. Designed in the French Gothic style, it includes a splendidly ornate chancel, with coloured marble inlays and the carvings of three angels playing different musical instruments. The more recent altar-rail kneeling-mat was worked by the ladies of the parish and includes a picture of one of the donkeys which were once used to deliver bread and milk up the steep village streets, both here and at neighbouring **Chalford.**

FROCESTER (2 J3) *4 mi. SW Stroud.* Small village lying beneath the Cotswold edge and centred upon a crossroads overlooked by the colourfully painted Royal Gloucestershire Hussar Inn. The 'new church' was largely rebuilt in the 19th century and is not of great interest to visitors. The remains of the 'old church' are about a mile to the west of the village, and consist of only a Victorian Gothic tower and spire. Frocester Court was once owned by the abbey of Gloucester and its tithe barn is one of England's finest specimens, being over 180 feet in length. The barn is open during all reasonable daylight hours. A large Roman villa has been excavated here, but its remains are not on view.

War Memorial, Frocester

FROCESTER HILL (2 J3) *4 mi. SW Stroud.* (Not shown on map.) A lovely open space on the Cotswold edge, with splendid views over the winding Severn Estuary. Gliders from the nearby club add further colour and interest. The best approach is from the adjoining **Coaley Peak Picnic Site.**

South Porch, Fulbrook

FULBROOK (1-2 H12) *1 mi. NE Burford.* Large village astride the A361 and only separated from Burford by the River Windrush and the water-meadows through which it flows. Its interesting Norman church stands in a quiet setting just to the north of the A361. It has a beautiful Norman south doorway, a fine 16th-century roof supported on well carved corbel figures, a series of solid 12th-century arcade capitals and an opulently colourful 17th-century monument in the chancel.

GATCOMBE PARK (1-2 K5) *5 mi. SE Stroud.* This handsome late 18th-century mansion, once owned by the political economist, David Ricardo, is now the home of the Princess Royal. The house is not open to the public, but the delightful park is used at least once a year for horse trials.

GLOUCESTER (1-2 G4) *7 mi. W Cheltenham.* Situated, like neighbouring **Cheltenham,** just below, and to the west of the Cotswold scarp, this city, the County Town of Gloucestershire, has a long and interesting history. In the years after their invasion of 43 AD, the Romans soon established a fort at the very end of the **Ermin Way,** at what is now Kingsholm on the north side of the city. This was used to house the famous 2nd Legion, but by the late sixties a new and larger fort had been built on the site of the present city centre, and which was by then already known as Glevum. By the end of the century the 2nd Legion had moved westwards to its new fortress at Caerleon to subjugate and control the Welsh tribes, and Glevum became a non-military colony. By the end of the 2nd century the city had grown to considerable importance and had become one of the four great *Coloniae* of Britain, along with Lincoln, York and Colchester.

As in the rest of Britain the departure of the Legions saw the eventual decline of Roman civilisation, and it was not until the Anglo-Saxons had firmly established themselves that Gloucester was reborn. The monastery of St Peter was established here as early as 681, a royal palace was built at Kingsholm probably in the late 9th century and St Oswald's Priory was founded in 909, by Ethelfleda, the Lady of the Mercians. She was probably also responsible for the building of the walls and streets. Although loosely based on Glevum's pattern of building, the present street plan owes less to the Romans than to the Saxons, with the streets of Northgate, Eastgate, Southgate and Westgate meeting at the Cross. At this time the whole of Anglo-Saxon England was divided up into shires and it was then that Gloucester became the capital of its own shire.

It was Edward the Confessor who established the tradition of holding a court here each Christmas, and William the Conqueror continued to do the same. It was here, in 1085, that William had *deep speech with his Witan* (his council of wise men), and it was at this meeting that the decision was made to start the great Domesday survey. It was only three years later that work was started on the new abbey church of St Peter, the fine building that was later to become the basis for Gloucester's great Cathedral. The Norman and Angevin kings continued to regard Gloucester as a place of great importance, and Henry II granted a Charter to the city giving it a status equal to that of Winchester and Whitehall. In 1216 the young Henry III was crowned here, and just over a hundred years later, in 1327, Edward II was buried here following his dreadful murder at **Berkeley Castle.**

Gloucester Cathedral

Although overtaken by Bristol as a commercial centre because of the distance of its port from the sea, Gloucester continued to flourish in medieval times, from its trade, its agricultural markets and from the number of pilgrims visiting the tomb of Edward II in the great abbey. Many churches were built and there were no fewer than three friaries in the city. Great changes took place during the Dissolution between 1536 and 1539: the friaries and the monastery were closed, and the great abbey church soon became a cathedral with its own diocese. With Henry VIII's daughter Mary on the throne the fortunes of the Protestant church went into reverse, and in 1555 Gloucester's bishop, John Hooper, was burnt at the stake in his own cathedral city.

Gloucester Docks

It was in the reign of Mary's sister, Elizabeth, that Letters Patent were granted establishing the City Docks, the basis of those that have survived to this day. In the century that followed the city had mixed fortunes. During the Civil War it successfully endured a long siege by the Royalists and this fact was not forgotten by Charles II who, after his Restoration, had the city walls and the castle demolished, and more importantly reduced the city's land holdings from 29,000 acres to only 400, thus cancelling a privilege hard won from his ancestor Richard III. The docks were relatively busy in the 18th century, but it was the opening of the Gloucester and Sharpness Canal in 1827 that brought renewed prosperity. However, by the mid-1860s the size of ocean-going ships had increased so much that the docks again went into a decline, and it is only recently that plans to revive them for leisure purposes have reached fruition.

To explore some of the best of Gloucester it is suggested that you first call at the Tourist Information Centre. Then go into Northgate Street to look at the New Inn with its beautiful galleried courtyard, and then turn right into New Inn Lane and right again into King's Walk, passing the remains of the Roman City Wall on the left. Cross Eastgate Street to Queen's Walk and head slightly to the left of Jubilee Gardens to visit the outstandingly interesting Gloucester Museum and Art Gallery, with its Roman mosaics and sculptures and, amongst other features, its special displays of furniture and paintings. Now turn right up Greyfriars passing the ruins of the 16th-century Greyfriars church on the right.

Turn left into Southgate Street by the largely Perpendicular Mary de Crypt Church, and soon fork right into Commercial Road, passing the Old Customs House which houses the Soldiers of Gloucester Museum. Now walk back to Commercial Road and turn left and then left again into Severn Road to visit the Gloucester Antique Centre, which has over sixty individual shops and a restaurant, all housed in yet another 19th-century warehouse.

The revitalised Gloucester Docks, with their cafes and restaurants and wealth of shops, are fascinating in themselves and during the summer holiday season individual and family guided tours are available on certain days. These start from the Mariners' Chapel and probably include a boat trip around the docks on the *Queen Boadicea II,* one of the 'little ships' that brought back troops from Dunkirk. Also walk around the dock area and visit one of the Victorian warehouses, including an exhibition of the docks' history and redevelopment. The National Waterways Museum which is housed in the nearby Llanthony Warehouse provides a fascinating variety of displays on the colourful history of canals and other inland waterways, with novel live exhibition areas outside and canal boats in the barge arm alongside.

Now walk back into Commercial Road, turn left into Barbican Road, and then into Bearland, where some of the city's finest 18th-century houses will be found, including Bearland House and Lady Bellgate House. Walk down Quay Street, turn right down

Lower Quay Street, and then right again into Westgate Street. Soon pass the Folk Museum, which is housed in Bishop Hooper's Lodging, a group of half-timbered buildings where the bishop is reputed to have spent his last night before being burnt at the stake.

Now turn left not far beyond St Nicholas's Church, down the narrow Three Cocks Lane which runs into St Mary's Street. Bishop Hooper's Monument, on the left, marks the spot where this brave but unfortunate prelate met his end. Now turn right through St

Mary's Gateway and into the Cathedral Close with its fine 16th-, 17th- and 18th-century houses and then visit the splendid Gloucester Cathedral. This is a triumphant blend of the Norman and high Perpendicular styles. A visit here should take at least two hours, but see especially the early Norman crypt, the great Norman pillars of the nave, the Norman chapter house, the splendid Perpendicular choir and cloisters, the beautifully vaulted Lady Chapel, the magnificent east window, and the massive 225-ft pinnacled tower. See also the outstandingly beautiful tomb of the murdered Edward II and the fascinating collection of carved misericords beneath the choir stalls. Coffees, teas and light lunches are available in the refectory.

The National Waterways Museum, Gloucester

After walking right round the Cathedral Close, leave College Green by College Court,. Now turn left into Westgate Street and return to The Cross, thus completing your walk around this most interesting city.

GLOUCESTERSHIRE WARWICKSHIRE RAILWAY ('The G.W.R.') (1 D8) *At Toddington, 3½ mi. NE Winchcombe.* (Not shown on map.) The long term aim of this preservation project is to reopen most of the former Great Western main line between Stratford-upon-Avon and Cheltenham. The line already connects Toddington, Winchcombe Station (nearer Greet than Winchcombe), Gretton Meadow, where there is a 7-acre Nature Reserve complete with Picnic Area, and Gotherington Station (No public access here). Plans are in hand to reach Cheltenham Racecourse, and then to concentrate on reopening the line northwards, through Broadway and on to Honeybourne Junction, where a link with the main lines may be possible once again. Steam and diesel-hauled trains both operate over the existing length of track. The restored Toddington Station has a book and souvenir shop and a cafeteria, and vintage locomotives and rolling stock are on display. As it grows in length, this line will become increasingly useful for walkers wishing to sample the delights of the Cotswold edge, either by using sections of the **Cotswold Way** or by planning their own routes.

THE GLOUCESTERSHIRE WAY (Not shown on map.) This 100-mile long-distance footpath runs between Chepstow and Tewkesbury and passes through Gloucester, Stow-on-the-Wold and Winchcombe.

GLYMPTON (1 F15) *3 mi. N Woodstock.* Much money has been spent over the years on this rebuilt 'Cotswold' village, which has mellowed most satisfactorily. The little River Glyme stumbles over a small waterfall by the bridge - a lovely cool place on a hot summer afternoon. The church lies behind the 18th-century mansion in lush Glympton

Park with its long serpentine lake, and the delightful walk to it, using the Ordnance Survey's Landranger Sheet 164, amply justifies a visit. See the splendid tomb of Thomas Tesdale, wool trader and benefactor of Oxford's Balliol and Pembroke Colleges, with Thomas and his wife on opposite sides of a prayer desk, all in alabaster.

Glympton Park

THE GOLDEN VALLEY (1-2 K4 etc.) *1 mi. SE Stroud, etc.* (Not shown on map.) This description is normally applied to the length of the Frome Valley that runs between **Chalford** and **Brimscombe,** but it appears to have derived its name from the prosperity brought here by the cloth weavers who were established all along the valley by the end of the Middle Ages. This prosperity increased with the building of mills in the years of the early Industrial Revolution, and was at its height in the early years of the 19th century. It was then that cloth manufacture began to move northwards to Lancashire and Yorkshire, and although light industry has now replaced some of the closed mills, much of this delightful valley now slumbers once again, and is 'golden' for very different reasons.

GREAT BARRINGTON (1-2 G11) *3 mi. W Burford.* This small village in the Windrush Valley has several pleasant 17th- and 18th-century houses. Many of these had been allowed to deteriorate in the middle years of the 20th century, but happily all have now been restored. The village is dominated by Barrington Park, a fine Palladian mansion built for Earl Talbot, Lord Chancellor in the reign of George II, possibly by William Kent. The house, which overlooks a beautifully landscaped park through which the Windrush flows, is not visible from the road, but the wrought-iron gates (which looked sadly neglected when we passed here last) on the road north towards Great Rissington and

Park Gates, Great Barrington

the exquisite temple visible through them provide tempting glimpses of otherwise hidden splendours. The largely Norman church lies on the edge of the park, and has an unusually high Norman chancel arch and several interesting monuments. These include a delightful memorial to Mary, Countess Talbot, by the fashionable 18th-century sculptor, Joseph Nollekens, and another one, to two children of the Bray family, previous owners of the manor of Barrington, with the little boy and girl being led heavenwards by an angel.

The bridge over the Windrush between the church and the Fox Inn was built by local master-mason, Thomas Strong (see also **Burford**). Traces of the great quarries in the area worked by the Strongs and the other family of master-masons, the Kempsters, are not easily found, for most of them were underground. They are all on private land, largely between the Windrush Valley and the A40 and well to the south of Great Barrington. See also **Taynton** and **Windrush.**

There is a good walk southwards, across the River Windrush to **Little Barrington,** and returning via the friendly Fox Inn. (The latter might make a good alternative starting point, but only if the landlord is willing to allow cars to be parked here, by those also using the inn.)

GREAT RISSINGTON (1-2 G11) *3 mi. SE Bourton-on-the-Water.* Situated on a gently sloping hillside, this widespread village looks westwards over the broad Windrush Valley. Its main street runs down from a small triangular green towards a fine 17th-century manor house. This and the nearby church are attractive buildings, both showing clear evidence of sympathetic restoration and care. The cruciform church has a 15th-century tower with pinnacles and battlements, and in the south transept there are three memorial tablets, that to John Barnard and his wife being especially pleasing. Do not miss the interesting little 15th-century carving of the Crucifixion which has been reset in the porch, nor the rather sad verse on the tablet to Thomas Cambray, which reads:

Whilst in this sad world I did remain
My latter days were grief and pain
Full fifteen years and something more
But now the Lord hath set me free
From grief and pain and misery

There is a pleasant walk southwards, over the fields, and then beside the River Windrush, to the village of **Windrush.** It is also possible to walk north to **Little Rissington** and onwards to Wyck Rissington to link on to the **Oxfordshire Way.** The massive airfield on the hill above the village is, at the time of writing, disused.

Manor House, Great Rissington

GREAT ROLLRIGHT (1 D13) *2½ mi. N Chipping Norton.* Windy upland village just over the county boundary from Warwickshire into Oxfordshire, with fine views south over a broad valley towards rolling hill country around **Chipping Norton.** There are no real features of interest here, apart from the Norman church. This has some grotesque gargoyles on its well proportioned Perpendicular tower and a Norman doorway whose tympanum has a fish inserted amongst various geometric carvings. The porch in which it shelters is two-storeyed and its cornice is richly carved with an assortment of animals, flowers and the heads of men and women. Inside there is much evidence of over-zealous Victorian restoration, but do not overlook the brass to John Battersby, rector here until his death in 1522, nor the pleasant roof, with the names of the churchwardens in the year 1814 on one of its beams.

Tympanum, Great Rollright

Walk north from here, down the scarp slope, across a valley, and beside a great wood, to the village of **Whichford** in Warwickshire, or eastwards to delightful **Hook Norton.** If driving westwards from Great Rollright, possibly to the **Rollright Stones,** do not miss the splendid panoramic views, to both north and south of the road.

GREAT TEW (1 D15) *5½ mi. E Chipping Norton.* This is largely a 'model village' established within extensive parkland overlooking the Worton Valley, which was, in part, the work of the landscape gardener, John Loudon, the manager of the estate from 1809 to 1811. It is for this reason that there are so many evergreen trees to be found in

'Tewland'. There are 'picturesque' stone cottages, a small inn, the Falkland Arms, and stocks on the village green, but it was all conceived so long ago that it no longer appears contrived.

Great Tew

Nothing remains of the fine manor house where, before his untimely death at the Battle of Newbury in 1643, the brilliant Lucius Cary, Viscount Falkland, once entertained poets and philosophers from Oxford. It has been replaced by an odd 19th-century mansion, built by the descendants of Matthew Boulton, partner of James Watt in Birmingham's famous Soho Foundry. Idyllic Great Tew therefore owes its very existence to wealth created by Black Country sweat in the early years of the 19th century. One of the Boultons, Mary, is remembered in the church above the manor, where there is a brilliant monument to her by the great 19th-century sculptor, Sir Francis Chantrey. The approach to the church is through a fine 17th-century gateway, thought possibly to be the work of Nicholas Stone, and up a delightful tree-lined path. There is a pleasant walk south-westwards from Great Tew, through Little Tew to the edge of Heythrop Park and then south to **Enstone.**

GREAT WITCOMBE (1-2 G5) *5 mi. SW Cheltenham.* Quiet village tucked away beneath the wooded Cotswold edge at **Birdlip,** with hills on three sides and reservoirs just below. Here are a few half-timbered cottages, a dignified little 19th-century school and school house, and an interesting church. This has a massive yew tree close to its attractive 18th-century porch, the latter being contemporary with the handsome tower. The interior is even more pleasing, with a Norman chancel arch, a barrel-vaulted ceiling to the nave, a medieval rood beam, and fragments of medieval glass in the north aisle windows.

There is fly-fishing available on the nearby reservoirs. **Witcombe Roman Villa** is less than a mile to the south-west and it is possible to walk there from Great Witcombe via a path beside the reservoirs.

GREAT WOLFORD (1 C12) *3 mi. NE Moreton-in-Marsh.* This modest village looks out towards neighbouring **Little Wolford,** across a valley through which the Nethercote Brook flows north to join the Stour, and so on to the Avon and Severn; but less than two miles away, streams flow south to join the Evenlode, which flows into the Thames. So, although the village stands less than four hundred feet above sea level, this is watershed country, and it was perhaps for reasons of strategy that a small Iron Age settlement was built here, the earthworks of which may be seen to the immediate south-east of the village. Wolford's medieval church was destroyed by fire in the early 19th century, and was replaced by a broad building, with a short chancel containing a number of monuments to the Ingram family. Its best feature is the tall spire, which is an outstanding landmark in this gentle south Warwickshire landscape.

GREET (1 D8) *1 mi. N Winchcombe.* This large hamlet has a pleasant manor farmhouse complete with a 17th-century dovecot, and a half-timbered house opposite, but both buildings have been overshadowed by considerable modern development. A short distance to the east, near the B4632, is the Winchcombe Pottery, which has been creating excellent craft work for many years. There is a modest shop and enthusiasts will probably be able to watch the potters at work. Less than half a mile to the west of the pottery there is a station on the **Gloucestershire Warwickshire Railway.**

GRETTON (1 D7) *1½ mi. NW Winchcombe.* Situated beneath 900ft-high Langley Hill, this small village has several half-timbered cottages prettily situated around the 15th-century tower of its otherwise demolished medieval church. Great care and attention was lavished upon its Victorian successor by the architect, John Drayton Wyatt, Sir Gilbert Scott's principal draughtsman. The end result, however, is not over-inspiring, and the interior lacks atmosphere. The nearby inn has for some years been known as the Bugatti, in recognition of the nearby **Prescott** Hill Climb, and the figure on the inn sign is that of Rivers Fletcher, the well-known Bugatti owner and driver. It is possible to walk southwards from Gretton, up over Langley Hill, to **Winchcombe,** or south-westwards to **Cleeve Hill.**

GRIM'S DITCH (1 F15 etc.) (Not shown on map.) A now disconnected series of banks and ditches, which once formed part of a defensive system built by an Iron Age (Belgic) tribe in the first part of the 1st century AD. The best sections are visible in **Blenheim** and **Ditchley** Parks.

GUITING POWER (1-2 9E) *5 mi. SE Winchcombe.* This delightful village is built around a

small sloping green, and is a fascinating example of the unconscious harmony created by Cotswold masons over the centuries. The cottages, shop and inns are all beautifully cared for. The Farmers' Arms in the village and the Hollow Bottom Inn on the road leading to Winchcombe, are both worth visiting, and form welcome breaks on a number of walks that can be taken in this area - north-westwards to **Guiting Woods,** south-eastwards down the Windrush Valley to **Naunton,** or south-westwards to **Hawling.** The church of St Michael has substantial Norman

Guitting Power

north and south doorways, but restoration by the Victorians has resulted in a certain lack of atmosphere within. However, there are pleasant views towards Naunton from its tidy churchyard.

GUITING WOODS (1-2 E8/9) *3 mi. SE Winchombe.* Extensive woodlands bordering the valley of the little Castlett Stream. They may be approached from **Guiting Power, Kineton, Temple Guiting** or **Farmcote.** There is a minute car park, overlooked by a handsome 17th- and 18th-century stone manor house standing above its own miniature park, which is approached by a minor road leading south-westwards from **Kineton.** This makes a very useful base from which to explore the area and a very minor road, signed as 'Unsuitable', runs northwards and then westwards from here partly beside the Castlett Stream, and this provides a fine, almost mud-free walk, even in the depths of winter. Use the Ordnance Survey's Outdoor Leisure Map, No 45 if you wish to explore this delightful area properly.

HAILES ABBEY AND HAILES (1 D8) *2 mi. NE Winchcombe.* Here beneath the Cotswold edge are the remains of a great abbey founded in 1246 by Richard, Earl of Cornwall, who had earlier vowed to do so, following his escape from a shipwreck off the Isles of Scilly. It was colonised by monks from Beaulieu in Hampshire, a Cistercian house founded by Richard's father, King John. Hailes's popularity as a place of pilgrimage was then assured by Richard's son Edmund, who gave the monks a relic of the 'Holy Blood of Christ', which had been authenticated by the Pope himself. From this time forth pilgrims poured into Hailes and it was only at the Dissolution of the Monasteries by Henry VIII that it suddenly ceased to have any significance.

Christmas Eve 1539 witnessed the final surrender of the abbey to the agents of the king, and according to legend its destruction was witnessed by the king's hated Commissioner, Thomas Cromwell, from **Beckbury Camp,** on the hillside above. The only remains that have survived are parts of the cloisters and various low walls, but the plan of the magnificent abbey church has been

Hailes Abbey

perpetuated by the planting of trees and the attractive site is well worth visiting. There is a small but interesting museum close by containing many medieval tiles, a beautiful series of roof bosses, many other finds from the excavation of the abbey and life-size figures of Cistercian monks.

The nearby parish church of Hailes, a small building nearly a hundred years older than the abbey, has ancient stone floors, medieval wall-paintings and stained glass, a 15th-century rood screen and attractive 17th-century woodwork. This delightful little building was sympathetically restored in 1961 and is still full of an atmosphere of the past.

Hailes is on the course of the **Cotswold Way,** and this can be used to climb up the hill on a pleasant bridleway to Farmcote. It is also possible to follow the Way over the fields to **Winchcombe,** along a path still known as the Pilgrims' Way. Motorists will find a pleasant, partly open road leading southwards up over Salter's Hill, following the course of the ancient **Salt Way,** and still known here as Salter's Lane.

HAILEY WOOD (1-2 K6) *4 mi. W Cirencester.* (Not shown on map.) This great area of woodland is a southern outlier of **Cirencester Park** and can be visited on the same terms (see **Cirencester Park** for details). The main London - Gloucester railway line runs through it, while beneath is the tunnel of the old **Thames and Severn Canal,** with several of its dangerous ventilation shafts and their attendant mounds still visible. This wood is crossed by the **Macmillan Way** from Sapperton and emerges by the hospitable **Tunnel House Inn,** from where it is possible to walk along the canal towpath to **Thames Head.**

HAMPEN (1-2 F8) *6½ mi. E Cheltenham.* Minute hamlet in unspoilt upland country to the south of the A436, on a bridle road running between **Salperton** and **Shipton Oliffe.** The long-vanished Banbury and Cheltenham Direct Railway ran just to the north of the hamlet, and its embankments and cuttings are still much in evidence hereabouts.

HAMPNETT (1-2 G9) *1 mi. NW Northleach.* This attractive village is thinly spread around a field-like village green, which gives birth to one of the Cotswolds' loveliest streams - the Leach. The church is largely Norman, but its interior was subjected to some very unusual stencil decoration in the 1880s. This work, largely carried out by Hampnett's

Norman Birds, Hampnett

vicar, detracts from the clean Norman lines, although it should be remembered that in medieval times most churches were decorated with a variety of patterns similar to this. Do not miss the carved birds on the capitals supporting the chancel arch - they are a fine example of late Norman work. Walk south-east from here down the valley of the infant Leach to **Northleach,** or south-westwards over the hills to **Yanworth** following the course of the **Macmillan Way.**

HAMPTON FIELDS (1-2 K5) *1 mi. SE Minchinhampton.* There is a pleasant row of 18th- and early 19th-century cottages in this small hamlet in partly wooded hill country. The Long Stone, the only surviving stone from an otherwise defunct long barrow, stands in a field to the east of the road from here to Minchinhampton.

The Long Stone

HARESFIELD BEACON (1-2 H4) *3 mi. NW Stroud.* (Not shown on map.) There is a topograph, or viewing table, near a car park in the Shortwood area, and beyond this a further car parking space for those who wish to walk along to the Beacon itself, a hill-top surrounded by the earthworks of an Iron Age promontory fort. There are splendid views over the Severn Estuary from this dramatic edge country, most of which is owned by the National Trust. **The Cotswold Way** passes through the area and a short distance along it to the north-east will be found the 'Cromwell Siege Stone', a simple monument commemorating the 5th of September 1643, the day when the Royalist siege of Gloucester was lifted, due to the imminent arrival of a strong Parliamentary force commanded by the Earl of Essex.

Topograph, Haresfield

HARFORD BRIDGE (1-2 F10) *4 mi. SW Stow-on-the-Wold.* Here is a pleasant little bridge across the Windrush, not far from a modest farmhouse. The Domesday Book records a village of Harford, but no trace of this remains. It was probably depopulated by sheep graziers in the 15th or early 16th century. There is a minor road near here, but it is far more pleasant to walk here from **Naunton,** and on down the Windrush Valley to **Bourton-on-the-Water.** Look out carefully for the flock of traditional Cotswold sheep which is usually to be seen grazing here - they were once known as 'Cotswold Lions'(see **Aldsworth).** Ancient Longhorn Cattle are also usually to be seen here, but if you fail to spot them, why not visit the **Cotswold Farm Park** (not far to the north of here), where there is an outstanding collection of rare breeds of farm animals.

HARNHILL (1-2 K8) *2½ mi. E Cirencester.* Compact village in flat country to the east of Cirencester, with a small conically towered Norman church standing almost in the garden of a largely Georgian rectory. The church's chief treasure is its Norman south doorway's tympanum which depicts St Michael locked in combat with a dragon, but there are also lovely fragments of medieval glass in the east window. This church was lucky enough to escape the attention of over-enthusiastic Victorian architects and was most sympathetically restored in 1909. Close by the church is a fine 16th-century manor house with an attractive square dovecot in its grounds.

HATHEROP (1-2 J10) *2½ mi. N Fairford.* This is a largely 19th-century estate village, the creation of Lord de Mauley, the owner of Hatherop Castle. The castle itself is a 17th-century manor house ambitiously enlarged and partly rebuilt in the 1850s, complete with battlements and other trimmings. This was the work of Henry Clutton, an architect much influenced by the eccentric William Burges, and also to some extent by the great French Gothicist, Viollet le Duc. The nearby French Gothic church was also the work of Henry Clutton and contains the

Hatherop Church

dramatic monument in white marble to Lady de Mauley, who died in 1844, twelve years before her husband.

Hawkesbury Church

HAWKESBURY (2 M3) *4 mi. S Wotton-under-Edge.* The tall-towered and mainly Perpendicular church stands almost alone, at the point where a wooded valley opens out from the hilly Cotswold edge. It all looks splendid from the outside, but once through the Norman north doorway one is greeted with a brutally scraped interior. However stop to look at the 15th-century stone pulpit and the monuments to the Jenkinson family, one of whom, the 2nd Earl of Liverpool, was Prime Minister at the time of Waterloo.

HAWKESBURY UPTON (2 M3) *4 mi. SE Wotton-under-Edge.* A rather bleak and indeterminate village, with two inns, one named The Duke of Beaufort and the other, rather appropriately, The Fox.

HAWLING (1-2 F8) *4 mi. SE Winchcombe.* Situated in high sheep country just to the east of the ancient **Salt Way,** this is a small, quiet village with a fine Elizabethan manor house next door to its church. The latter was largely rebuilt in 1764 and was probably still in such good order in the 19th century that it escaped the more ruthless 'restoration' experienced by so many other churches at that time. It has a handsome Georgian pulpit, an unusual set of 17th-century brass plaques to various members of the Stratford family and a colourful little ceiling beneath its tower, this being the only medieval part of the church to survive. There is a pleasant, partly unfenced road running eastwards from here to **Guiting Power,** and for walkers there is a bridleway leading northwards over open wold country to Deadmanbury Gate on the western edge of **Guiting Woods.**

HAZELTON (1-2 K6) *4½ mi. E Nailsworth.* This fine 16th- and 17th-century manor house and farmstead stands on the site of a 12th-century priory and is just visible to the north of the road between **Rodmarton** and **Cherington.** Windmill Tump Long Barrow, to the south of the road, is a classic chambered long barrow complete with a false entrance between two projecting horns, similar to that at **Belas Knap.** It is on private ground.

HAZLETON (1-2 G9) *2½ mi. NW Northleach.* An unspoilt village situated high up on the wolds, on the line of the ancient **Salt Way.** The church has Norman origins, although its tower and most of its windows are 15th-century Perpendicular. There is a fine Norman south doorway and chancel arch, and a massive 13th-century font. Walkers will enjoy the attractive bridleways eastwards to **Turkdean,** north-eastwards to **Notgrove** and northwards to **Salperton.**

HETTY PEGLER'S TUMP (or Uley Long Barrow) (2 K3) *On B4066, 1 mi. N Uley.* (Not shown on map.) A Neolithic chambered long barrow about 180ft long, surrounded by a dry-stone revetting wall and containing a central passage of stone with three burial chambers. In the care of English Heritage, it may be visited at 'any reasonable time'.

Hetty Pegler's Tump

HIDCOTE BOYCE (1 B10) *2 mi. NE Chipping Campden.* Here is a pleasant hamlet below the western slopes of high Ilmington Downs. It has a single, gently sloping street bordered by flower-filled cottage gardens. Some distance to its north, the road is overlooked by Hidcote House, a delightful manor house which was built in 1663, probably by Francis Keyte of neighbouring **Ebrington**. This has attractively curved gable-ends and mullioned windows, and pretty fan-tailed doves are usually to be seen flying to and from their nesting boxes overlooking the gateway. It is possible to walk from here, up onto Ilmington Downs and back down through Hidcote Bartrim (see below).

HIDCOTE MANOR GARDEN, Hidcote Bartrim (1 B10) *2 mi. NE Chipping Campden.* This was given to the National Trust in 1948 by the great horticulturist, Major Lawrence

Hidcote Manor Garden

Johnson, who had by that time devoted forty years of his life to its creation. When he came to Hidcote in 1905 there was only the minute hamlet of Hidcote Bartrim, and a 17th-century manor house in company with a cedar tree, a clump of large beeches and a few walls. The garden that we see today was therefore created from eleven acres of largely open Cotswold hill country. In fact Major Johnson made not one garden but a series of small gardens, separated by now mellowed walls and by hedges of hornbeam, yew, green and copper beech, box and holly. Amongst these magnificent hedges are to be found the Fuchsia Garden, the White Garden, the Bathing Pool Garden, and, in contrast to these formal creations, a wild garden beside a stream. These are enriched by grass walks and lawns, mellow brick gazebos and wrought-iron gates through which one can glimpse distant views of Bredon Hill and the Malverns, across the blue haze of the valleys through which the Avon and Severn flow. See also the Theatre Lawn, which is usually the scene for an open-air Shakespeare play at some time each summer, the Long Walk in the Kitchen Garden, which contains a fine collection of old French roses, the alley of lime trees, and the fine avenue of beech trees. The National Trust describes Hidcote as 'one of the most delightful gardens in England', and it would indeed be hard to dispute this claim. The Trust has one of it's excellent gift shops here, and refreshments available include coffees, lunches and cream teas.

Walk down to **Mickleton,** via neighbouring **Hidcote Boyce,** and back up the hill via **Kiftsgate,** where there is another delightful garden. This walk can also be extended by taking a track up the hill from Hidcote Bartrim which leads over the top of Ilmington Downs, from where it is possible to walk down into nearby **Hidcote Boyce,** and return across fields to the start. But do not use the National Trust's car park, which is for the use of those visiting the garden.

Farm at Hilcot

HILCOT AND PINCHLEY WOODS (1-2 G7) *5 mi. SE Cheltenham.* This is a delightful and little-known area of woodland in a valley which gives birth to the Hilcot Brook, a tributary of the River Churn. Public footpaths are few, but the roads approaching from **Withington, Andoversford, Seven Springs** and **Colesbourne** are normally quiet enough to be used for walking. Upper Hilcot farmhouse is half-timbered - an unusual feature in this countryside of Cotswold stone, and perhaps a reflection of this hidden valley's rich timber resources in days gone by.

HILLESLEY (2 M3) *2½ Mi. S Wotton-under-Edge.* Modest village on the Cotswold edge, with a severe little Baptist chapel and an ambitious Victorian church - the work of a capable amateur architect, the Rev. Benjamin Perkins. Walk eastwards along a minor road and the then north-eastwards up a valley bridleway to **Tresham.**

HINCHWICK (1 D10) *4 mi. NW Stow-on-the-Wold.* An early 19th-century manor house and a few cottages, on the line of the Romans' **Ryknild Street,** at the southern end of a tranquil, wooded valley, with a series of small lakes amongst the trees (please do not trespass). This valley should contain the upper reaches of the little River Dikler, but although it must have its origins on Bourton Downs, it remains underground and it is not until it reaches **Donnington Brewery** that it finally emerges for good at the head of a beautiful lake, by now in sufficient volume to justify a large

Early Spring near Hinchwick

mill-wheel. Use a path north from Hinchwick, leading up the dry valley, and over the wold country of Bourton Downs.

HOLWELL (1-2 H11) *2½ mi. SW Burford.* Quiet hamlet in open wold country with pleasant farm buildings not far from a small church, which was entirely rebuilt in 1895. The interior is not of great interest, apart from the pulpit which has delightful 17th-century Flemish panels built into it, depicting various scenes from the Nativity.

HONINGTON (1 B12) *1½ mi. N Shipston-on-Stour.* A most attractive village centred around a wide, tree-shaded green, with a beautiful assortment of houses and cottages in timber, mellow brick and stone, blending together to produce a highly satisfying scene. Honington is approached from the A3400, Stratford to Shipston road, by a small road leading over a pretty five-arched bridge with balls upon its parapets. This is probably contemporary with the late 17th-century Honington Hall, an exceptionally handsome mellow brick mansion visible well over to the left in parkland beside the River Stour. The Hall was built in 1685 by a London merchant, Sir Henry Parker, and is enriched by a series of oval recesses between the upper and lower windows, in which busts of the twelve Caesars sit most comfortably. The Hall was lovingly restored in the mid-1970s, and incorporates a wealth of richly contrived 18th-century plasterwork, especially in its entrance hall and octagonal Saloon.

Apart from its 13th-century tower, the adjoining church is contemporary with the house, and its elegantly decorated interior reminds one of a Wren City church. It was also restored in the 1970s and contains several handsome monuments to members of the Parker and Townsend families. See especially the self-important but sumptuous monument to Sir Henry Parker and his son Hugh, a piece of work that typifies the spirit of the age in which they lived. In contrast, there are two monuments by the 19th-century sculptor Sir Richard Westmacott, less exciting, but also less worldly - the one to Lady Elizabeth Townsend, depicting a mourning male figure by an urn - a typically poignant Westmacott treatment. There is a pleasant little road north from Honington, to the village of Halford, with views over the River Stour from its northern end.

HOOK NORTON (1 D14) *5 mi. NE Chipping Norton.* A large village situated in remote hilly country that once yielded great quantities of ironstone. The old ironworks have

long since vanished, but other evidence of Hook Norton's past importance as an ironstone centre may still be seen - a series of dramatic piers , the only remains of a massive railway viaduct that once spanned the broad valley to its east, carrying the long-vanished Banbury and Cheltenham Direct Railway. There is also a Victorian brewery here (its red-brick fabric an unusual intrusion into the Cotswold scene) which still brews the most delectable Hook Norton Ale. This

Viaduct Piers near Hook Norton

beer, like the village in which it is brewed, is known far and wide as 'Hooky', to all those who know a thing or two about real ale.

This village, with its orange-brown stone and thatched roofs, is well worth exploring. 'The Green' and 'East End' are both very pleasant, but we particularly favour the terrace in the centre of the village, with the Bell Inn at one end and the church at the other. The latter is a large building of Norman origin with a finely pinnacled Perpendicular tower and a spacious, pleasantly bare interior, in which is a fascinating Norman font complete with sculptured figures of *Adam and Eve, Sagittarius the Archer,* and other signs of the Zodiac. Walk south-east from Hook Norton, across the broad valley over which the viaduct once ran, and up over the hill to the delightful little village of **Swerford** in the next valley.

HORLEY (1 B15) *3 mi. NW Banbury.* Situated on the slopes of a valley just below open ironstone country so typical of north Oxfordshire, Horley is a delightful, small village with its church poised at the top of a street lined with old stone houses and cottages. The church, with its Norman tower and chancel, was exceptionally well restored as recently as 1949, when a rood loft and screen were added. In the north aisle will be found Horley's greatest treasure, an unusually well preserved 15th century wall painting of St Christopher fording a stream. With its details including two anglers both of whom have made a catch, this still seems to breathe the very spirit of late medieval England, and is well worth seeing. Walk up the valley from here, to **Hornton,** and then on over the hills to **Ratley** and **Edgehill,** to link onto the **Macmillan Way.**

HORNTON (1 A14) *4 mi. NW Banbury.* Here, to the north of the church, were the quarries that gave their name to Hornton stone, the slightly orange, toffee-coloured ironstone that has given the towns and villages of this area their unique flavour. Hornton is a quiet, pleasing village in a hollow at the head of a small stream flowing south-eastwards in the general direction of the River Cherwell. It has a small green, many stone houses and cottages, some of them thatched, two 17th-century farmhouses and a manor house of the same period. The church dates back to the 12th century, although the tower and many other features are Perpendicular. Like the church at neighbouring

Horley, it has a medieval wall painting - the one here being a late-l4th-century 'Doom' depicting *the Last Judgement.* The purpose of Doom paintings was to instil into the illiterate parishioners, a fear of hellfire and damnation if they transgressed in any way from the required God-fearing standards required of them. The 'Doom' at Hornton is comparatively mild in its content, but many others that survive (including that depicted at **Oddington**) are still convincingly horrifying and it is no wonder that the church was so successful in maintaining its hold over the simple peasant mind for so long. Walk north from here, to **Ratley** and **Edgehill,** or south-eastwards, down the valley to **Horley.**

HORSLEY (1-2 K4) *1 Mi. SW Nailsworth.* An unexceptional village in high country on the busy B4058, with fish breeding ponds in the valley between here and Nailsworth. Its priory has long since vanished and the only remains of the medieval church is its tower. The rest of this rather impressive church was designed in 1838 by Thomas Rickman, who is perhaps better known as the original classifier of the styles of English architecture - *Early English, Decorated and Perpendicular.* There is a fine walk south-westwards up a wooded valley to **Kingscote,** or south-eastwards over hilly open country to **Chavenage.**

HORTON AND HORTON COURT (2 N2) *5 mi. S Wotton-under-Edge.* Situated beneath the wooded Cotswold edge, the lovely manor house of Horton Court is in the care of the National Trust. Its fine Norman hall and its detached 16th-century ambulatory are both open to the public. The latter was built by William Knight, who was Henry VIII's envoy to the Pope when the king was attempting to obtain a divorce, and its elegant Renaissance style, complete with the medallion heads of four emperors, must have been inspired by Knight's visit to Rome. The nearby church has a well proportioned Perpendicular tower and a

Horton Court

vaulted porch of the same period. In the pleasantly white-painted interior are a Jacobean pulpit and two handsome 18th-century wall monuments, the one to Anne Paston being most tenderly worded.

Round House at Hyde

HYDE (1-2 K5) *1½ mi. NE Minchinhampton.* Upper Hyde hamlet, with its Ragged Cot Inn, overlooks the **Golden Valley,** and Lower Hyde, in the valley itself, has a delightful little 'round house' built beside the **Thames and Severn Canal,** a restored stretch of which runs here. These round houses were built for the canal's maintenance men, known as 'lengthmen', as each was responsible for the upkeep of a certain length of the waterway.

ICOMB (1-2 F11) *2½ mi. SE Stow-on-the-Wold.* Situated beneath 800ft-high Icomb Hill, this village has a pleasant variety of houses and cottages, almost all of which are a delight to the eye. The small church has a blocked-up Norman north doorway and an Early English chancel, but all has been rather heavily restored. However, visitors should not overlook the effigy of Sir John Blaket, a 15th-century knight in armour upon a fine tomb chest, and almost certainly the builder of Icomb Place, the medieval manor house hidden away from view at the southern end of the village. A path leads south from the vicinity of the church to join the **Oxfordshire Way** in less than a mile. Use this to walk eastwards to **Bledington,** and then down the Evenlode Valley to **Bruern Abbey** and **Shipton-under-Wychwood.**

Font at Idbury

IDBURY (1-2 F12) *4½ mi. SE Stow-on-the-Wold.* Situated on the western slopes of the broad Evenlode Valley, and not far to the east of the earthworks of a large Iron Age settlement, Idbury is a minute village with far-ranging views across to the Oxfordshire Cotswolds. The lovely Tudor manor house was once the editorial headquarters of that delightful little magazine, *The Countryman,* as it was then the home of the publication's founder, Robertson Scott. There is a tablet over the door inscribed, *Oh more than happy countryman, if he but knew his good fortune.* There is also a more poignant reminder of the Scott connection on a wall by the roadside nearby inscribed, *This tree is planted in proud memory of Peter Scott, A.F.C., of Idbury, who died in 1943, in Canada.* It is at least good to know that *The Countryman* continues to flourish, with its editorial office having been in Sheep Street, **Burford** for many years now.

The interior of Idbury's largely Perpendicular church has an unspoilt medieval flavour, with a blocked-up Norman doorway, a beautiful 15th-century nave roof supported on corbel figures, and a pulpit made up from three medieval bench-ends. See also the medieval bench-ends still serving their original purpose, the 19th-century box pews, the unusual 'walk-through' squint and the particularly lovely octagonal font. In the churchyard will be found the tomb of Sir Benjamin Baker, the civil engineer who designed the original Aswan Dam and the still-famous Forth Railway Bridge. There is a bridleway heading eastwards from here into the Evenlode Valley, joining up with the **Oxfordshire Way** at **Bruern Abbey.**

IDLICOTE (1 B12) *3 mi. NE Shipston-on-Stour.* Delightfully situated on a small hill, with a tree-shaded pool and views eastwards, over flat valley countryside to the dark outline of Edge Hill, Idlicote is little more than a hamlet, but it does have a small church. This has Norman origins, but its Norman doorway is filled with a Georgian door, and this provides a foretaste of the interior, which is full of 18th-century flavour, with a little west gallery, a three-decker pulpit and a 17th-century ogival font cover. There is also a pleasant 17th-century chapel, with Tuscan columns dividing it from the chancel. Idlicote House, off the drive to which the church lies, is a dignified early-19th-century building, while close to it, is a fine 18th-century octagonal dovecote, which once provided shelter for no fewer than 1002 nesting birds. The best walk from Idlicote is southwards, over Idlicote Hill, past St Dennis Farms, and across to Brailes. By turning right before reaching St Dennis, it is possible to make a circular walk, taking in the lovely village of **Honington.**

ILMINGTON (1 B11) *5 mi. NE Chipping Campden.* A most attractive stone village lying beneath Windmill Hill, the most northerly bastion of the Cotswolds, and still very 'Cotswold' in flavour. It spreads itself comfortably below the hill slopes, and to be properly savoured should be explored on foot. Here will be found a wealth of old houses and cottages, many beside small paths which stray away from the road that encircles the village. There is a lovingly restored manor house, the beautiful gardens of which are normally open to the public at least twice a year. There are also two very pleasant inns, the Howard Arms and the Red Lion.

It is possible to walk around the village taking in many of its best features, including the church, beyond a quiet little pathway, overlooking two pools in a field. This is a largely Norman building, with Norman north and south doorways and chancel arch, and Norman windows in the aisle. Once beyond the 16th-century porch, one comes upon splendid oak pews and other furnishings. These were all installed in the 1930s, and are the work of master-craftsman, Robert Thompson, whose descendants still produce their stout oak furniture in his original workshops in the little village of Kilburn, beneath the steep slopes of the far-off North York Moors. All of Robert Thompson's work, and that of his descendants too, includes a unique signature, an individually carved mouse. Can you find the eleven mice that he carved upon the Ilmington oak? However, during your search for the mice, do not overlook the severely classical monument to Francis Canning and his wife, by the early 19th-century sculptor, Sir Richard Westmacott, other examples of whose work will be found at **Honington** and at Preston-on-Stour, near Stratford-

Ilmington Church

upon-Avon. Westmacott, much in the spirit of his times, was very fond of weeping figures and classical urns, and these features will be found in all three of the village churches concerned. The unusual lantern-like structure by the south porch is an early 19th-century monument to members of the Sansom family.

There is a pleasantly quiet road running south from Ilmington, along the eastern slopes of Windmill Hill to **Charingworth,** with fine views over the Vale of Red Horse to the distant line of Edge Hill.

INGLESHAM CHURCH (1-2 K11) *1 mi. S Lechlade.* Situated by a farm beside the Thames, this charming little building was sensitively preserved by a man to whom we owe so much - William Morris. His work has left the medieval flavour of Inglesham undisturbed, and it is well worth visiting. Be sure not to miss the hauntingly beautiful 13th-century Madonna and Child. The River Coln flows into the Thames not far away, and it was here also that the **Thames and Severn Canal** ended its long run over the Cotswolds to join the Thames.

JURASSIC WAY (Not shown on map.) Now used as the title of a long-distance path across Northamptonshire, this is also the name that some archaeologists have given to the prehistoric 'ridgeway' running south-westwards from the mouth of the Humber to Salisbury Plain and the coast beyond. Although its course through the Cotswold area is not at all clear it appears to have followed the high ground some distance behind the long west-facing scarp - from the Rollright Stones in the east, to the hills above Bath in the far south-west. Some of its course is still followed by modern roads, and much of it was also used by medieval traders, especially those transporting wool by pack animals to the port of Bristol (see **Campden Lane.**). For more information on this and other ancient trackways, read G.R. Crosher's excellent book, *Along The Cotswold Ways.*

KELMSCOT (1-2 K12) *2½ mi. E Lechlade.* Lying just to the north of the Thames, this small village will for ever be associated with the man who lived at the lovely manor house here from 1871 until his death in 1896 - William Morris, craftsman, poet, social reformer and visionary. In a letter to a friend in 1871, Morris wrote:

I have been looking about for a house for the wife and kids, and whither do you guess my eye is turned now? Kelmscot, a little village about two miles above Radcot Bridge - a heaven on earth; an old stone Elizabethan house - and such a garden! close down on the river, a boat house, and all things handy.

The manor, an Elizabethan building with 17th-century additions, still bears the stamp of Morris's powerful personality, besides containing furnishings, wallpapers, and fabrics designed by him, and pictures by his friends Rossetti and Burne-Jones. It is now owned by the Society of Antiquaries of London and is open to the public.

A stone carving on the village's Memorial Cottages depicts Morris sitting beneath trees, and the nearby Morris Memorial Hall, designed by Ernest Gimson (see **Daneway**), was opened by George Bernard Shaw. The small cruciform church contains much evidence of its Norman origins, and in the churchyard will be found Morris's tomb which, like the Memorial Cottages, was designed by Philip Webb.

Walk from Kelmscot, starting near the Plough Inn and crossing the Thames to **Buscot Park,** or going across Buscot Weir to **Buscot.** It is also possible to walk on along the north bank of the Thames to St John's Bridge and **Lechlade,** using the **Thames Path.**

KEMBLE (1-2 K7) *4 mi. SW Cirencester.* This large village astride the A429 grew in importance in the years when it was a junction on Brunel's busy railway line to the west: hence the number of 19th-century buildings to be found here. The branch lines from it to Tetbury and Cirencester are long gone, but the little station here is still a favourite with those travelling to London from the southern Cotswolds. The line of the old **Thames and Severn Canal** passes about a mile to its north, and not much further away is the source of the Thames at Trewsbury Mead - known as Thames Head. The church was largely rebuilt in the 19th century, but retains some interesting older features. The whole of the south transept was brought from nearby **Ewen,** where it had served as a chapel. There is also a beautiful Norman inner doorway, and hidden behind the organ is an effigy of a 13th-century knight in chain mail. It is possible to walk south-eastwards from here to **Poole Keynes** and the western fringes of the **Cotswold Water Park,** or northwards to the **Thames Head** - the source of the River Thames.

KENCOT (1-2 J12) *4 mi. NE Lechlade.* This pleasant village to the immediate north of **Broadwell** has the misfortune to lie close to the airfield at Brize Norton and noise here is a problem. However, flying does not go on all the time, and Kencot is an otherwise quiet village with an interesting little church beyond a small triangular green. This building has an unusual turret stair and a Norman south doorway with a tympanum depicting *Sagittarius the Archer* (quite a favourite in this area - see also **Hook Norton** and **Salford**). The interior was restored in 1962, and, as a modest notice proclaims, *this was made possible by the generosity of Edith Bundy of San Francisco.* There is an attractive little early-19th-century gallery, a Jacobean pulpit and a 17th-century monument, to Mary Oldisworthy and Elizabeth Mountsteven.

Dovecot at Kiddington

KIDDINGTON (1 F15) *4 mi. NW Woodstock.* Here is a largely 19th-century mansion, Kiddington Hall, overlooking a landscaped lake in the Glyme valley. The little church is prettily sited beside the mansion, but it has been so heavily restored that very little atmosphere remains. Do not overlook the beautifully roofed, circular dovecot just beyond the churchyard wall (but do not trespass beyond the wall).

KIFTSGATE COURT GARDEN (1 B10) *3 mi. NE Chipping Campden.* This is perhaps not as well known as neighbouring **Hidcote Manor Garden**, but it should on no account be missed. Kiftsgate Court, situated on the very edge of the Cotswold scarp above **Mickleton** is a largely Victorian house, with an 18th-century portico which was moved piece by piece up from Mickleton Manor on a specially constructed light railway. Most of the garden was created in the years following the First World War, by Mrs Heather Muir, and she was no doubt helped and inspired by her neighbour and friend, Major Johnson, the creator of nearby **Hidcote Manor Garden.** Kiftsgate Garden's steep hillside setting is more dramatic than Hidcote's, and Mrs Muir took full advantage of this in her splendid design.

Mrs Muir's daughter and granddaughter, Mrs Binny and Mrs Chambers, have carried on the Kiftsgate tradition, and today the garden continues to evolve. There are paths, flower-beds, shrubs and trees on the terraced areas above the scarp, and a steep cliff with pine-trees, and winding paths leading to a swimming pool on a grassy terrace at its foot, with views down a wooded combe to the Vale of Evesham. Come here in summertime, when the air is heavy with the scent of roses, and the blue swimming pool, viewed through the pine-trees from the steep hillside above, brings a hint of the Mediterranean to this lovely garden enfolded in the Cotswold hills. Teas are available here. Walk from here, down to **Mickleton** or link on to the walks from **Hidcote Manor Garden.**

Kiftsgate Court

THE KIFTSGATE STONE (1 C10) *1 mi. W Chipping Campden.* (Not shown on map.) This rather unexciting monolith lies half hidden in woodland just to the north-west of the road towards Broadway, on the hill to the west of **Chipping Campden.** It marks an ancient 'moot' or meeting place, where people used to gather to organise their affairs and dispense justice (often of a very rough nature), and this was in fact the original administrative centre of the Kiftsgate Hundred. 'Hundreds' were sub-divisions of shires, part of a system of local government which grew up in Saxon times, and one which was so firmly established by the time of the Norman conquest that it was absorbed into the Norman framework of administration. Traditions attached to the Kiftsgate Stone itself were indeed so strong that its use ceased only in the years following the proclamation of George III in 1760, the last occasion which was celebrated here.

KILKENNY AND COLD COMMON (1-2 F7) *1½ mi. SW Andoversford.* Here at Cold Common on the A436, just to the west of the Kilkenny road junction, is a large car park and picnic area, with information points. There are wide views over the surrounding countryside, and an attractive minor road running southwards into the **Hilcot and Pinchley Woods.**

The Lower Ford, Kineton

KINETON (1-2 E9) *5 mi. E Winchcombe.* The attractions of this hamlet lie mainly in the two nearby fords spanning the little tree-lined Windrush, which flows southwards from its source above **Cutsdean.** The lower of the two fords is easily negotiated, but do not try the upper one. There is a Donnington Brewery pub here - the Half Way House. Head westwards from Kineton to cross another ford, before arriving at a crossroads in miniature parkland, which makes an excellent base for exploring **Guiting Woods.**

KINGHAM (1-2 E12) *4 mi. SW Chipping Norton.* Lively village in the broad Evenlode Valley, with wide greens at the northern end, and at the southern one, a very handsome 17th-century rectory. Beyond the rectory, the small tower of Kingham church looks out across the Evenlode meadows. The unusual stone pew-ends and backs were installed in the church as part of a restoration in 1853 and are elegant but rather stark. Do not miss the monument to the Rev. William Dowdeswell, who built the splendid rectory, nor the monument to Lieutenant-Colonel Davis, showing a soldier leaning on his tomb with a reversed rifle. See also the brass to Katherine James (1588), depicting her kneeling figure surrounded by children. Use the **Oxfordshire Way** to walk westwards across the

Evenlode Valley to Gawcombe and over to **Wyck Rissington,** or to walk southwards down the valley to **Bruern Abbey** and **Shipton-under-Wychwood.**

KINGSCOTE (2 L3) *4 mi. E Dursley.* Agreeable village in high country, with an over-restored 13th-century church. This has a Perpendicular tower and there are several interesting monuments in its churchyard including a triangular stone pyramid. A tablet in the church recalls that it was here, in 1788, that Catherine Kingscote was married to Doctor Edward Jenner of Berkeley, the discoverer of vaccination - *a marriage which brought him much happiness.* Walk southwards from here, down a valley to **Newington Bagpath, Lasborough** and **Boxwell;** or north-eastwards to **Horsley** and **Nailsworth.**

KING'S STANLEY (1-2 J4) *2½ mi. W Stroud.* This village lies beneath the Cotswold edge and is rather overpowered by modern development. The fine old Stanley Mill, which was built in the early years of the 19th century, stopped making cloth some years ago, but there are hopes that it will be restored. At the north end of the village there is a partly Norman church in a churchyard with clipped yews.

KINGSWOOD (2 L2) *1 mi. SW Wotton-under-Edge.* This village beneath the Cotswold edge has an early-18th-century church, which was over-restored and partly rebuilt in 1900. All that survives of the great Cistercian abbey of Kingswood is its 16th-century gatehouse, which is tucked away between various old houses behind the village's main street. This gateway, which is in the care of English Heritage, was completed only a few years before the rest was destroyed during the Dissolution of the Monasteries in 1539. It is therefore one of the youngest examples of monastic building in the country. It has fine vaulting beneath its entrance arch and a pleasantly beamed room above.

Kingswood Abbey Gatehouse

LANGFORD (1-2 K12) *3 mi. NE Lechlade.* This quiet village looks southwards over flat Thames Valley farmland to the distant line of the Berkshire Downs beyond. Langford's church is a treasure-house of early medieval art and architecture and should not be missed. Built into the south porch are a rare and beautiful Saxon carving of the Crucifixion, and a 14th-century carving with the figures of Mary and John. There are also other fascinating figures carved on the central tower, which itself was probably built by Saxon craftsmen working soon after the Norman conquest. The Norman and Early English arches beneath the tower of this cruciform church are unusually lofty, and it is thought that its ambitious conception was possibly due to the parish having been in royal hands (as it certainly was by the time of the Domesday Survey of 1086). Do not miss a visit to this exceptionally interesting church.

Langford War Memorial

LARK STOKE AND ILMINGTON DOWNS (1 B11) *1½ mi. W Ilmington.* At 850 feet above sea level, this is the highest point in Warwickshire, and one of the northern bastions of the Cotswolds. Despite the presence of a small TV transmitting station, this is still reasonably good walking country, and there are fine open views northwards over the Avon valley, and eastwards to the wooded silhouette of Edge Hill and the rolling Northamptonshire uplands that lie beyond. Lark Stoke received a separate entry in the Domesday Book (1086), but there is now no trace of any ancient village on these windy hillsides, nor in the woodlands below. Walk south from here to **Ebrington,** and then south-west to **Chipping Campden;** or make a small circular walk by taking in Hidcote Boyce and Hidcote Bartrim, calling in of course at the splendid Hidcote Manor Garden. Motorists can use a narrow, partly unfenced road, leading up from the minor road between **Ilmington** and **Mickleton.**

LASBOROUGH (2 L3) *4 mi. SW Nailsworth.* A dignified 17th-century manor house and a small Victorian church overlook the quiet valley in which lies Lasborough Park, a fine 18th-century mansion built by James Wyatt. A drive or a walk as far as the church makes a pleasant diversion from the busy A46.

LATTON (2 L9) *1½ mi. NW Cricklade.* Mercifully this small village has now been by-passed by the modern road that veers away from the course of the old **Ermin Way.** It lies in water-meadow country near the old **Thames and Severn Canal**, with one of the canal's little 'round houses' nearby (see **Hyde**). The stout Norman church was over-restored by the renowned Victorian architect, William Butterfield, and regrettably lacks any feeling of the medieval past. However, there are pleasant stone floors and an amusing series of corbel figures supporting the nave roof.

LAVERTON (1 C9) *2 mi. SW Broadway.* Large hamlet beneath the Cotswold edge, with several pleasant farmhouses. There are paths from here to **Buckland** and **Stanton,** and a pleasant bridleway up the hill linking onto the **Cotswold Way,** and going beyond to **Snowshill.**

LEAFIELD (1-2 G13) *4 mi. NW Witney.* This long, straggling village stands on high ground between the Evenlode and Windrush valleys and just to the south-west of the much depleted **Wychwood Forest;** in medieval times it must have stood near it centre. The tall spired church was built by Sir Gilbert Scott in 1860 and has an austere but rather grand interior. It looks out across a long green, with a medieval cross which was restored by the villagers in 1873 in thanks for *their deliverance from the scourge of smallpox.* There are fine views southwards to the distant line of the Berkshire downs.

Cottages at Leafield

LECHLADE (1-2 K11) *9 mi. S Burford.* Here on the southern borders of the Cotswolds, the Rivers Coln and Leach join the Thames, and **Inglesham,** just above Lechlade, marks the head of its navigation. After 1789 it was possible to trans-ship to narrow boats (see also **Buscot**), for it was in that year that the **Thames and Severn Canal** was opened. It was also from Lechlade and nearby Radcot (see Maps 1-2 K13) that much of the stone quarried in the Burford area was shipped down river for the building of St Paul's Cathedral and a multitude of other buildings in London and Oxford. Lechlade church was itself built almost entirely of stone from Burford's neighbour, **Taynton.**

This small market town is still busy with the comings and goings of boats, but now they ply for pleasure only. There are two fine bridges here - 18th-century Ha'penny Bridge with its little square tollhouse overlooking the boatyard at the southern end of the town, and St John's Bridge, dating from as early as 1228, in meadows well to the south-east. In summertime, many boats moor on the river banks between the two bridges, and there is a busy Riverside Parking and Leisure Area just upstream from Ha'penny Bridge, and reached from the A361 to its south. For those wishing for more tranquillity, small boats may be hired from the Riverside Boatyard to explore the narrow, shallow river meandering past **Inglesham** up towards Hannington Bridge. There is also a path leading south-westwards beside the south side of the river almost as far as the point where the **Thames and Severn Canal** joined the river. This confluence is marked by a little 'round house' (see **Hyde**).

The town itself, which to its credit appears to make few other concessions to tourism, is centred upon its small triangular Market Square. This is overlooked by dignified 18th- and early 19th-century buildings, including the handsome mellow-brick New Inn, with

its archway entrance reminding the visitor that Lechlade was once a busy coaching stop. The Square is dominated from its far corner by Lechlade's fine Perpendicular Parish Church, with its tower topped by a slender spire - described by the 16th-century antiquary John Leland in his famous *Itinerary*, '*as a pratie pyramis of stone*'.

Ha'Penny Bridge, Lechlade

The interior is handsomely proportioned, with a high clerestory and a magnificent chancel roof with carved bosses. See also the beautifully carved door leading to the vestry, the 15th-century brass of wool merchant John Townsend and his wife, and the beautifully executed monument to Mrs Anne Simons (1769). It was the churchyard at Lechlade that inspired the poet Shelley to compose his *Summer Evening Meditation*, and there are few better places to stop awhile than this quiet corner.

Do not let the charms of the Square and the churchyard deter you from exploring the three streets that stem from it - Burford Street, running northwards, High Street to the west and St John Street to the east. All three are blessed with a wealth of pleasant 17th-, 18th- and early 19th-century buildings and are well worth visiting.

There is a Trout Farm on the A361 just to the north of the town, beyond the River Leach and the flooded gravel pits beside it, one of the latter providing opportunities for sailing. These 'lakes' are at the far, eastern end of the **Cotswold Water Park.** Just beyond is the hamlet of Little Faringdon, which has a small Norman church with several interesting features, notably the sculptural details to its north arcade capitals - very probably by the same craftsman who worked at **Langford, Fulbrook** and **North Cerney.**

In addition to the walk upstream from Ha'penny Bridge, referred to above, it is possible to walk south-eastwards across the meadows to St John's Bridge, where there is a cheerful inn, The Trout, and the highest lock on the Thames, St John's. This is busy with colourful boats and boating people all summer long, and there is a fine view from here across the meadows to Lechlade Church.

LECKHAMPTON (1-2 F6) *1 mi. S Cheltenham.* This large suburb of Cheltenham is situated on its southern fringes beneath the steep quarries of Leckhampton Hill (see **The Devil's Chimney**). Despite Cheltenham's proximity Leckhampton has retained a flavour of its own. The church of St Peter is pleasantly sited, with its slender 14th-century tower and spire viewed against a backdrop of the hills. Almost all the rest of the church was rebuilt in the 19th century, but there are interesting monuments to be seen, including the fine effigies of Sir John Giffard and his lady (1327), and the attractive brass of Elizabeth Norwood (1598), complete with husband, nine sons and two daughters. In the churchyard will be found a monument to Edward Wilson, one of Captain Scott's ill-fated companions on their journey to the South Pole in 1912.

LEDWELL (1 E15) *7 mi. N Woodstock.* Delightful hamlet tucked away in a quiet cul-de-sac leading from a cross-roads just north of **Sandford St Martin**. It has a small green overlooked by thatched stone cottages, with a Victorian well-head and cast iron pump and, some distance away, a little Primitive Methodist chapel dated 1856. Lord Deloraine, the third son of the ill-fated Duke of Monmouth had a mansion here, but it has long since vanished. He is buried in the churchyard at neighbouring **Sandford St.Martin**. Walk north-west and then west, to **Great Tew,** or north-eastwards to **Over Worton**.

LEIGHTERTON (2 M4) *4 mi. SW Tetbury.* An attractive village in high country, with a hospitable inn called the Royal Oak and a church which was heavily restored in the 19th-century and which has, unusually for the Cotswolds, a timber-framed belfry. There is a pleasant duckpond at the southern end of the village and there are footpaths across the fields, south-eastwards to **Westonbirt Arboretum** and westwards to **Tresham.**

LEONARD STANLEY (2 J3) *1 mi. S Stonehouse.* There are fragmentary remains of a priory in some of its farm buildings and the village's fine church owes much to its monastic origins. This looks out over a small green with a few brick and stone cottages and beside it there is a lovely 18th-century fronted farmhouse. The church is cruciform and has a beautiful interior with four Norman arches at the tower crossing and exquisitely carved capitals to the chancel vaulting shafts, together with many other interesting features. There are pleasant walks southwards up the steep wooded slopes of **Frocester Hill.**

Romanesque Sculpture, Leonard Stanley

LIDSTONE (1-2 E14) *3 mi. SE Chipping Norton.* A hamlet on the steep southern slopes of the Glyme Valley. The little Talbot Arms has gone long ago and there is now no special reason to visit Lidstone. However it is enviably sited, looking out across to the woodlands of Heythrop Park and well removed from the busy A44.

LITTLE BARRINGTON (1-2 H11) *3 mi. W Burford.* A very pleasing village with most of its houses grouped around a sloping, bowl-shaped green, which was originally a quarry. At least two cottages have re-set medieval stone doorways. The church, away from the centre on the east side of the village, has a Norman doorway and nave, and a Norman tympanum depicting *Christ in Majesty* over the outside of a blocked-up doorway in the north aisle. Do not miss the charming early 18th-century memorial tablet built into the outer east wall of the porch. To the north-east of the village there is an inn of character called The Fox which overlooks an old bridge across the Windrush built by local master-mason, Thomas Strong (see **Burford**). The Inn for All Seasons, an attractive hotel and restaurant, is situated about half a mile to the south, on the busy A40.

Walk via the Fox Inn to **Great Barrington,** returning via Barrington Mill. The Fox Inn

might make an alternative starting point, but only if the landlord permits the parking of cars by those also intending to use the inn's services. It is also possible to walk westwards from here across the fields to the village of **Windrush,** and from there northwards up the Windrush Valley to **Great Rissington.** For those not wishing to walk, there is a quiet little road down the Windrush Valley from Little Barrington to **Burford,** with beautiful views of the meandering river in the meadows beyond.

Memorial Tablet, Little Barrington

LITTLE COMPTON (1 D12) *4 mi. SE Moreton-in-Marsh.* Situated in a sheltered hollow between Barton Hill and the main Cotswold edge, this pleasant village, Warwickshire's southernmost, is over the watershed into the `land of the Thames'. This great river may seem very far away, but the stream on which Little Compton lies flows west to join the Evenlode below Moreton-in-Marsh, where this river is itself near the start of its quiet journey to join the Thames' just above Oxford. The little church retains its 14th-century tower with saddleback roof, but the rest of the building dates from the 1860s, and is not of great interest to visitors. In the churchyard there is a gravestone carved by one of the 20th century's outstanding sculptors, Eric Gill; a simple but fine example of his craft. The lovely 17th-century manor house next to the church was the home of Bishop Juxon, who had the unenviable task of attending Charles I at his trial and subsequent execution on the scaffold outside the Banqueting Hall, Whitehall. During their walk to this place of execution, Juxon was observed by the king to be weeping, and the king is supposed to have exclaimed, *Leave all this my Lord; we have no time for it.* This terse comment appears at least to have

The Manor, Little Compton

stopped Juxon's tears, and after some years he received substantial consolation, for when his monarch's son Charles II was finally crowned in 1660, he was appointed Archbishop of Canterbury - a post he held until his death, sadly only three years later.

If you pass through Little Compton during 'opening hours', call at the Red Lion. This cheerful inn serves Donnington Ale - real ale which is brewed at the delectable little **Donnington Brewery,** a short distance to the north of Stow-on-the-Wold. Walk northwards from Little Compton, on the quiet road over Barton Hill to **Barton-on-the-Heath,** or over the fields on a path parallel to the road, passing Salter's Well Farm.

Little Rissington

LITTLE RISSINGTON (1-2 F11) *1½ mi. E Bourton-on-the-Water.* Situated on the eastern slopes of the Windrush valley, this small village has pleasant views out over several flooded gravel pits, some of which are now nature reserves (see **Bourton-on-the-Water**). The church, which is approached by a pathway over fields, was restored twice in the 19th century and is not of great interest apart from its Norman south doorway. In the neat churchyard will be found the graves of several young men who were killed while flying from the great airfield on the hill above. This was once the RAF's Central Flying School, and the original home of the Red Arrows Display Team, but has now been closed for many years. There is a good bridle road southwards to **Great Rissington,** and it is also possible to walk northwards to **Wyck Rissington,** to link onto the **Oxfordshire Way,** or westwards, down to **Bourton-on-the-Water,** passing one of its gravel-pit lakes.

LITTLE ROLLRIGHT (1 D13) *2 mi. NW Chipping Norton.* Here, in a quiet setting beneath

the hills, are a fine 17th-century manor house, a modest rectory of the same period, a few cottages, and a delightful little church. This is a largely Perpendicular building, but its squat tower and south window date from the 17th century. It has a simple interior, with pleasant Perpendicular windows and two gorgeous 17th-century monuments - canopied tomb chests to members of the Dixon family which make it clear that the Dixons were persons of considerable substance, probably sheep graziers. Do not miss a visit to this very satisfying

Monuments at Little Rollright

little building. Although most visitors will arrive at the fascinating **Rollright Stones** by car, it is also possible to reach them by walking north-eastwards over the fields from Little Rollright.

LITTLE SODBURY (2 N2) *2 mi. NE Chipping Sodbury.* The fine medieval manor house where William Tyndale (see **North Nibley, Slimbridge** and **Tyndale Monument**) was almost certainly tutor in 1522-3, lies to the south of this small village. Its unexceptional church is claimed to be based upon the plans of the Tyndale Chapel behind the manor house and the handsome 19th-century pulpit has a figure of Tyndale carved upon it. Little Sodbury lies on the **Cotswold Way** and this can be used to walk south to **Old Sodbury,** passing through the ramparts of Sodbury Camp - a very impressive Iron Age hill fort.

LITTLE WASHBOURNE (1 D7) *4 mi. NW Winchcombe.* This small hamlet has a minute Norman church prettily sited in an orchard, with a bellcote and a completely unspoilt Georgian interior. There is a Norman chancel arch, and a Norman lancet window in the chancel, but the principal attractions of Little Washbourne church are its two-decker pulpit and its lovely 18th-century box pews, each with its own candle-holder. Visitors wishing to sample the simplicity of 18th-century England can do no better than to sit for a few moments in this charming little building.

Little Washbourne Church

LITTLE WOLFORD (1 C12) *4 mi. NE Moreton-in-Marsh.* A hamlet of Victorian estate cottages and unexciting council houses, situated in gently undulating countryside, with views towards the spires of **Todenham** and **Great Wolford,** over the valley through which the little Nethercote Brook flows, on its way to join the Stour a mile or so to the north. Any dullness is relieved by tantalising glimpses of Little Wolford's fine Tudor manor house. This is in a pleasing blend of stone and timber-framing - appropriate in an area which lies between the ancient forest country of Warwickshire and the bare stone uplands of the Oxfordshire Cotswolds. Walk south and east, up the valley, past Pepperwell and Kings Brake Farms, to **Long Compton**, and return via an unfenced road across **Weston Park.**

LODGE PARK (1-2 H10) *2½ mi. SE Northleach.* This charming little mid-17th-century building standing in open wold country was commissioned by the hunchback John 'Crump' Dutton of nearby **Sherborne Park.** It was designed in the French style, probably by Valentine Strong, the Little Barrington quarry-owner, as a grandstand from which Dutton's guests could watch the coursing of deer by greyhounds. It was converted into a dwelling only in 1898, and was bequeathed some years ago to the National Trust, along with most of the Sherborne Estate. Read more about Lodge Park in James Lees-Milne's delightful book, *Some Cotswold Country Houses.*

Gateway, Lodge Park

LONGBOROUGH (1 D10) *2½ mi. N Stow-on-the-Wold.* Attractively sited village on a hill slope looking out eastwards over the broad Evenlode Valley, with a pleasant inn called the Coach and Horses, many neat houses and cottages and a church which has Norman origins and which once belonged to **Hailes Abbey.** It has a 13th-century tower with an added upper stage in the best Perpendicular tradition, complete with pinnacles and gargoyles. The sunken path to the south porch is overlooked by the beautiful Decorated-style windows of the 14th-century south transept. This houses the very grand 17th-century monument to Sir William Leigh, complete with his wife and children, and a monument to a 14th-century knight and his lady, for whom this transept was probably built. The north transept, added after the demolition of nearby **Sezincote** church, is sealed off and houses the tomb of Sir Charles Cockerell, the builder of **Sezincote**. This church contains several other items of interest, but make a point of looking at the beautiful 14th-century font - a tall richly sculptured piece. Walk north from here to **Sezincote,** and on to **Bourton-on-the Hill** and **Batsford,** with fine views over the Evenlode Valley from many points along the way.

South Porch and Transept, Longborough

LONG COMPTON (1 D12) *4 mi. NW Chipping Norton.* This attractive stone village stretches out along the A3400 for over half a mile, to the very foot of the long hill that climbs up over the Cotswold edge, across the county boundary from Warwickshire into Oxfordshire. There is considerable modern building at its northern end, and the main road is always busy with traffic; but despite this Long Compton has much to offer. It has a cheerful inn, many trim houses and cottages, and a church whose handsome Perpendicular tower looks westwards over a large bumpy field which must have been the site of the original village. The church's lovely south porch is approached by a yew-lined path leading from a delightful little two-storeyed lych gate, which is believed to be a small timber-framed cottage with its lower storey removed. The core of the church is 13th-century, but externally it appears to be almost entirely Perpendicular. See the nave roof, the charming little Perpendicular south aisle chapel, and in the porch the pathetically worn effigy of a lady. For a full account of life at Long Compton and in the countryside that surrounds it, read Edward Rainsberry's delightful book, *Through the Lych Gate*, published by the Roundwood Press, but unfortunately now out of print.

The best walk from Long Compton uses the **Macmillan Way** and leads across fields north-eastwards to **Whichford,** skirting the southern edge of the great Whichford Wood. There is also a good walk leading south-westwards over a spur of the hills (also partly using the **Macmillan Way**), and down into **Little Compton.**

LONG HANBOROUGH (1 G15) *2 mi. SW Woodstock.* This is stretched out along the busy A4095, with much modern development. However the George and Dragon looks pleasant and there is a quiet green beside the road northwards to Combe. The Oxford Bus Museum is in the Old Station Yard at the eastern end of the village. This houses over 40 vehicles, from Oxford trams to buses of the 1970's.

LOWER KILCOTT (2 M3) *3½ mi SE Wotton-under-Edge.* Quiet little hamlet tucked away in the steep, edge country, with a small 18th-century water mill, with some of its machinery still intact. *(Not open to the public.)* Follow the **Cotswold Way** south-westwards from here to visit the **Somerset Monument.**

LOWER LEMINGTON (1 C11) *1½ mi. NE Moreton-in-Marsh.* This is now no more than a

Lower Lemington Church

quiet little hamlet with a farm, a few houses and a small church - all spread around an open field-cum-farmyard. However, the undulating fields surrounding it conceal the remains of a larger medieval village, and on the road to its south there is a substantial 16th- and 17th-century manor house. The little church in its stone-walled churchyard has a small bellcote where the nave roof meets that of the chancel, and a narrow Norman doorway within its porch. The chancel was damaged during the Civil War, but the exceptionally narrow Norman chancel arch, with minute squints on either side, has survived. There are pleasant old Commandment Boards, an early Norman tub font, an 18th-century two-decker pulpit and a small 17th-century brass to two brothers, Charles and Peter Greville. The nearby Lemington Fishing Lakes provide angling opportunities.

LOWER SLAUGHTER (1-2 F10) *1½ mi. N Bourton-on-the-Water.* Most of this delightful and much visited village seems to have been planted upon the banks of its stream, the little River Eye, the two sides of which are linked by a series of small, simply built bridges. The water-mill with its pond and its mellow-brick chimney provides a fitting entrance for the stream, whose departure is marked by graceful willows, as it hurries away to join the River Dikler just to the east of Bourton-on-the-Water. The manor house, now much altered, was built in about 1650 by Valentine Strong, the quarry-owner of Little Barrington, and in its grounds is one of Gloucestershire's largest

The Mill, Lower Slaughter

dovecots. The nearby church was rebuilt in 1867 and is not of great interest to visitors.

Lower Slaughter is perhaps a little too trim, and there are now two hotels in the village, but it is still well worth visiting. Explore both Lower and Upper Slaughter, which are linked by a delightful footpath beside the little River Eye. There is another pleasant walk from here, southwards across the fields to **Bourton-on-the-Water** and it is also possible to use the **Macmillan Way** to walk south-westwards to **Cold Aston** and **Turkdean.**

LOWER SWELL (1-2 E10) *1 mi. W Stow-on-the-Wold.* Much of this tidy, well built village is astride the still-busy B4068, once the main Stow to Cheltenham road. It has a pleasant 17th-century inn, the Golden Ball, and a small hotel close by. In the valley at its eastern end there is a bridge over the little River Dikler, which has here just completed its short journey through the park of Abbotswood, a fine early 20th-century house designed by Sir Edwin Lutyens. Abbotswood Gardens are particularly lovely and will possibly be open to the public on one or two Sunday afternoons in spring and early summer. To the left of the road up to Stow, a short distance beyond the bridge, will be found Spa Cottages, built in a slightly oriental style and thought to have been inspired by S.P. Cockerell's work at **Sezincote.** There is an inscription on one of them stating that a chalybeate spring was discovered here in 1807, and it was intended that this feature should be the basis for a spa - a plan that appears never to have fully materialised.

Memorial, Lower Swell

Lower Swell's church lies to the north of the village, on the road to Upper Swell. The original Norman building now forms the south aisle and this still retains the former Norman chancel arch, which is enriched with a splendid series of animal carvings. The Norman south doorway is equally interesting, and has a tympanum above it depicting a dove eating fruit from a 'tree of life'.

LUCKINGTON (2 N4) *7 mi. SW Malmesbury.* Small village astride the B4040 with a minute lock-up, an inn called The Royal Ship, and away to its east a church with 13th-century origins sitting in a churchyard above. The church's near neighbour, Luckington Court is a delightfully mellow Queen Anne house. The **Macmillan Way** follows the course of the Avon for a short distance here although it soon veers south towards **Castle Combe,** some five miles southwards.

House at Luckington

MACMILLAN WAY LONG DISTANCE FOOTPATH (Not shown on map.) This fully waymarked, 290-mile coast-to-coast path runs from Boston in Lincolnshire to Abbotsbury in Dorset. It runs right across the area covered by this guide - from **Warmington** to **Castle Combe,** a distance of just over 70 miles.

MADMARSTON HILL (1 C14) *4 mi. W Banbury.* Site of an Iron Age hill fort with the course of a Roman road running through Swalcliffe Lea to the south of it. The line of this road runs through the site of an extensive Roman settlement, and it is interesting to note that the area is known as 'The Blacklands', the same description as that for the area north of Kings Sutton, where there was also a Roman settlement. This is probably due to a certain rich quality in the soil caused by previous human habitation. Walk northwards from here to **Shutford** and **Shenington,** or eastwards to **Broughton.**

MALMESBURY (2 M6) 5 mi. SE Tetbury. An unspoilt hilltop market town above the upper reaches of the Bristol Avon, not far from its source on the southern fringes of the Cotswolds. Visitors to its abbey, founded in the 7th century, must have brought considerable prosperity to the town, but by the time of the Dissolution, weaving had become the main source of wealth, as at Bradford-on-Avon and nearby **Castle Combe.** The fabric of the abbey was largely Norman and its abbey church was a vast cruciform building. At the Dissolution the Abbey was sold to a prosperous local clothier, called Crump, who set up his looms in parts of the building. However the nave and the south porch of the abbey church soon became the parish church and we are therefore much indebted to Master Crump for the saving of this remarkable building. The Norman interior, the original nave, is most impressive and its blank east wall reminds us that there was once so much more here, allowing us to imagine the spire that once stood above the crossing just beyond - a spire apparently even taller than Salisbury's. This unfortunately fell down in 1500 and was not replaced. See especially the 15th-century tomb (now empty) of King Athelstan, grandson of Alfred the Great.

Today however the church's outstanding feature is its Norman porch. This is entered beneath a large archway, sculptured richly enough to give a hint of the treasures within. Here are some of the finest Romanesque carvings in England - a *Christ in Majesty* in the tympanum above the inner south door, with the wonderfully elongated figures of six apostles on the facing side walls. After looking at these marvels, walk through an arched gateway into the little Market Square where there is an attractive Perpendicular Market Cross, which, as Henry VIII's antiquary, John Leland states in his *Itinerary, 'was for poore folkes to stande dry when rayne cummeth'*.

Apart from these survivals from medieval times, there is a wealth of 17th- and 18th-century buildings in Malmesbury, many of which are now host to bright and friendly shops and inns. For this reason alone, the town is well worth visiting, but before exploring its many quiet corners, pay a visit to the helpful Tourist Information Centre in the ground floor of the Town Hall in Market Lane. This is also the location of the Malmesbury Athelstan Museum, where there are, amongst other items, displays relating to lace-making, rural life and local industry.

MARSTON MEYSEY (2 L10) *3 mi. SW Fairford.* A long, thin village in flat country not far from the monster runway of Fairford airfield, once used by *Concorde* in the years of its flight-testing. The church is Victorian and not of great interest to visitors, but there are many lovely old tombs in its churchyard. Well to the south of the village there is one of the round houses built for the maintenance men of the long-vanished **Thames and Severn Canal.** This is reached on foot from Marston Meysey, and there is a path beyond, across water-meadows to Castle Eaton on the Thames.

Canal Round House Nr Marston Meysey

House at Maugersbury

MAUGERSBURY (1-2 E11) *¹⁄₂ mi. SE Stow-on-the-Wold.* Quiet hamlet on the south-eastern slopes of Stow-on-the-Wold's hill, with attractive views across to Icomb Hill. There are several pleasant farmhouses, but no features of special interest apart from St Edward's Well, which is situated in an overgrown late 18th-century garden (on private ground) on either side of the now blocked-off road between the village and the Foss Way, and which is supposedly connected by a tunnel under the road. It is not certain with which St Edward the well is supposed to be connected - Edward, King and Martyr, Edward the Confessor, or Edward the Hermit - the latter being a shadowy local figure from early Christian times. The same mystery surrounds this 'St Edward connection' at **Stow-on-the-Wold.** The **Macmillan Way** comes through Maugersbury and this can be used to walk to **Lower Slaughter.** There is also a good bridle road southwards from Maugersbury to **Icomb.**

MEYSEY HAMPTON (1-2 K9) *2 mi. W Fairford.* This very trim village has a semi-circular green overlooked by a small inn, the Mason's Arms, and a fine Georgian manor house. The 13th-century cruciform church was probably built by the Knights Templar and is a neat looking building. Within its rather cold interior will be found four well sculptured tower arches, handsome triple sedilia with a piscina in a fourth niche, and a very engaging 17th-century monument incorporating the effigies of physician James Vaulx, his two wives and their many offspring. Vaulx, a doctor with a considerable reputation,

was once asked by James I, who was considering a change of physician, how he had come by his great skill. But when he was told by Vaulx that he had acquired it by practice, that somewhat dour monarch is supposed to have replied,

Then, by my soul, thou hast killed many a man and shalt na' practise on me. Alas, poor Vaulx!

Vaulx Monuments, at Meysey Hampton

MICKLETON (1B10) *3 mi. N Chipping Campden.* This almost town-like village has considerable modern development on its fringes, and is rather disturbed by traffic on the still-busy B4632. However, it lies in a fine setting immediately beneath the Cotswold edge, and has several attractive stone houses and cottages in addition to those of thatch and half-timber. The little Victorian Memorial Fountain close by the Three Ways Hotel is an interesting feature - an unusually restrained piece of work by William Burges, the architect of Cardiff Castle and Castle Coch, two supreme examples of the High Victorian Gothic.

Turn up beside handsome 'Cotswold-Queen Anne' style Medford House, to visit the church, which lies on the southern edge of the village, with pleasant views up towards the wooded Cotswold edge. This has a fine 14th-century tower and spire, and a most unusual 17th-century two-storeyed porch. Inside will be found a 12th-century crucifix or rood (over the north aisle chapel altar), some stout, late Norman arcading, and a monument to the 18th-century architect, builder and quarry-owner, Thomas Woodward of Chipping Campden, erected by his grandson, Edward. There is considerable evidence of Victorian restoration in the shape of the east window and most of the woodwork, but Mickleton church has retained an atmosphere that makes a visit here well worthwhile.

There is a pleasant but challenging circular walk leading up the hill from the church to **Kiftsgate, Hidcote Manor Garden,** and then up on to Ilmington Downs, before going down again through **Hidcote Boyce** to return to Mickleton. There is also a walk leading southwards, over the hill to **Chipping Campden,** passing close to the southern entrance to **Campden Railway Tunnel.**

Memorial Fountain, Mickleton

MIDDLE DUNTISBOURNE (1-2 J7) *4 mi. NW Cirencester.* A hamlet in the lovely Duntisbourne Valley, with a rather deep ford overlooked by farm buildings.

MILTON-UNDER-WYCHWOOD (1-2 G12) *4 mi. N Burford.* This widespread village in the broad valley of the Evenlode has much modern development on its fringes, and a church designed by G.E.Street, the Victorian architect perhaps best known for his work on the Law Courts in the Strand. Church, lych-gate, school and school-house all bear witness to his very considerable skill. The long village street beyond the Quart Pot Inn has a series of shops and houses, but apart from the little stone bull's head above the butcher's shop, there is nothing of great interest here.

MINCHINHAMPTON (1-2 K5) *1½ mi. NE Nailsworth.* Situated on the eastern fringes of

Minchinhampton Common, high above valleys once prosperous with the production of cloth, this is an especially attractive little Cotswold town. It is centred upon its High Street and old Market Square, the chief features of which are the late 17th-century Market House supported on stone columns, the handsome Crown Hotel, and the Post Office, a genuine Queen Anne building.

The interesting church, with its truncated spire, looks over the Market Square, but at the same time stands slightly aloof from it. It was given to Caen's Abbaye aux Dames by William the Conqueror, and then in 1415 passed to Syon Abbey, in whose hands it remained until the Dissolution. The present building dates from the 12th century and is full of interest. See especially the fine 14th-century south transept with its Decorated-style tomb recesses and effigies, the vaulting beneath the tower and also the outstanding series of monumental brasses.

Minchinhampton

There are old cloth mills in the valleys to the south, notably at Ball's Green, where the great Longfords Lake once provided water for power and washing at the long closed Longfords Mill. See also **Hampton Fields** and **Gatcombe Park.**

MINCHINHAMPTON COMMON (1-2 K5) *1 mi. NW Minchinhampton.* (Not shown on map.) Owned by the National Trust, this 590-acre sweep of turf country is situated on high country between the deep Frome and Nailsworth Valleys. It is a favourite with walkers and horse riders alike, and there are fine views on every side and interesting archaeological remains, including The Bulwarks, parts of an Iron Age defensive system, and Amberley Camp, an Iron Age settlement. Whitfield's Tump is a long barrow, so named because it was from here that one of the founders of Methodism, the famous preacher George Whitfield, addressed a large crowd in 1743, despite having been assaulted in Minchinhampton a few hours earlier.

MINSTER LOVELL (1-2 H13) *2½ mi. W Witney.* A trim stone and thatch village set in the lovely Windrush Valley, with a small hotel called the Old Swan not far from its bridge across the stream. The church, standing at the eastern end of the village, was once in company with a small priory (hence the village's name), but this was dissolved in 1414, as it had by then become an alien house in the ownership of Ivry Abbey in distant Normandy. The fine cruciform, 15th-century church has beautiful vaulting beneath its central tower, and some benches and

The Old Manor House, Minster Lovell

stained glass both of which may be contemporary with the church. See also the tomb of a knight - probably William Lovell, the builder not only of the church, but also of the adjoining manor house.

The splendid 15th-Century manor house of the Lovells, Minster Lovell Hall, has been a ruin since it was dismantled in 1747, but its setting on the willow-bordered banks of the Windrush is incomparable and it is well maintained in its present form by English Heritage. It was built as a fortified manor house, much like a small castle, and its quarters, ranged around a quadrangle, include a great hall with solar and kitchens. Its circular dovecot is situated in an adjoining farmyard. Francis, the 13th Lord Lovell, was associated with the ill-fated Lambert Simnell Rising in 1487, and following its failure it is thought that he sought refuge in a secret room at Minster Lovell. The location of this room was apparently known only to one trusted servant, and when, so the story goes, he suddenly died, his master was trapped, and in due course starved to death. During repairs to the house in 1708 the skeletons of a man and a dog were found in a secret room, and this discovery appears to bear out the story of Lord Lovell's disappearance unless it was thought up by the 1708 repairers to explain their macabre find, in a manner similar to the story of the Bisley Boy ? (see **Bisley**)

Another of the village's Lords of the Manor also met an unpleasant, but in this case, well-deserved end - on the gallows. This was a certain Mr Freeman, who lived here in some style in the early 1800s, until it was discovered that he was the highwayman responsible for a large number of hold-ups on the toll roads of Oxfordshire and the Cotswolds.

It is possible to walk from the car park well to the south-west of the Old Swan Hotel, up the village street, through the churchyard beyond the far side of the manor house ruins, and soon over a footbridge crossing the Windrush. Go down the valley from here to the delightful hamlet of **Crawley** and then return over slightly higher ground to Minster

Miserden

Lovell. This walk is nearly three miles long, but well worthwhile.

MISERDEN (1-2 H6) *7 mi. NW Cirencester.* A very trim, largely 19th- and 20th-century village, with a small octagonal shelter built around a massive sycamore tree and overlooked by the hospitable Carpenter's Arms. The church, standing in a churchyard enriched with yew and beech, has late Saxon origins but was heavily restored in the 1880s. See especially the elaborately carved and gilded reredos and the splendid series of 17th-century monuments. The War Memorial was designed by Sir Edwin Lutyens, who also carried out extensive work at Misarden Park, an Elizabethan mansion with lovely gardens overlooking the wooded Frome Valley to the immediate east of the village. There are the earthworks of a motte and bailey castle in the valley to the immediate west of the River Frome. These probably mark the site of a castle built soon after the Norman Conquest, and already ruined by the end of the 13th century. Follow the path from Miserden, eastwards across the valley to **Winstone,** passing close to these earthworks, although they are on private land. Return to Miserden through parts of Misarden Park, but please keep to the right-of-way. There is also a longer walk southwards to **Edgeworth** and on to **Sapperton.**

MORETON-IN-MARSH (1 D11) *4 mi. N Stow-on-the-Wold.* The intrepid late 17th-century traveller and diarist, Celia Fiennes, (see also **Broughton and Broughton Castle**) visited Moreton several times, as she had a widowed aunt living there. Her succinct description of 'Morton Hindmost' as a *little neate stone built town, good Innes for traveller* could hardly be bettered today. As Mistress Celia pointed out, it lay on the main route from London and Oxford to the cities of Worcester and Hereford, and the centre of Wales; and this probably accounted even more strongly for Moreton's prosperity than did its position astride the Foss Way.

Morton in Marsh

It appears that this *little neate stone built town* was also once called Moreton Henmarsh, the Henmarsh being low-lying country much frequented by coots and moorhens; but we still find Celia's 'Morton Hindmost' an even more endearing name. The origins of the town are somewhat obscure, but the oldest part grew up around the church, a former chapel of ease for nearby **Bourton-on-the-Hill**. The present Parish Church, lying to the east of the High Street, and south of Oxford Street, is almost entirely Victorian, and is not of great interest to visitors. However, the elegant 18th-century house to its immediate east should not be overlooked.

Almost all of interest in Moreton-in-Marsh is situated on its High Street, with a series of stone built shops, houses and coaching inns facing each other across the broad Foss Way, but unfortunately divided by incessant traffic passing along it between the Midlands and the South-West. The Manor House Hotel and the Redesdale Arms are both pleasing buildings, and the White Hart Royal Hotel claims the distinction of having provided shelter for Charles I - on 2nd July 1644. The little 16th-century Curfew Tower on the corner of Oxford Street has a bell dated 1633, and this was rung each evening until as recently as 1860. On the other side of the High Street is the dominant feature of Moreton-in-Marsh, the confidently neo-Tudor Redesdale Market Hall, built in 1887 to the designs of Sir Ernest George, who was soon to carry out a similar commission for Lord Redesdale - the design of a 'Cotswold-Elizabethan' mansion, at nearby **Batsford Park.** There is an Information Centre at the Library in Jameson Court, just off the Foss Way at the Stow-on-the-Wold end of the town.

The coming to Moreton in 1843 of Brunel's Oxford, Worcester and Wolverhampton Railway brought a connection with the outside world that some of Moreton's neighbours must have envied at the time, and a certain robust quality appears to have survived here to this day (see also the **Stratford and Moreton Tramway**). So despite the traffic, do take time off to walk down both sides of Moreton's long High Street - there are several interesting and attractive shops, and the tree-lined greens at the northern end are especially pleasing. The Wellington Aviation Museum, just out of the town, on the A44 road to Broadway, displays a most interesting collection of World War II aviation memorabilia in the museum itself and, in the garden at the rear, the centre-section of a Wellington bomber showing its unique geodetic framework. There are also a wide variety of paintings and books on sale.

The best walk from Moreton-in-Marsh is north-westwards, up over the hills to **Blockley**, skirting the southern edge of **Batsford Park,** and possibly calling in to look round the **Batsford Park Arboretum.** To make a long circular walk, move south-west from **Blockley,** via Dovedale and Bourton Downs, to **Hinchwick,** and then head east, making some use of public roads to return to Moreton, skirting to the south of **Sezincote.**

N**AG'S HEAD** (1-2 5K) *3 mi. E Nailsworth.* (Not shown on map.) This delightful little hamlet takes its name from an inn that used to be here. It has a row of small houses looking southwards over a quiet valley, some with interesting architectural detail. Walk eastwards from here, over the fields to **Cherington,** and beyond to **Hazelton** using part of the **Macmillan Way.**

Nag's Head

NAILSWORTH (1-2 K4) *4 mi. S Stroud.* The centre of this modest cloth town stands at the union of two valleys, and is much dominated by the busy A46. There is a mid-20th-century clock tower at its centre and its old cloth mills have been put to new uses. Egypt Mill, on the A46, has been restored, with two of its great water-wheels and attendant gearing, and is now a restaurant. Nearby Ruskin Mill now houses a lively Arts and Crafts Centre complete with cafe and working water wheel. On the slopes above the valley bottoms there are a multitude of attractive streets and alleyways, which will amply repay those who explore on foot. See especially the steep little Chestnut Hill, with Stokes Croft at its foot, and the Quaker Meeting House a short distance beyond - both attractive 17th-century buildings. Also do not miss a visit to the Selsley Herb Shop at Wheelwright's Corner, with its attractive little forecourt. The late Victorian church is not of great interest to visitors. It is possible to walk southwards from here, over open hill country to **Chavenage** and **Beverston.**

NAUNTON (1-2 E9) *5 mi. W Stow-on-the-Wold.* This is a delightful, elongated village, spread out along the floor of the deep Windrush Valley, and looking like a model from the B4068 on its hillside above. The church has a handsome Perpendicular tower with pinnacles and gargoyles, and although time has not dealt as kindly as it

Dovecot at Naunton

might with the interior, this has a beautifully carved early 15th-century stone pulpit and an interesting font of the same period. There are also two small 17th-century brasses in the chancel and a wall tablet to Ambrose Oldys who died in 1710, with 'better fortune' than his father Dr William, who, the tablet relates, was *barbarously murdered by ye rebells* in 1645. Rest awhile at the little bridge over the Windrush near the lovely Old Rectory, before walking down the village to the hospitable Black Horse Inn, passing on the way a charming 17th-century dovecot overlooking the stream to the right. Walk north-west from here, up the Windrush Valley to **Guiting Power,** or south-east to **Harford Bridge** and then down the Windrush Valley to **Bourton-on-the-Water.**

NETHER LYPIATT MANOR (1-2 J5) *2 mi. SE Stroud.* (Not shown on map.) An especially lovely 17th-century manor house standing close to a minor road junction, and looking westwards over Stroud from a hilly edge. Read more about this house and its various fascinating owners in James Lees-Milne's delightful book, *Some Cotswold Country Houses.*

NETHER WORTON (1 D15) *6½ mi. SW Banbury.* An immaculate farm, a very grand 17th-century manor house, much restored in about 1920, and a little church close by. This and a few cottages make up Nether Worton, a deliciously quiet hamlet sheltering beneath wooded Hawk Hill, in the valley of the little River Tew. The medieval church has a modest 17th-century tower, and a pleasant interior, the contents of which include a Jacobean communion rail, and a wall monument by the sculptor Henry Westmacott. This gentleman was the thirteenth child (no less) of his better-known

Near Nether Worton

father, Sir Richard Westmacott, who was as prolific a sculptor, as he was a father.

NEWARK PARK (2 L3) *2 mi. E Wotton-under-Edge.* This was originally a hunting lodge, built in Elizabethan times by the Poyntz family, on the edge of a cliff looking eastwards over the valley of Ozleworth Bottom. It was converted in 1790 into a four-square castellated country house by the redoubtable architect, James Wyatt, who provided a new south front incorporating a Gothick porch. Owned by the National Trust, it is being rehabilitated by the Trust's tenant and is, at the time of writing, only open on a restricted basis.

Newington Bagpath

NEWINGTON BAGPATH (2 L3) *4 mi. E Wotton-under-Edge.* Minute hamlet in a quiet valley overlooked by the circular earthworks of a medieval castle and a small church beside them. Visitors may find this isolated church locked and the churchyard will probably be overgrown. However, there are pleasant views over the valley and a feeling of utter tranquillity not often encountered today. The church's squat tower has an attractively hipped roof, and a Jacobean pulpit together with medieval choir stalls and reredos. Little else appears to have survived the restoration of 1858. There is a fine circular walk from here taking in **Lasborough** and **Ozleworth.**

NORTH CERNEY (1-2 H8) *4 mi. N Cirencester.* Pleasant village in the Churn Valley, with the hospitable Bathurst Arms set in a streamside garden and looking across the busy A435 to the little saddleback tower of a largely Norman church. This was exquisitely restored and refurnished in the early years of the 20th century, much of the work being carried out under the direction of F.C. Eden, the fruits of whose peculiar genius the writer first encountered at the village of Blisland on the remote western fringes of Bodmin Moor. Eden's work includes the porch gates, three stained-glass windows, a vestment press, the rood loft and screen, and the reredos. See also the Norman south doorway, the roof with its fascinating corbel figures of monks, kings and queens, the handsome gallery, the fine 15th-century stone pulpit, the beautiful medieval glass, and the lovely 18th-century monument to Thomas Tyndale in the Lady Chapel. This list tells but half the story, so be prepared to spend time here - it will be well rewarded. There is a fine late 17th-century rectory opposite the church, and handsome Cerney House is just beyond. It is possible to walk northwards from this village, beside the River Churn to **Rendcomb,** or southwards to **Baunton.**

North Cerney

NORTHLEACH (1-2 G9) *10 mi. NE Cirencester.* In the Middle Ages this was one of the Cotswolds' most important wool trading centres and acknowledged only Cirencester and Chipping Campden as its superiors. Situated in the valley of the infant River Leach just to the east of the Foss Way, and now happily bypassed by the busy A40, this attractive little town has regained the tranquillity it enjoyed before the coming of the motor car. It is now probably less busy than it was in the days following Thomas Telford's diversion of the main road to bring coaches through the town - a move that placed it on the great coaching route between London, Oxford, Gloucester and South Wales. The town's small square stands just above the road, to the east of the church, and is a focal point of the modest High Street, itself lined with pleasant houses, shops and inns dating from the 16th to the early 19th century, a few of them half-timbered. The Dutton Almshouses 'for women' were built by Thomas Dutton of neighbouring **Sherborne** in 1616, and of special interest to visitors is Keith Harding's World of Mechanical Music at Oak House in the High Street, where there are regular demonstrations of mechanical musical instruments, musical boxes and automata.

Northleach Church

However Northleach's outstanding feature is its magnificent 'wool church' which was entirely rebuilt in the 15th century - a splendid example of the Perpendicular style. It has a fine tower and the elegantly pinnacled south porch is one of the finest in England. The interior is beautifully proportioned and well lit by clerestory windows. Its contents include a lovely 15th-century goblet-shaped pulpit, and new seating designed by Sir Basil Spence, and made in the furniture workshops of Gordon Russell at Broadway. The outstanding monumental brasses commemorate the great wool merchants of Northleach, men whose wealth rebuilt the church and enriched its fabric - Thomas Busshe, Merchant of the Staple of Calais, John Taylour, Thomas Parker, William Midwinter, John Fortey and Thomas Fortey. These families grew rich on trading in Cotswold wool, and many of them enjoyed a significant position not only in the commerce of England, but in that of Europe generally.

At the crossing on the Foss Way, just to the west of the town, there is a late 18th-century 'house of correction' or prison. This was built by the philanthropist and prison reformer, Sir George Onesiphorus Paul, a member of the prosperous family of Huguenot clothiers from Woodchester, who built Highgrove House at **Doughton,** the present home of the Prince of Wales. Sir George was also the builder of three other similar prisons, but despite his reforming zeal a treadmill was still installed at Northleach and this must have provided a punishing means of exercise for the still unfortunate prisoners. The prison building now houses a most interesting museum of rural life, including a restored 18th-century cell block, and this museum is known as the Cotswold Countryside Collection. There is also a small Tourist Information Centre here. Walk north-west from here up beside the little River Leach to its source on **Hampnett** village green, and return over slightly higher ground. It is also possible to walk south-eastwards down the valley of the Leach to **Eastington.**

NORTH LEIGH (1-2 G14) *2½ mi. NE Witney.* A sprawling village with much modern development. The interesting portion lies to the north, with a character inn called the Harcourt Arms and the church not far beyond, beside a handsome 17th-century rectory. The church has an exceptionally beautiful north aisle chapel with stone screen and vaulting, and an altar tomb with effigies. See also the 'Doom' wall paintings over the chancel arch.

 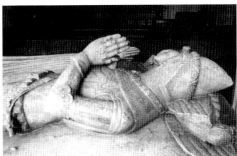

Effigies at North Leigh Church

There is an attractive bridleway southwards beside Eynsham Park, over the A40 and onto a footpath beyond it to South Leigh.

Mosaic at North Leigh Roman Villa

NORTH LEIGH ROMAN VILLA (1 G15) *3½ mi. W Woodstock.* (Not shown on map.) Situated in gentle wooded countryside not far from the banks of the River Evenlode, are the remains of a large 4th-century Roman villa on a site first occupied in the 1st century. First excavated as long ago as 1813, these remains, which are in the care of English Heritage, surround a courtyard and include living quarters with mosaics and a bath (not often viewable!). It is possible to walk northwards from here, over the Evenlode to **Stonesfield**, a village once noted for its Cotswold stone tiles.

NORTH NIBLEY (2 L2) *2 mi. SW Dursley.* This small village is situated just below the **Tyndale Monument,** and claims, like **Slimbridge**, to be the birthplace of William Tyndale, the priest who first translated the New Testament into English. It has a largely Perpendicular church on its western edge, with fine views over to Stinchcombe Hill. This building has an unusually attractive 19th-century French-Gothic chancel, which was designed by J.L. Pearson, the architect best known for his creation of Truro Cathedral. Do not miss the 17th-century wall monument to Grace Smyth complete with coloured heraldry. There is a path south-eastwards, up the hill by the **Tyndale Monument,** and southwards past the woodlands which contain the extensive earthworks of an Iron Age settlement known as Brackenbury Ditches.

NORTHWICK PARK (1 C10) *1 mi. N Blockley.* A large 16th- and 17th-century mansion built on the site of a vanished medieval village, in a great park on the slopes of the hills to the north of Blockley. It has an east front built in 1732 to the designs of the great advocate of Palladianism, Lord Burlington, and both house and outbuildings have now been extensively restored and converted into houses and flats. The nearby encampment, built during the last war, is now used as a `business centre', and although not of great beauty, provides valuable local employment.

NOTGROVE (1-2 F9) *3 mi. N Northleach.* Situated in high wold country, but just sheltered from the worst excesses of the north winds, this modest village spreads thinly around a rough green, with church and rebuilt manor house at its southern edge. These two buildings are at the end of a tree-lined driveway and both look over a valley containing the headwaters of the little Sherborne Brook, which rises in the village. The small, stone spired, largely Norman church has a primitive Saxon crucifix on its exterior south wall, while the heavily restored interior is enlivened by a colourful 20th-century tapestry

Saxon Crucifix

representing the outline of the reredos that it covers. There is Norman arcading, a Norman tub font, two effigies of medieval priests, and a large monument to various members of the Whittington family, the descendants of Sir Richard (Dick) Whittington. The best walk from here runs south-westwards to **Hazleton.**

NOTGROVE LONG BARROW (1-2 F9) *4 mi. N Northleach, 1½ mi. NW Notgrove.* In the care of English Heritage, this long barrow is situated in high country to the immediate south of the A436. Most of the earth covering

Notgrove Long Barrow

the burial chambers has long been removed, and the massive stones that remain provide an interesting impression of what the gallery and chambers must once have looked like. However, for 'prehistoric flavour' most visitors will still prefer **Belas Knap** or **Hetty Pegler's Tump.**

NYMPSFIELD (2 K3) *4 mi. NE Dursley.* Small village sheltering near the head of a valley just to the east of the Cotswold edge. It used to lie on the old Gloucester-Bath coach route and in the mid-18th century there were no fewer than five inns here. The pleasant Rose and Crown Inn has survived to this day, and is not far from the 19th-century church, which has a Perpendicular tower complete with gargoyles, a turret stair and a handsome clock-face. The nearby Nympsfield Long Barrow (in the care of English Heritage) is open to the sky, and provides a good opportunity to see the layout of a typical Cotswold long barrow. This can best be visited from the nearby **Coaley Peak Picnic Site**. On a high ridge, not far to the east of the village, there is a dramatically large wind generator which was revolving merrily when we called here last. It is hoped that it is not the precursor of that most intrusive of features - a so-called 'wind-farm'. Perhaps the term 'wind-farm' is intended to persuade us that this is an acceptable countryside adornment? The writer, for one, is not convinced !

OAKRIDGE **(1-2** J5) *4 mi. E Stroud.* Small village above the steep slopes of the **Golden Valley,** with a lively little inn called the Butchers Arms. At the south-western end of the village, below a pleasant triangular green, is the church which was built in 1837 when Thomas Keble held the living here. It has a lofty, well restored interior, but no features of outstanding interest to the visitor. The little Oakridge Village Museum is only open infrequently, but worth visiting.

ODDINGTON (1-2 E11) *2½ mi. E Stow-on-the-Wold.* An attractive village spread thinly on the lower slopes of the hill between **Stow-on-the-Wold** and the River Evenlode, and made up of Upper and Lower Oddington. It has several very pleasant houses including early 17th-century Oddington House, which was extensively remodelled in the early 19th century, and the nearby Old Rectory, which has had very much the same history. There are two inns, the Fox in 'Lower', and the Horse and Groom in 'Upper'. There is also an unassuming mid-19th-century 'new' church, but the village's best feature is some way off.

Font at Oddington Church

This is the old church of St Nicholas, which lies by itself at the end of a quiet road south of the village, although there is a long bridleway onwards from here to **Bledington.** It is also just off the course of the **Macmillan Way.** This remote church has had a number of illustrious owners, ranging from the Abbot of Gloucester to the Archbishop of York and various kings of England, and it is known that Henry II stayed at Oddington several times. This distinguished ownership resulted in relatively ambitious building in the 13th and 14th centuries, and thanks to its being largely unused in the 19th century, it has remained wonderfully unspoilt. See especially the Jacobean pulpit on its turned newel post, the lovely old chancel roof, the 15th-century font and Oddington's greatest treasure - its extensive and horrific late 14th-century 'Doom' wall painting. A few minutes' study of this fascinating relic of medieval times will show how easy it must have been for the clergy of the day to keep their primitive flock in a truly 'God-fearing' frame of mind.

OLDBURY-ON-THE-HILL (2 M4) *6 mi. SW Tetbury.* A hamlet to the immediate north of Didmarton, with a small church beside an extensive farm. Within the white painted interior of the church are high backed pews and an 18th-century two-decker pulpit, in very much the same style as neighbouring **Didmarton.**

OLD SODBURY (2 N2) *1½ mi. E Chipping Sodbury.* Small village on the A342 with a large, partly Norman church in a churchyard astride the **Cotswold Way**, with many trees and good views westwards to Chipping Sodbury. The much restored Norman south doorway provides an appropriate introduction to a similarly restored interior, largely the result of mid-19th-century 'restoration'. However the two medieval effigies in niches in the north transept should not be missed - one in wood and one in stone. There is a castellated tower some 300 yards to the south-east of the church, which is one of a series topping ventilation shafts of a railway tunnel beneath the hill here.

Cottages at Over Worton

OVER WORTON (1 D15) *7 mi. S Banbury.* There is a delightful open road between here and **Nether Worton,** overlooked by a Victorian church beautifully situated in a clump of trees. To reach this church, walk past thatched cottages in colourful gardens, in front of a dignified Georgian manor house and pass the base of a medieval cross marking the entry to Over Worton's quiet churchyard. There are flowering trees and entrancing views from the churchyard over the bumpy landscape hereabouts, but the church itself has no special features of interest.

OWLPEN (2 K3) *3 mi. E Dursley.* A delightful group of buildings in a deep hollow beneath

Owlpen Manor and Church

woodlands. Here is a fine 15th-century manor house with 16th-, 17th- and 18th-century alterations, a small Victorian church above it, and a little 18th-century mill not far away. All this is framed by clipped yews and backed by steep woods above - a perfect example of a small Cotswold estate. The present condition of the manor house owes much to the work of the architect Norman Jewson, a disciple of Ernest Gimson and the Barnsley brothers (see **Daneway**), who bought and restored it in the 1920s, but who then sadly could not afford to live in it. The interior still contains unique 17th-century wall hangings and, appropriately, much Cotswold Arts and Crafts furniture. There is a restaurant in the medieval tithe barn.

The Oxford Canal North of Banbury

The interior of the nearby church is enriched by much painting and mosaic work, and there are no fewer than eight monumental brasses to members of the Daunt family, dating from 1542 to as late as 1803. Read more about Owlpen in James Lees-Milne's most interesting book, *Some Cotswold Country Houses.* There is a pleasant walk from here, northwards to the village of **Nympsfield**.

OXFORD CANAL (Not shown on map.) *This runs very much on the eastern fringes of the Cotswolds, but is so much in harmony with the area that we felt that it should be included.* This was one of a series of waterways conceived by James Brindley, the pioneer canal builder and was planned to run between Hawkesbury in the Coventry coalfields and the Thames at Oxford. It opened in 1790, about a year after the **Thames and Severn Canal.** The section between Napton in Warwickshire and Cropredy, north of Banbury, is a continuous delight, especially as Brindley made such great use of contours when crossing summit levels. From Cropredy southwards Brindley made use of the River Cherwell, both as a feeder of water and in places, for actual navigation, and this again adds to the charm of this unique waterway. The towpath has been much improved in recent years and it is now possible to walk the whole length of the canal on the well-signed 'Oxford Canal Path' all the way between Hawkesbury Junction, near Coventry, to Oxford.

OXFORDSHIRE CIRCULAR WALKS (Not shown on map.) Reference to these walks will be found on the relevant Ordnance Survey maps of the area. One of these is a walk with many varying circuits around the Windrush Valley to the west of **Witney** - from 2 1/2 to 13 miles in length.*(Details of this and other Oxfordshire Circular Walks may be obtained from The Countryside Service, Oxfordshire County Council, Holton, Oxford OX33 1QQ.)*

THE OXFORDSHIRE WAY (Not shown on map.) This 65-mile field path links the Cotswolds and the Chilterns. It starts from Bourton-on-the-Water, and then heads through or past Wyck Rissington, Bledington, and Shipton-under-Wychwood. From here it runs down the Evenlode Valley, passing Charlbury, North Leigh Roman Villa, and the northern edge of Blenheim Park, before leaving the area covered by this guide, on its way to the Chilterns. *Guides to this walk are published by the CPRE, and by Oxfordshire County Council - see Oxfordshire Walks, above.)*

OXHILL (1 A13) *5 mi. NE Shipston-on-Stour.* A tidy, stone village in the 'Vale of Red Horse', with views south-eastwards to the scarp face of the Oxfordshire Cotswolds, where the Red Horse itself must have once been clearly visible, on its hilly site above the straggling village of **Tysoe**. Oxhill has an attractively signed, stone-built inn, the Peacock, and many pleasant farmhouses and cottages; and the character of the village is not overawed by modern building on its northern edge. The interesting, largely Norman church has Norman north and south doorways, the south being a much richer specimen. The tower is Perpendicular, and there is a fine 15th-century roof to the nave, and a fascinating Norman font, ornamented with the rather scrawny figures of Adam and Eve at the 'Tree of Life'. See also the fine 15th-century rood

Ozleworth Bottom

screen across the tower arch, and in the south-eastern part of the churchyard, the grave of a female negro slave. She died in 1705, the property of 'Thomas Beauchamp, gent. of Nevis' who was probably a sugar plantation owner, and who almost certainly married one of the local rector's twin daughters. Walks across the relatively flat countryside around Oxhill are not exceptionally interesting, but the best one runs north along a largely unfenced minor road to the A422, and then across fields to Pillerton Hersey.

OZLEWORTH (2 L3) *2½ mi. E Wotton-under-Edge.* This small group of buildings is situated in a delightfully quiet, well wooded valley overlooked by both the National Trust's **Newark Park** and a tall but less beautiful concrete communications tower. It is possible to walk up the short drive towards handsome 18th-century Ozleworth Park and round behind it to visit the little Norman church. Standing in a circular churchyard, this has a very rare central hexagonal tower. Ozleworth Bottom, the valley running south-westwards from here, once sheltered several water-mills. These were first used for the grinding of corn or fulling, but in the 16th and 17th centuries they were converted into cloth mills. Little trace of these now remains. Walk eastwards from Ozleworth, up another beautifully wooded valley to **Lasborough** and **Newington Bagpath.**

Painswick Church

PAINSWICK (1-2 H4) *3 mi. N Stroud.* Painswick is situated on a high spur between two valleys, with a series of old mills on the stream in the valley to its south-west. These mills were once used for the production of cloth, and it was both the wool trade and the dyed-cloth industry that brought prosperity to this delightful little town in the 17th and 18th centuries, the latter witnessing its peak. The dyeing of cloth had become a speciality here owing to the purity of its streams and especially its spring water. Before starting to explore the town try to pay a visit to the Tourist Information Centre at the Library to the south-west of the church, on Stroud Road. The church's 15th-century tower is topped by a fine 17th-century spire, and also houses a peal of twelve bells. The interior, with its vaulted nave ceiling and painted chancel ceiling, is remarkably uncluttered. It does, however, contain a number of interesting monuments including a 15th-century tomb-chest in Purbeck marble in St Peter's Chapel. This was used for a second time for the body of Sir William Kingston, Constable of the Tower of London at the time when the unfortunate Anne Boleyn was beheaded. The third and final users of the tomb lie upon it in effigy - 17th-century Doctor John Seaman and his wife, with a pile of law books between them.

However, it is Painswick's churchyard that attracts the majority of visitors. Here is a splendid colonnade of architecturally clipped yew trees, most of which were planted in 1792. Legend has it that only ninety-nine will grow at any one time, as the Devil always kills off the hundredth. Some have become so intertwined over the years that it is now impossible to confirm or deny the truth of this charming story. The annual clipping service is held on the Sunday following the patronal festival. During this open-air service children join hands (clipping means 'embracing') and encircle

Painswick's Rococo Garden

the church while singing a traditional hymn. Tradition also ensures that the children wear flowers in their hair, and that for their part in the ceremony they each receive a 'Painswick Bun' and a coin.

Painswick churchyard is also noted for its splendid series of 17th- and 18th-century Renaissance-style table tombs, many of which were carved by Joseph Bryan and his two sons, John and Joseph. John Bryan was also responsible for the handsome pair of gate-piers at the north-east entrance to the churchyard. See also the headstone to freemason, Thomas Hamlett, complete with a display of mason's tools. The stocks in nearby St Mary's Street were installed here in the mid-19th century *for the punishment of those who carry on carousels to the annoyance of neighbours.*

In the streets around the church will be found a rich array of houses, shops and inns, almost all of which are built of Painswick's creamy grey-white stone, and many of which are also embellished with pleasing architectural details. Take time to stroll round Painswick, a small town which was fortunate to grow up at a time when prosperity brought such perfection. This feeling of pleasant affluence is also reflected in the most attractive hilly countryside around it, which is rich in elegant houses and enviably lovely cottages. Half a mile to the north, to the left of the B4073, Gloucester road, will be found the delightful Painswick Rococo Garden, the 18th-century Painswick House's six-acre garden, which is being restored to the original form as depicted in an 18th-century painting by Thomas Robins.

It is possible to walk north-eastwards from **Painswick,** up the valley and into lovely **Cranham Woods,** or south-westwards, down the valley to busy **Stroud.** Painswick is also situated astride the **Cotswold Way,** and this can be followed north to **Prinknash,** or south to **Stonehouse** and on to **Dursley.**

PAINSWICK BEACON (1-2 H4) *1½ mi. N Painswick.* (Not shown on map.) About 250 acres of common land - pleasant, open country with pine trees, old quarries and a golf course nearby. It can become very crowded on Sunday afternoons. The **Cotswold Way** passes just below it, to the east.

PETTY FRANCE (2 N3) *8 mi. SW Tetbury.* A hamlet astride the busy A46 with two pleasant hotels. The name *Petty France* was probably derived from Westminster's area of the same name, although another theory points to there being a camp for French prisoners-of-war here during the Napoleonic Wars.

PITCHCOMBE (1-2 H4) *2 mi. N Stroud.* Appropriately named village on a steep hillside, with lovely Pitchcombe House standing close to a terrace of older houses looking southwards. The church was entirely rebuilt in the 19th century and is a dignified if rather dull building relieved only by the handsome table tombs and clipped yews in the churchyard - both these being in the best Painswick tradition.

POSTLIP (1-2 E7) *1 mi. W Winchcombe.* Here is a fine Jacobean manor house, Postlip Hall, charmingly situated at the head of the Isbourne Valley below the bare heights of **Cleeve Common.** In its grounds is a small Norman chapel, now used as a Roman Catholic church. This has a Norman south doorway and chancel arch, and a 16th-century roof. The nearby 15th-century tithe barn has a little stone figure on its western gable-end which is said to represent Sir William de Postlip, who lived in the reign of King Stephen. Legend has it that whenever Sir William hears the midnight chime, he comes down off his gable to drink at the nearby well. A little further down the valley, nearer to Winchcombe, is a papermill, which has been making fine quality papers since the mid-18th century, taking advantage of the pure, iron-free waters of the little River Isbourne. There are good walks up over **Cleeve Common** from Postlip, going for a short time through open country rather like parts of the Peak District and quite unique in the Cotswold area.

POULTON (1-2 K9) *3 mi. W Fairford.* A small village in flat country with no outstanding features. It has a modest little inn overlooked by an equally modest late 17th-century manor house. The nearby church and school were both built by the redoubtable Victorian architect William Butterfield. Within the church's large, rather bare interior will be found a water-colour painting of the charming little church that was swept away with such Victorian zeal. Two crossroads on the road north are marked on the Ordnance Survey's Landranger map as 'Betty's Grave' and **'Ready Token',** but the reasons for these place-names are unfortunately far from clear.

PRESCOTT (1 D7) *2½ mi. W Winchcombe.* Small hamlet beneath steep Nottingham Hill, which is itself topped by the ramparts of an Iron Age settlement. Prescott is renowned throughout the world of motor sport as the site of the Prescott Speed Hill Climb. This is operated by the Bugatti Owners' Club and meetings are held here about seven times a year. Walk south from Prescott, up over Nottingham Hill, and on to **Cleeve Hill**.

PRESTBURY (1-2 E7) *1½ mi. NE Cheltenham.* Sheltering beneath the steep western scarp face of Cleeve Hill, this large, busy village is now almost part of Cheltenham. Its old houses are built either of stone or of timber, and the little half-timbered King's Arms is a particularly attractive inn. Nearby Prestbury Park has been the site of Cheltenham's world-famous racecourse since 1823, and the great jockey Fred Archer trained here while living at the King's Arms - an inscription here informs the passer-by that Archer 'who trained on toast, Cheltenham water and coffee, lived at this Prestbury inn'.

The church was over-restored by G.E.Street in 1864, but several medieval features have survived, including a Perpendicular tower, 15th-century arcading and chancel arch, and a double piscina in the Lady Chapel. 'The Priory', a nearby house of 14th-century origin, reminds the visitor that the long-vanished Priory of Llanthony at Gloucester, once owned both this and the church. There are two steep lanes heading eastwards up on to

Cleeve Hill, to link with the **Cotswold Way.** Once up on **Cleeve Common**, walking possibilities are limitless.

PRESTON (1-2 K8) *1 mi. SE Cirencester.* A minute village in flat country to the immediate west of Cirencester's bypass. It has a small church approached by a narrow pathway bordered with pollarded limes. The 14th-century triple bellcote is worth noting, and the contents of the church's over-restored interior include a stout, cylindrical Norman font.

PRINKNASH ABBEY (1-2 G5) *2½ mi. NE Painswick.* This establishment dates from 1928, when a Benedictine community moved here from Caldey Island, off the Pembroke Coast, having handed over Caldey to the Cistercians. The 'old abbey' was built in the 14th century as a grange and hunting lodge for the abbots of Gloucester, but inevitably passed out of monastic hands at the Dissolution. Writing to a friend in 1774,

Prinknash Abbey

Horace Walpole tells that, *Yesterday I made a jaunt to Prinknash. I wished you there. It stands on a glorious but impracticable hill, in the midst of a little forest of beech and commanding Elysium.* Coming here today, he would no doubt be surprised by the lines of the new abbey, but he would not be disappointed with its setting or the magnificent views out over the Vale of Gloucester to the distant Malverns.

The new abbey was completed in 1972 using stone from the quarries of Guiting, and is an unashamedly modern structure owing little to the traditions of the medieval building that it replaced. Clay was discovered here when the foundations of the new abbey were being dug, and this material soon became the basis for Prinknash's main commercial activity - its well-known pottery. However, vestments, incense, stained glass and iron-work are also created here. It is possible to visit the abbey church, the walled garden, and nearby tearoom. The adjoining Prinknash Bird Park is also well worth visiting, and consists of nine acres of parkland, with numerous species of waterfowl, West African Pygmy Goats, and a herd of Fallow Deer.

Norman Doorway

Quenington

QUENINGTON (1-2 J10) *2 mi. N Fairford.* A highly attractive village, with many pleasant houses and cottages on slopes above the little River Coln. Notable amongst these is Quenington Court, a largely 19th-century house on the site of a preceptory of the Knight's Templar, which later passed into the hands of the Knights Hospitaller. This has an interesting 13th-century gatehouse, and

a circular dovecot which is probably about the same age. The little church nearby was over-restored in the late 19th century, but its Norman north and south doorways, each with a richly carved tympanum, should on no account be missed. The tympanum over the south doorway depicts *The Coronation of the Virgin,* and that over the north doorway *The Harrowing of Hell.* Both are outstanding examples of Romanesque art. Explore part of the Coln Valley by taking in some of neighbouring **Coln St Aldwyns** and walking on north-westwards from the latter, beside the Coln to **Bibury.**

Quinton

QUINTON, UPPER AND LOWER (1 A11) *2 mi. NE Mickleton.* There is a large ex-military housing estate here, but most of Lower Quinton remains unspoilt, with a village green overlooked by several thatched, timber-framed cottages, a handsome mellow-brick 17th-century house with Cotswold stone tiles, and a well restored inn, the College Arms. This displays the arms of Magdalen College, Oxford, which still owns much land in the area. All is overlooked by the splendid 130ft-high spire of Quinton church. This has Norman south arcading and a Norman font, and many interesting features from the centuries that followed, including a Perpendicular clerestory, and the effigy of a knight who fought at Agincourt, Sir William Clopton, and a fine brass of his widow, Lady Clopton. On Sir William's death, this lady took a vow of widowhood, and is believed to have lived as an anchorite, or hermit, in a cell nearby. It is probably to her that we are indebted for the clerestory and the splendid spire.

It is possible to walk across the fields to Upper Quinton, where there is an early timber-framed manor house with very close vertical timbers. To the south of Upper Quinton is Meon Hill, one of the northern outliers of the Cotswolds. There are memories here of suspected witchcraft in comparatively recent times, and the hill's summit is crowned by the ramparts of an Iron Age settlement.

RADWAY (1 A14) *7 mi. NW Banbury.* Delightful Hornton-stone village beneath the partly wooded slopes of Edge Hill. Many of its houses and cottages are thatched, and at the far end of the village there is a small green enriched by a tree-shaded pool and overlooked by further cottages and a little 19th-century chapel. The small spired church was built on a new site in 1866, to replace a brick building at the other end of the village. Its contents are not of great interest, apart from a monument brought here from the old church, to Captain Kingswell, a Royalist officer, killed at the Battle of Edgehill in 1642 (see **Edgehill**), and a plain wall monument to Sanderson Miller, who died in 1780. Miller was squire of Radway, and owner of Radway Grange, the handsome stone building in its own park, not far from the church. He was an outstanding 'gentleman architect', and one of the pioneers of the Gothick style, being at least three years ahead of the better known Horace Walpole, who was soon to begin his famous improvements to Strawberry Hill. Miller was responsible for a fascinating series of architectural works, from Wiltshire to East Anglia, including (in the area covered by this guide) **Adlestrop Park, Upton House** and **Wroxton.** He made considerable alterations to his own home, the Elizabethan Radway Grange, and built the Edgehill Tower on the ridge above his park, marking the spot where the Royal Standard was raised at the Battle of Edgehill. He also planted the hanging woods above the park. The large statue of Caractacus, which now stands in the garden of Radway Grange, was originally intended for the Edgehill Tower but found to be too large for its niche there. Radway Grange was, in Sanderson

Miller's time, a centre of fashion and intellect, and Fielding read the manuscript of his novel *Tom Jones* to Miller and his friends Lord North, the Earl of Chatham and Sir George Lyttleton in the Grange's dining room. It is sad to relate however that Miller spent many of his later years confined in the Lincolnshire asylum of Doctor Willis, the physician famed for his treatment of the madness of George III.

Ramsden

If possible, walk up the hill from Radway into Miller's hanging woodlands and beyond them to his Edgehill Tower (now an inn). It is unfortunately not possible to walk north-westwards over the Edgehill battlefield site, as this is occupied by the Ministry of Defence.

RAMSDEN (1-2 G14) *3 mi. N Witney.* Pleasant village on the line of the Romans' **Akeman Street** and not far to the south of **Wychwood Forest.** Its cross-roads are marked by an unusual stone war memorial and this is overlooked by the Royal Oak Inn and an attractive row of cottages, all in Cotswold stone. The church is Victorian and not of great interest to visitors.

RANDWICK (1-2 J4) *1½ mi. NW Stroud.* The lower parts of this village are now almost a suburb of Stroud, but the rest is full of character. It is attractively sited on steep hillsides beneath Standish Wood. There is an inn called the Vine Tree and, sitting below the road in a tree-shaded churchyard, a largely Victorian church, which has retained its Perpendicular tower. This church is the focus of 'the Randwick Wap', an ancient ceremony, the first part of which is held on the first Sunday in May. Three cheeses are carried here on litters decorated with flowers, and after being blessed during a short service they are rolled three times round the church before being cut up and distributed by officers in ceremonial dress. On the following Sunday, the second part of the ceremony takes the form of a mock mayor-making. There are the earthworks of two round barrows and a long barrow in Standish Wood (most of which belongs to the National Trust), just above the village. There is a path near the church heading up into this wood, thus providing a link with the **Cotswold Way,** which passes through it.

READY TOKEN (1-2 J9) *5 mi. E Cirencester.* There was once an inn at this, the point where the Romans' **Akeman Street** is crossed by the **Welsh Way.** No doubt it was a popular stopping point for the ever-thirsty Welsh drovers, especially in summertime when the dust from the great herds of cattle must have parched many a Welsh throat. Why the name 'Ready Token'? There appears to be no clear answer to this question.

Rendcomb Font detail

Rendcomb Font

RENDCOMB (1-2 H8) *5 mi. N Cirencester.* Situated on the slopes of the beautifully wooded Churn Valley, this is a small estate village at the gates of Rendcomb Court, a

19th-century Italianate mansion, which has been a boarding school since 1920. The Court was built most meticulously by the famous contractor Thomas Cubitt to the designs of Philip Hardwick, an architect much influenced by the ideas of Sir Charles Barry.

Close to the school is Rendcomb's largely Perpendicular church, which was built by Sir Edmund Tame, the prosperous **Fairford** wool merchant. Sir Edmund was the son of John

Rendcombe Court

Tame, the builder of the magnificent church at Fairford, and there are definite similarities between the two buildings, especially in the carving of their screens. The stained glass, although only fragmentary, is clearly the work of craftsmen influenced by the Renaissance to a far greater extent than those at slightly earlier Fairford. See also the little sculpture of the Crucifixion over the east gable, the fine 15th-century south door, which is contemporary with the church itself, and the outstandingly beautiful Norman font, with figures of eleven apostles beneath arcading in high relief, and the figure of Judas left uncarved. This font is thought to have come from Elmore, a village on the banks of the Severn below Gloucester. Before leaving do not overlook the cross in the churchyard - a 19th-century head on a stout medieval base.

Walk south from here, down beside the Churn to **North Cerney** and **Baunton,** or go south-westwards to **Woodmancote** and **Duntisbourne Rouse** following the **Macmillan Way.**

ROBINS WOOD HILL COUNTRY PARK (1-2 G4) *2 mi. S Gloucester.* Robins Wood Hill,

an outlier of the Cotswolds, lies entirely within the boundary of the city of Gloucester, and the 250-acre country park is owned by the City Council. There is a small Visitor Centre, also horse trails, nature trails and footpaths. At the very top of the hill there is a viewing topograph which helps to identify the features that can be seen on distant horizons. The best approach to the park is by turning off the St Barnabas Roundabout on the ring road, onto Reservoir Road. The rest of the hill is owned by the Gloucester Country Club, which provides a wide range of sporting facilities, including a golf

Rodborough Common

course and one of England's highest dry-ski slopes. Matson House, below the north-eastern slopes of the hill, was the headquarters of the Royalists during their siege of Gloucester, and the top of the hill above must have provided the besiegers with a superb vantage point.

RODBOROUGH (1-2 J4) *1 mi. SW Stroud.* This scattered village is now a hilly suburb of
Stroud, and much walking up and down its sloping streets is required to appreciate its remaining character. Its manor, burnt down in about 1900, was once the home of Sir George Onesiphorus Paul, the local prison reformer of Huguenot descent (see also **Doughton, Northleach** and **Woodchester**). Up on windy Rodborough Common, well above the village, Rodborough Fort is a prominent landmark. This was built in 1761 as a

'pleasure-house' by local dyer, George Hawker, but having been entirely rebuilt in 1870 it now looks typically Victorian. There is a good caravan site here, pleasant walks over to the south side of the common and wide views out over the still-busy valleys below. Well beyond the village, on the southern edge of the common, there is a comfortable hotel called 'The Bear at Rodborough'.

Rodmarton Churchyard

RODMARTON (1-2 K6) *4½ mi. NE Tetbury.* This has a small green overlooked by quiet cottages and an attractively spired church. Pollarded trees create a 'lych-gate' effect over the churchyard gate, and there are several pleasant tombs in the churchyard. Unfortunately the interior was ruthlessly scraped by Victorian 'restorers', but there are old stone floors, several handsome 18th- and 19th-century monuments, and the brass of a 15th-century lawyer dressed in his cap and gown. The nearby manor house was built for Claud Biddulph, between 1909 and 1926, to the designs of Ernest Barnsley, one of a group of artists and craftsmen much influenced by William Morris's 'Arts and Crafts' philosophy (see also **Daneway**). As part of Biddulph's and Barnsley's plan, the house was built entirely by estate workers and local specialist craftsmen, using local materials but no machinery and nothing modern. Its furniture includes items by Ernest Barnsley himself, his brother Sidney, and their friend Ernest Gimson. Read more about the building of this fascinating house in James Lees-Milne's *Some Cotswold Country Houses. (Rodmarton Manor is not open to the public.)*

ROEL GATE (1-2 E8) *3½ mi. SE Winchcombe.* Lonely cross-roads about 900 feet above sea level, with fine views down the 'Sudeley Valley' to **Winchcombe.** Roel Gate lies on the **Salt Way,** at one of the highest points on its course between Droitwich and the
Thames. There is a seat here, in memory of Arthur Edwin Boycott - *Pathologist, Naturalist and Friend* - 1877-1938, and it would be hard to find a finer place at which to be remembered.

There is an Iron Age settlement at Grim's Hill, half a mile to the west, and a mile and a half in the opposite direction lies Roel Farm, an old manor house which provided shelter for Lord Chandos, his family and retainers from **Sudeley Castle,** during the troubled times of the Civil War. A village of Roel is recorded in the Domesday Book, but this was probably depopulated in the 14th century when great sheep runs were established here and elsewhere in the Cotswolds by the Abbot of Winchcombe, and no trace of it remains apart from slight undulations in a field next to the farm.

The King Stone

THE ROLLRIGHT STONES (1 D13) *2½ mi. NW Chipping Norton.* These consist of three separate features. 'The King's Men' are a Bronze Age stone circle about a hundred feet in diameter, and date from between 2000 and 1800 BC. This group is situated to the immediate south of a minor road between the A3400 and the A44. 'The Whispering Knights', are the remains of a Bronze Age burial chamber, standing four hundred yards to the east of the circle, and finally 'the King Stone', is an isolated 'standing stone', nearly opposite 'the King's Men', and almost certainly associated with them, although its exact purpose is not known. These features all lie in fine upland country, and there are splendid views, especially northwards from the King Stone. The ridge on which these stones are situated is believed to have carried one of Britain's earliest and most important tracks - the so-called **Jurassic Way**, leading south and west along the limestone belt from the shores of the Humber, to Salisbury Plain and the coast beyond. For further reading on the subject of trackways in this area, see G.R.Crosher's *Along the Cotswold Ways*.

The 18th-century antiquary, William Stukeley, referred to the Rollright Stones as being *corroded like wormeaten wood by the harsh jaws of time*, but despite their exposed upland setting they still survive. In earlier times they were the subject of a legend relating to a king intent on the conquest of England, who was confronted here by a witch who spoke thus:

> *If Long Compton thou canst see,*
> *King of England thou shalt be.*

Unfortunately for the king and his followers this proved to be impossible at the time, and the witch continued :

The Whispering Knights and the Kings Men, Rollright Stones

> *As Long Compton thou canst not see*
> *King of England thou shalt not be.*
> *Rise up stick, and stand still, stone,*
> *For King of England thou shalt be*
> *none.*
> *Thou and thy men hoar stones shalt*
> *be,*
> *And I shall be an eldern tree.*

And so, it is sad to relate, the king, his men and his knights were all turned into stone, and the witch into an elder tree.

ROUSHAM HOUSE AND GARDENS (1

E16) *6 mi. NNE Woodstock.* A Jacobean mansion enlarged and enriched by William Kent in 1783, and still in the hands of the family who

Sculpture at Rousham

built it - the Dormers, latterly the Cottrell-Dormers. While the house with its fine collection of portraits and furniture is of considerable interest, a visit to its landscaped gardens is a quite unique experience.

These were laid out by William Kent, and are the only surviving example of his landscape design, still including many of the features which proved so enticing to 18th-century visitors. Horace Walpole was one of these visitors and described the garden as *the most engaging of all Kent's works.* Sited amongst woods along the rushy tree-shaded banks of the River Cherwell, the garden's various features include ponds, cascades in Venus' Vale, the Cold Bath, and the seven-arched Praeneste. This is a lovely classical summer-house with views across the valley to a sham ruin on the skyline - known, like several other examples in various parts of the country, as an 'eyecatcher'.

Ryknild Street, south of Condicote

See also the lovely flower borders in the old walled garden, the 16th-century dovecot with revolving ladder, and the nearby church with its fine Cottrell-Dormer monuments. To quote from the descriptive leaflet, *Rousham is uncommercial and unspoilt with no tea room and no shop. Bring a picnic, wear comfortable shoes and it is yours for the day.* Need we say more, apart from asking readers to leave their dogs at home and to bring no children under 15. There is no better place to visit on a hot summer's day.

RYKNILD STREET (Not shown on map.) This Roman road was an important route running northwards from the **Foss Way** near **Bourton-on-the-Water,** and down the Cotswold edge between **Saintbury** and **Weston Subedge.** From here it ran across the Midland plain, past Birmingham and Derby, and ended up at Templeborough near Sheffield. Its line across Bourton Downs is not easy to spot on the ground, although there are slight humps to be seen where it crosses a minor road running eastwards from Snowshill towards the A424. These provide a fascinating clue which has been substantiated by excavation at Bourton Far Hill Farm, a short distance to the south. Apart from this, the best section of road for walkers is the track known as Condicote Lane which runs southwards from **Condicote** almost to **Upper Slaughter.**

SAINTBURY (1 B9) *2 mi. NE Broadway.* Small village poised on the slopes of the Cotswold edge, with a single street leading up from a medieval wayside cross on the B4632, past a series of enviably lovely stone houses and cottages, to the slender-spired church at its top. There are fine views from the church's north porch which itself shelters a pleasant early Norman doorway complete with patterned tympanum. The interior is delightfully unspoilt, with light flooding in onto old benches through the clear glass of the Perpendicular west window. There is a lovely old roof to the nave, a fine 15th-century font complete with an ogee-shaped 18th-century wooden cover, and several other attractive items including fragments of 17th-century wall-painting.

ST KENELM'S WELL (1 D8) *1 mi. E Winchcombe.* (Not shown on map.) This is a 19th-century reconstruction of a Holy Well connected with St Kenelm, the martyred boy prince, who was murdered in AD 819 in the far-off Clent Hills, and whose shrine at Winchcombe Abbey brought it such prosperity. The well lies about a quarter of a mile north of the road up from **Winchcombe** which passes the rear of **Sudeley Castle.** The footpath is muddy and possibly unsigned, and the going is steep, but the views are worthwhile and the spring feeding the well still flows. It is possible to walk on from here to the top of Salter's Hill, and then down Salter's Lane, following the line of the **Salt Way,** to **Hailes Abbey.**

SALFORD (1 D13) *2 mi. NW Chipping Norton.* This modest village just off the busy A44 has no special features apart from its church. This was largely rebuilt by the very competent Victorian architect, G.E. Street, although it is not one of his better works. However, there is the base of an old cross in the churchyard, an interesting Norman font with interlaced arcading, and a crudely carved tympanum over the north doorway which may represent *'Sagittarius the Archer'*. This subject was quite a favourite in the Cotswolds - see also **Kencot** and **Hook Norton.** It is possible to walk eastwards from Salford across the fields to **Chipping Norton.**

SALPERTON (1-2 F9) *4 mi. NW Northleach.* Here is a minute village in a quiet fold of the hills between the A40 and the A436, and on the probable line of both the **Salt Way** and **Campden Lane,** the latter being a wool trading trackway between **Chipping**

Salperton Manor

Campden and the southern Cotswolds; the two medieval trading routes appear to have converged here. The name Salperton is almost certainly derived from the early English *salt-paeth*, the salt path.

Nearby Salperton Park is a 17th-century manor house much altered in the 19th century. The adjoining church has a small tower complete with painted clock-face. The church is Norman in origin and has many Norman features, including its chancel arch. To the north of the tower arch is a late-medieval wall painting of a skeleton with a scythe and arrow - *Death, the Grim Reaper perhaps?* There is a coat of arms of George III, and a handsome 18th-century wall monument to John Browne with a draped coffin, urns and cherubs. Salperton Park is private property, but there appears to be a public path to the church in front of the house (please check locally if in doubt). Do not miss the attractive 17th-century table-tombs in the churchyard. Walk southwards from Salperton to **Hazleton** following the probable course of the **Salt Way,** and then eastwards along a good bridle road to **Turkdean.**

THE SALT WAY (Not shown on map.) Several trackways across the Cotswolds were used by medieval traders in salt, and some Cotswold manors even had their own salt-workings in the Droitwich area. However, the best-known of these tracks, known as the

Stanford St Martin

Salt Way, linked the main workings at Droitwich with the head of the navigable Thames in the vicinity of Lechlade, from whence the salt could easily be moved down-river to London. Study of the Ordnance Survey's Landranger Sheets 150 and 163 will soon reveal its approximate course, as it is still referred to as the Salt Way in several places, sometimes following modern roads, sometimes bridleways and at others just ill-defined pathways. For more details on this fascinating subject read G.R. Crosher's book, *Along the Cotswold Ways,* and J. Finberg's *The Cotswolds.*

SANDFORD ST MARTIN (1 E15) *6 mi. N Woodstock.* Delightful village of stone and thatch in the valley of the little River Dorn. Here is a snug manor house, well hidden from the road and, opposite the church, Sandford Park, a lovely 18th-century mansion with extensive parkland and gardens *(not open to the public).* Just to its south there is a village cross overlooked by a substantial 16th- and 18th-century farmhouse and beyond this a number of pleasant houses and

cottages line the street. The church is largely Decorated and Perpendicular, although the chancel was rebuilt in 1856 by the Victorian architect G E Street, who also built the lychgate. Lord Deloraine, the third son of the Duke of Monmouth (see **Ledwell**), is buried in the churchyard beneath a low, tunnel-like mound with low stone walling at either end. It is said that the coffin in which Lord Deloraine was buried had glass ends, this being due to his claustrophobia. However, following two occasions when foxes went to earth in the vault, it was sealed for all time and the mystery remains.

SAPPERTON (1-2 J6) *5 mi. W Cirencester.* Situated just beyond the western extremities of the great **Cirencester Park** and poised above the deep Frome Valley, this is a trim little village, with an inn of great character called the Bell, and an attractive terraced road beyond its church. This lies at the lower end of a long path sloping beneath yew trees. It is a largely 18th-century building, having round-headed windows with their original glass, and a very stylish interior which has utilised much Jacobean woodwork removed from Sapperton House, itself demolished in about 1730 to make way for the western end of Cirencester Park's Long Ride. There are two very fine monuments here, both with life-size figures - one to Sir Henry Poole and his family and the other to Sir Robert Atkyns, the noted county historian and author of *The Ancient and Present State of Gloucestershire.* In the churchyard outside will be found the base and shaft of an 11th-century cross, and, beneath trees on either side of a sloping path, the tombs of the three artist-craftsmen who carried on the traditions of William Morris in the surrounding area - Ernest Gimson, and the brothers Ernest and Sidney Barnsley (see also **Daneway**). For further memories of the life and work of these three and their fellow craftsmen, read the account by their best-known disciple, the architect Norman Jewson, entitled *By Chance I Did Rove.* This was originally published in 1920, but was reprinted in 1973.

Monuments at Sapperton

    The Thames and Severn Canal runs in a tunnel beneath the village, to emerge at its north-western end at **Daneway** in the valley below. The best walk from Sapperton runs north-eastwards along the valley slope to lovely 17th-century Pinbury Park (see **Edgeworth**), once the home of Sir Robert Atkyns, and for a few years at the beginning of the 20th century, that of Ernest Gimson and the Barnsleys. The walk then returns through woods down beside the infant Frome. Sapperton lies astride the **Macmillan Way** and this can followed southwards through the splendid **Hailey Wood** to the **Tunnel House Inn** and beyond to **Tarlton.**

SARSDEN (1-2 F13) *3 mi. SW Chipping Norton.* A quiet hamlet in rolling, wooded parkland, with a few thatched cottages, two round barrows, a medieval wayside cross, and a beautiful late 17th-century mansion in a park landscaped by Humphry Repton. Beside the mansion is a church rebuilt in 1760 - an austere building with little of interest for the visitor.

SELSLEY AND SELSLEY COMMON (1-2 J4) *2 mi. SW Stroud.* Small hillside village which is almost a suburb of Stroud. It has an interesting church, which was paid for by the prosperous mill-owner Samuel Marling. Despite his wish that this should resemble the church of Marling in the Tyrol, which he had recently visited, it was designed more in the French-Gothic style much favoured by his talented architect, G.F. Bodley (see also **Bussage** and **France Lynch**). This church contains stained glass by almost all the leading figures of the Pre-Raphaelite circle, including William Morris himself, Philip Webb, Ford Madox Brown, Edward Burne-Jones and Dante Gabriel Rossetti, and for this reason is well worth visiting. In Water Lane, to the south-east of the village, will be found the attractive Selsley Herb and Goat Farm. As their leaflet states, *goats and herbs don't mix,* but visitors may look round the orchard where the goats are kept, and of course visit the delightful herb garden. There is a barn shop and light refreshments are available. Selsley Common extends along a ridge south-westwards from the village and is a fine open stretch of country, with many picnic possibilities and a series of extensive views.

SEVENHAMPTON (1-2 F8) *4 mi. S Winchcombe.* This modest village has a small ford across the infant Coln, a river which rises about a mile to its north. The ford is overlooked by a few cottages and not far away there is a Norman church. This was much altered and improved by the benefaction of a rich wool merchant, John Camber, who died in 1497, and whose likeness is well portrayed on a memorial brass to be found within. Flowering rock plants

Sevenhampton

line the path to the south door, which is sheltered by a handsome little porch, and the base of John Camber's Perpendicular tower provides a fascinating architectural story, with flying buttresses within the body of the church, and vaulting high up above the tower crossing. The interior has been over-restored, but there are several interesting monuments to be seen. It is possible to walk northwards from here, up the head of the Coln Valley, over the watershed to **Charlton Abbots,** and down to **Winchcombe.**

SEVEN SPRINGS (1-2 G6) *3 mi. S Cheltenham.* Although this has sometimes been claimed to be the 'highest source of the Thames', it is in fact only the source of its attractive tributary, the Churn. It consists of a rather muddy little pool, apparently still fed by seven springs, and is situated beside the A436 where there is a much-used lay-by. Walk south from here down the Churn Valley to **Coberley,** then eastwards to **Upper Coberley** before returning to Seven Springs. The course of the **Cotswold Way** passes within a few yards of Seven Springs, and this can be used to walk north and north-west to Charlton Kings Common and the **Devil's Chimney.**

SEZINCOTE (1 D10) *2½ mi. SW Moreton-in-Marsh.* In medieval times there was a small village here, but its church was destroyed by Cromwell's forces, apparently because the estate was in the hands of an ardent Royalist family. In 1795 Sezincote was purchased by Colonel John Cockerell, a 'nabob' recently returned from Bengal. He died only three years later, leaving the estate to his younger brother Charles, who had served with him in the East India Company. Charles, who became a Baronet in 1809, and a Member of Parliament for Evesham, built a new house, employing another brother, Samuel Pepys Cockerell (the family were distantly related to the diarist), as his architect.

S.P.Cockerell, who had already designed nearby **Daylesford** for Warren Hastings, was Surveyor to the East India Company. He worked closely with Thomas Daniel, an artist who had also recently returned from India, and together they created a magnificent house in the Indian manner. This was at least in part inspired by the extensive works of the 16th-century Mogul Emperor, Akbar, who had deliberately mixed Islamic and Hindu styles in an attempt to integrate the diverse cultures of the two races. The result achieved at Sezincote is unique - a grand house in the authentic Mogul style in a rural English setting, the beauty of which was further enhanced by the outstanding landscape artist, Humphry Repton, who helped to create the lovely water gardens and lakes on the gently sloping hillside that gives birth to the River Evenlode. In contrast Sezincote offers a most elegant classical interior, which has been beautifully restored in the mid-20th century, and a visit here should certainly not be missed.

Sezincote was visited in 1806 by the Prince Regent who was staying with the

Marquess of Hertford at Ragley, near Alcester, at the time, and it is thought that he was so impressed by Sezincote's style that he advanced his plans for the 'Indianisation' of his Pavilion at Brighton. Sadly, however, the commission was given to the Prince's favourite architect, John Nash, rather than to Cockerell. For a delightfully nostalgic account of Colonel and Mrs Dugdale's frequent house-party weekends at Sezincote in the early 1930s, read John Betjeman's long poem, *Summoned by Bells*. This is extensively quoted in James Lees-Milne's highly informative book, *Some Cotswold Country Houses.*

SHEEPSCOMBE (1-2 H5) *1½ mi. E Painswick.* A long village beautifully situated on both sides of a quiet valley beneath luxuriantly wooded hillsides. In the 18th century this was a cloth-weaving village and a few of the cottages still have the large three-light windows which were built to provide the maximum possible light for the weavers. In the early years of the 19th century there was no church here, but there were no fewer than eight unlicensed alehouses. Its inhabitants had by then mostly become factory workers at the

Brookland Mill, and they had acquired a reputation throughout the district for drunkenness and riotous behaviour. However, by 1825 a church had been built and a Sunday School opened, and Sheepscombe soon became known as the 'Peaceful Valley'. This almost miraculous transformation appears to have been a permanent one. Today there is one inn - the little Butcher's Arms - complete with a colourful carved sign, and across the valley, immediately above a sloping green, the quaint little church still stands proudly, with its minute tower attached to an ornate west end. Walk northwards from Sheepscombe, up through woods and over to **Cranham.**

SHENINGTON (1 B14) *5 mi. W Banbury.* Large stone and thatch village grouped around a wide green, standing over five hundred feet above sea level, and looking across the valley of the Sor Brook to its smaller neighbour, **Alkerton.** It has an attractive little inn, the Bell, which is noted for its bar meals. The church has a Perpendicular west tower, and a porch of the same period, but it is otherwise largely in the Decorated style. It was heavily restored in 1879 by an architect, who was not always so ruthless - J L Pearson, the

Trophy Sign, Shenington

builder of Truro cathedral. Here are shiny tiles, pitch pine pews and scraped walls, but better features include a 13th-century chancel arch, medieval ornamentation of the south aisle arcade capitals, and the sculptured figures of a man and his ox on the outside of the south wall.

Shenington lies on the **Macmillan Way** and this can be followed northwards up the valley of the Sor Brook or southwards to **Epwell,** Ditchedge Lane and **Traitor's Ford.**

Haycroft Bottom near Sherborne

The countryside hereabouts is the Oxfordshire Cotswolds at its best - high rolling countryside intersected by deep valleys running south towards the distant Thames.

SHERBORNE (1-2 G10) *4 mi. S Bourton-on-the-Water.* The village has been part of the Sherborne House Estate for centuries. The site was once owned by the abbots of **Winchcombe,** who had a substantial farm here. Apparently the abbot would spend most of the month of May at Sherborne to supervise the shearing of the vast flocks gathered in from his abbey's great sheep runs, which stretched over the Cotswolds from **Snowshill** and **Roel Gate,** through **Charlton Abbots** and **Hawling.** At least one wool-buyer from Italy is known to have visited Sherborne in 1436, and until the English clothiers took up most of its output, the majority of the abbey's fleeces would have been exported to Italy and Flanders.

Following the Dissolution of 1539, the Sherborne estate was purchased in 1551 by Thomas Dutton, who at once built himself a fine house here. His grandson John 'Crump' Dutton, the hunchback Royalist colonel, who at the end of the Civil War was clever enough to convince Cromwell that he had only served the king under duress, employed Valentine Strong, quarry-owner and builder of nearby Taynton, to enhance the original building (see also **Lodge Park,** another house built for him, probably also by Strong).

Using stone from underground quarries (or mines) in the park, Sherborne House was regrettably rebuilt in the 19th century, largely by Lewis Wyatt, but also by Anthony Salvin, the architect who is best remembered for his extensive rebuilding work at Windsor Castle. The house was a boarding school for some years, but has now been converted into flats. The estate remained in the hands of the Dutton family, latterly the Lords Sherborne, but it was generously bequeathed to the National Trust some years ago. There is an interesting display relating to the Sherborne Estate at Ewepen Barn, which is up a short drive off a minor road leading north, off the A40 towards Sherborne village. There is a car park and picnic area here and a series of waymarked walks across parts of the park. The restored water-meadows beside the Sherborne Brook are of particular interest.

The church lies close to the park, but although its tower and spire are medieval, the rest was rebuilt during the first half of the 19th century. However, its well-proportioned interior was refurnished in the 1930s, and also contains a splendid series of monuments to various members of the Dutton family. See especially the fine monument to Sir John Dutton by the celebrated sculptor, John Rysbrack, and the one to John Lennox Dutton, by Richard Westmacott the elder. The village itself is delightfully situated in the valley of the little Sherborne Brook, not far from its confluence with the more important River Windrush. It is divided into two parts, to the east and the west of the park, and both have a number of attractive houses and cottages not far from the brook. At the eastern end of the village there is a cottage with a small reset Norman arch. Walk eastwards from here, down the valley to **Windrush** and **Little Barrington.**

Sherston Porch

SHERSTON (2 N4) *5 mi. W Malmesbury.* A large village just to the north of the infant Bristol Avon, with a wide main street, Sherston was a borough by the 15th century and the variety of beautiful stone houses and inns still bear witness to its past prosperity. Although only just over the Gloucestershire border into Wiltshire, Sherston seems to already have a 'West Country' flavour. Its church has a handsomely vaulted Perpendicular porch and a fine tower, surprisingly built as late as 1730. Sherston is astride the **Macmillan Way** and this can be used to walk south-westwards down the Avon Valley to **Luckington** and then on to **Castle Combe,** a distance of about eight miles.

SHILTON (1-2 H12) *2½ mi. SE Burford.* This charming village is tucked away in the quiet valley of the Shill Brook, just below the busy B4020 and only a mile away from the garrison town of **Carterton** and the adjoining airfield of Brize Norton. Apart from the noise of aircraft overhead, Shilton is near perfection, with a stream, a pond edged with chestnut trees and a forded road leading up beside a farm and a dovecot. It also has rose-decked cottages, flower-filled gardens and a small but very friendly inn - the Rose and Crown. Church and rectory lie to the south of the village, and in the church, which has many Norman features, will be found an exceptionally beautiful font enriched with

14th-century carvings on all four sides depicting scenes from the Passion, with the Evangelists at each corner.

SHIPSTON-ON-STOUR (1 B12) *7 mi. NE Moreton-in-Marsh.* 'Sheepstown', as its name implies, was once an extremely important market for sheep, and its many delightful houses from the 17th, 18th and 19th centuries bear witness to a prosperity lasting for at least three hundred years. That it continued to thrive in the 19th century must have been due in part to the enterprise of the local canal and railway promoter William James of Henley-in-Arden, who in 1826 completed a tramway linking the canal wharfs of Stratford-upon-Avon with Moreton-in-Marsh, with a branch line to Shipston opening ten years later (see **Stratford and Moreton Tramway**). Eventually, in 1889, many years after Brunel's main Oxford, Worcester and Wolverhampton line came through Moreton-in-Marsh, part of the tramway was converted into a railway branch line between there and Shipston. Another factor contributing to Shipston's continuing prosperity was its position astride a busy north-south coaching route, and a number of its old coaching inns survive to this day, amongst them those in the very pleasant High Street, Shipston's little market square. This is just far enough away to escape the busy traffic of the A3400, Stratford to Oxford road. Shipston today is a busy little shopping town, with its shops attractive enough to tempt customers from far and wide.

St Edmund's Church has retained its 15th-century west tower, but is otherwise the creation of Victorian architect, G.E.Street. The interior is not of outstanding interest, but do not miss the very unusual conversion of a sounding-board from an earlier pulpit into an octagonal table. There is also a handsome little monument to another person to whom Shipston must have owed some of its prosperity, John Hart, who died in 1747 - *A considerable Improver and Promoter of Manufacture in this his native Town.* There is an attractive walk, partly beside the River Stour, to **Barcheston,** and on to **Willington,** and also one south-westwards across the fields to **Todenham.**

SHIPTON OLIFFE (1-2 G8) *6 mi. E Cheltenham.* Long straggling village on a small

Shipton Solers

tributary of the Coln with a small ford, a Methodist chapel in bright red brick looking startlingly like a Victorian railway station, and a pretty church overlooking ornamental gardens by the stream. This little church with its 13th-century bellcote has been rather tidied up inside, but has a colourful Royal Coat of Arms in plaster relief, blocked-up Norman doorways, remnants of medieval wall-paintings and old oak pews which were originally in the church at neighbouring Shipton Solers. It is possible to walk north-eastwards from here to **Hampen** and on to **Salperton.**

SHIPTON SOLERS (1-2 G8) *5½ mi. E Cheltenham.* This is smaller than its neighbour Shipton Oliffe, but there are delightful glimpses of the manor house's stream-side gardens, and the little 13th-century church this is situated just above the road and was very sympathetically restored in 1929. Its contents include a 17th-century pulpit complete with sounding board and a plain 15th-century font. The Frogmill Inn, well to the west of the village, was once a well used coaching halt on the Gloucester to London road and is now a hotel and restaurant. Walk south from Shipton Solers to Cleevely Wood, and then walk beside the stream to **Withington.**

SHIPTON-UNDER-WYCHWOOD (1-2 G12) *4 mi. NE Burford.* This large village was once the centre of the great **Wychwood Forest** and a large fair was held here each year. Shipton is situated in the broad valley of the River Evenlode and has several very pleasant old houses, including handsome 17th-century Shipton Court behind its high wall. The largely 15th-century Shaven Crown Hotel was once a guest house run by the monks of **Bruern Abbey,** and is claimed to have held a licence since the year 1384. This fine old building has a central hall and a carriage entrance opening onto a partly cobbled yard. It was at the Shaven Crown that the fascist leader Sir Oswald Mosley and his wife Diana (one of the 'Mitford Girls' of nearby **Swinbrook**) were detained by the authorities for a short time during the Second World War.

The Shaven Crown looks out across a fine, wide village green to Shipton's tall-spired church. This has a Norman tower and a 15th-century vaulted porch opening into a large, rather bleak interior, this condition being partly due to the heavy-handed work of Victorian architect, G.E. Street. It does, however, contain a handsome 15th-century stone pulpit, a large font of the same period, and a charming Tudor wall monument with husband and wife at a prayer desk with their children in attendance. At the southern end of the village will be found the hospitable Lamb Inn a small hotel and restaurant.

Shipton-under-Wychwood

About two miles to the south-east is the farmhouse of Langley, a largely mid-19th-century building on the site of a royal hunting lodge. Most of the Tudor monarchs stayed here when hunting in **Wychwood Forest,** and it was certainly used by the Royal Court for this purpose as late as 1614.

The Gibbet Tree, to the east of the A361, about two miles south of Shipton, was the single oak tree where the bodies of two of the notorious Dunsdon brothers were hung in chains in 1785, following their earlier hanging at Gloucester. These three brothers, named Tom, Dick and Harry, were highwaymen who had acquired a notoriety not far short of Dick Turpin's, and the writer suspects that it is to them that we may owe the oft-used phrase, 'Tom, Dick and Harry'. They were born at nearby **Swinbrook,** but appear to have worked from Icomb, using an old underground quarry beneath their cottage to stable their horses and to store their loot.

Shipton-under-Wychwood is on the course of the **Oxfordshire Way,** and this can be used to walk north-westwards up the Evenlode Valley to **Bruern Abbey** and **Bledington,** or eastwards down the valley to **Charlbury.**

SHORTHAMPTON (1-2 F13) *2 mi. W Charlbury.* A quiet hamlet overlooking the broad valley of the Evenlode, with a farm, a few cottages and a wonderfully unspoilt little medieval church. This appears to have been overlooked by all those zealous Victorian 'restorers', and its 18th-century high-backed pews and two-decker pulpit have survived intact. There is also a most interesting series of wall paintings of the 15th, 16th and 17th century, including a unique depiction of *The Miracle of the Clay Birds.* Shorthampton lies on the **Oxfordshire Way** and this can be followed westwards to **Ascott-under-Wychwood** and **Shipton-under-Wychwood,** or eastwards to **Charlbury.**

SHURDINGTON (1-2 G6) *3 mi. SW Cheltenham.* This large village below the Cotswold scarp is now almost a suburb shared between Cheltenham and Gloucester, and its peace is shattered by traffic on the A46. However, the church lies away from this busy road, with yew trees lining the long path to its south porch. This is overlooked by a slender 14th-century spire, which is even more graceful than its contemporary at nearby **Leckhampton.** Inside its much restored interior there is fine rib vaulting

Shurdington

below the tower, and beneath it a pleasant 14th-century font, but otherwise there is little of interest to the visitor here. It is possible to walk south-eastwards, up Shurdington Hill, to link onto the **Cotswold Way.**

SHUTFORD (1 B14) *4½ mi. W Banbury.* Quiet village on steep slopes amidst small bumpy hills. The prettily signed George and Dragon inn is comfortably sited almost beneath the church. This has a miniature pinnacled tower, Perpendicular in period, Norman arcading, a pleasant oak screen, also Perpendicular, and early-19th century box pews. The largely 16th-century manor house has an unusually tall, projecting staircase tower, and it is believed that the upper storey of the house once had an eighty foot gallery (not an uncommon feature in houses of this period), where Lord Saye and Sele, of nearby Broughton Castle, used to drill local troops before the outbreak of the Civil War. There is a bridle-road south from here, beside Madmarston Hill, to **Swalcliffe,** and on beyond, south-westwards to **Hook Norton.** Alternatively there is a path up the valley of the little Sor Brook to **Shenington.** There is also an attractive, partly unfenced road running east and south-east to **Broughton,** with its beautiful moated castle.

Cottages at Sibford Ferris

SIBFORD FERRIS AND SIBFORD GOWER (1 C14) *6 mi. W Banbury.* These two together with Burdrop, a minute hamlet sandwiched between them, make up a large village, with Ferris to the south, and Gower to the north, of a quiet valley running south-westwards to the Stour. Burdrop has a colourful little inn called the Bishop Blaize looking out over the valley. Ferris has a large Quaker boarding school including one or two elegant 18th-century houses, and a short unfenced road with fine views, leading south-westwards, past Woodway Farm. Gower has a largely unremarkable Victorian church, which is however worth visiting on account of the charming little monument to Mrs Isabelle Stevens (1907) by her son Frank Lascelles, who lived at the manor house and who was, in his day, well known for the great pageants that he used to organise. Gower also has a wealth of Hornton stone and thatched cottages, and a pleasant inn called the Wykeham Arms.

It is possible to walk westwards from here, across the fields to link onto the **Macmillan Way** along Ditchedge Lane, an old 'green road', which forms the border between

Norman Tympanum, Siddington

Warwickshire and Oxfordshire, following it southwards to the point where it crosses the Stour at **Traitor's Ford.**

SIDDINGTON (1-2 K8) *1 mi. SE Cirencester.* Now almost a suburb of Cirencester, Siddington has somehow managed to preserve its individuality in the area immediately surrounding its tall-spired church. Much of this was rebuilt by the Victorians, but there is a splendid Norman south doorway with beak-head decoration and an outstanding tympanum depicting *Christ in Majesty*. There is also a beautiful Perpendicular north aisle chapel with a fine roof supported on angel corbels. Unfortunately for Siddington, the lovely 15th-century glass from here was transferred to Cirencester church, where it now forms the central feature of the massive east window. The cylindrical Norman font is so tall that it is thought to have been used at one time for adult baptisms. While visiting the church do not miss the pleasant 16th-century barn overlooking the churchyard. Siddington is on the course of the long-closed **Thames and Severn Canal**. Traces of this may be seen to the south of the village and it is in fact still possible to use part of its old towpath to walk southwards to **South Cerney.**

SLAD (1-2 J5) *2 mi. NE Stroud.* Strung out along the B4070 on the side of a valley dropping down into Stroud, this small village is now inevitably linked with the poet and author, Laurie Lee. His childhood years in the village are brilliantly recalled in his book, *Cider with Rosie.* Despite its fame Slad has remained remarkably unspoilt, so let us help to keep it this way by trying not to linger too long here. The small Victorian church is certainly for architectural enthusiasts only. There is a pleasant, winding road westwards from here to **Bisley.**

SLIMBRIDGE and THE WILDFOWL TRUST (2 J2) *12 mi. SW Gloucester.* This modest sized village lies in flat, non-Cotswold country between the M5 and the shores of the Severn Estuary, and like Berkeley Castle should really be outside the scope of this guide. There are, however, two reasons why it has been included. Firstly it has a fine 13th-century church - one of the area's best examples of the Early English style. The three-stage tower is topped by a tall, beautifully proportioned spire, and the 13th-century architectural detail within is full of interest. William Tyndale, the first translator of the New Testament into English, was probably born at Slimbridge, in the year 1484, but the **Tyndale Monument**, erected to his memory in the 19th century, stands on the Cotswold edge some miles to the south, above **North Nibley,** as this village also claims to have been his birthplace.

Having looked round the church, drive beyond the village, cross the broad waters of the Gloucester and Sharpness Canal, and head for the place that has brought world-wide fame to the name of Slimbridge - the Wildfowl Trust's splendid reserve, a few hundred yards short of the Severn Estuary. Established by Sir Peter Scott in 1946, this organisation was originally called the Severn Wildfowl Trust. It has four aims - education, research, conservation and recreation - and thanks to the dedication of Sir Peter and his successors, these aims have been achieved with outstanding success. The Wildfowl Trust, as it is now called, has established similar reserves at Peakirk, Cambridgeshire; Martin Mere, Lancashire; Washington, Tyne and Wear; Arundel, Sussex; and Llanelli in South Wales. At Slimbridge and all the above reserves there is a combination of tame waterfowl from all over the world, and wild native species in their natural habitat. At two other reserves - Caerlaverock, Dumfries and Welney, Norfolk, there are no tame birds, but there is an abundance of wild ones.

At any time of the year a visit to Slimbridge will prove to be a delight, for here is the world's largest and most varied collection of wildfowl, including colourful flocks of all six of the world's species of flamingoes. There is also a tropical house with humming birds flitting amongst jungle foliage. In winter the skies are alive with swans, geese and ducks, and they can be observed from comfortable hides. The visitor centre has exhibitions, displays and a 100-seat cinema. There is also a gift shop and excellent restaurant. A visit here will help to support the fine aims of the Wildfowl Trust.

SNOWSHILL (1 D9) *2½ mi. S Broadway.* This charming hillside village is situated at the head of a quiet valley, on slopes just below Oat Hill, one of the high points along the Cotswold edge. Hardly any two of Snowshill's roof lines are on the same level, and there are beautifully framed views over the Avon Valley and to the Midland Plain beyond. Viewed from the little road above it, the church sits comfortably into the hillside and appears to be almost part of the earth itself. It was rebuilt in the mid-19th century and is not of great interest, although its contents does include a good Perpendicular-style octagonal font, and a pulpit constructed of 17th-century carved panels. A series of attractive houses and cottages are grouped around the small sloping churchyard and village green, while below the church will be found a busy and welcoming inn, the Snowshill Arms.

Not far beyond the inn is the National Trust's Snowshill Manor - a beautiful Tudor building with a William and Mary south front. It is set in lovely terraced gardens which overlook orchards below and farmland which rises beyond. Once owned by the abbey of Winchcombe, and then by Catherine Parr, the last of Henry VIII's

Snowshill Manor

six wives, it was purchased just after the First World War by Charles Paget Wade, whose family had amassed great wealth from sugar plantations in the West Indies. An architect, artist, craftsman, eccentric and scholar, he first restored the manor, and then proceeded to fill it with a most extraordinary collection. As a result the house is packed from ground floor to attic with a fascinating collection of bygones - toys, telescopes, sedan chairs, ship models, clocks, musical instruments, weavers' and spinners' tools, Japanese armour and even bicycles. Each of the many rooms in which the collection is housed bears a name beautifully painted above its door - names like *Nadir, Meridian, Seraphim, Dragon, Admiral, Top Gallant* and *Seventh Heaven.* Mr Wade, who gave Snowshill Manor and its contents to the National Trust in 1951, lived in extreme simplicity, never having electric light in the house, and sleeping in an adjoining cottage in a Tudor cupboard-bed. However, very late in life he married, and eventually retired to the West Indies, where he died in 1956. The house and its contents, and the delightful gardens which surround it, make a visit here very rewarding, but try to avoid peak times. There is a car park, restaurant and shop close by, at the lower, northern end of the village. One item of local interest not to be seen in the manor's collection is a device claimed to be the world's earliest sewing machine. This is to be found in the Science Museum in South Kensington, but it was made at Snowshill in the year 1842 by a certain Charles Keyte, known to his friends rather appropriately as 'Schemer Keyte'.

There are a number of walks from Snowshill - to **Buckland, Laverton, Stanton** and **Stanway.** The best starting point for walks in this area is a small car-parking space on the course of the **Cotswold Way**, which can be reached by a narrow public road running from the village, first westwards and then north-westwards.

SOMERFORD KEYNES (2 L8) *4 mi. S Cirencester.* A pleasant stone village with a hospitable inn and, in a park-like setting between its manor and rectory, a most interesting church with Saxon origins. The tall, narrow doorway in the north wall has been reopened, and with its single stone arch may be over a thousand years old. Inside will be found a fragmentary carving which may be Danish in origin, showing the confrontation of two strange beasts. However, many visitors will find the elegant 17th-century monument to Robert Strange, complete with bewigged effigy, more to their liking. Somerford Keynes lies just to the east of the infant River Thames, and it is possible to walk northwards close beside it to the pleasant hamlet of **Ewen,** making use of the **Thames Path.**

The Keynes Country Park, well to the east of the village, is one of the main features of the very extensive **Cotswold Water Park,** and details of its facilities will be found under this heading.

The Somerset Monument

THE SOMERSET MONUMENT (2 M3) *3½ mi. S Wotton-under-Edge.* This high stone tower, with its slightly oriental flavour, was designed by the architect Lewis Vulliamy in 1846 for the Duke of Beaufort, and commemorates General Lord Robert Somerset, a member of the Beaufort family who served under Wellington at Waterloo. It may be possible to climb the 144 steps to a platform, from where views ranging from Flat Holm in the Bristol Channel to the Forest of Dean and the distant mountains of Wales may be obtained. *(Enquire locally.)* The monument lies on the course of the **Cotswold Way,** and this provides a good walk north-eastwards to **Lower Kilcott.**

SOUTHAM (1-2 E7) *3 mi. NE Cheltenham.* Situated beneath Cleeve Hill's steep scarp slopes, Southam has grown considerably in the last few years, with many new houses being built for those working in nearby Cheltenham, of which Southam is almost a suburb. Worth visiting is the small Norman church, which had fallen into disuse by the mid-19th century before being partially rebuilt, much restored and also richly furnished, by Lord Ellenborough, who had retired to Southam after a term as Governor-General of India. Lord Ellenborough lived at Southam Delabere, an Elizabethan mansion nearby which he enlarged, adding a neo-Norman keep and a Gothic tower. It is now a hotel. There is a steep walk from Southam up onto **Cleeve Hill,** linking with the **Cotswold Way.**

SOUTH CERNEY (1-2 K8) *3 mi. SE Cirencester.* A large village on the banks of the River Churn, only about four miles above its confluence with the Thames at **Cricklade.** It is also on the edge of the large gravel pits which, now flooded, are part of the extensive **Cotswold Water Park.** Two lakes near the village are devoted to fishing and a third to sailing. The village itself is of considerable interest, with an 18th-century octagonal gazebo by the River Churn, a number of pleasant old houses in Church Lane and Silver Street, and a walk near the George Inn with the delightful name `Bow-Wow'. The large church dates back to the Norman period and above the Norman south doorway are sculptured details of *The Christ in Glory and The Harrowing of Hell.* The large central tower was once topped by a spire, but this was dismantled in 1862, during restoration work carried out by the architect J.P. St Aubyn. See also the fragments of a 12th-century rood, with the head and foot of a crucifix, one of the earliest and most outstanding pieces of wood-carving in the country.

Do not miss a visit to The Butts Farm, a working farmstead well to the north-east of the village. This has a wide variety of animals and should be especially popular with young children. The course of the **Thames and Severn Canal** passes to the north of the village, and it is possible to use the old towpath, to walk north to **Siddington** or south-eastwards to **Cerney Wick,** where there is a canal 'round house' (see **Hyde**), and on to **Cricklade.**

South Newington

SOUTH NEWINGTON (1 D15) *6 mi. SW Banbury.* Situated in the valley of the little River Swere, this delightful village has an inn on the main road called the Wykeham Arms. Much of the rest of the village lies beyond a small trim green which is overlooked by South Newington's exceptionally interesting church. This has a handsome Perpendicular porch with canopied niche, a cylindrical Norman font with a zigzag band, a Jacobean pulpit, and a series of box pews (all as originally numbered - an unusual survival in this area). There are also a number of interesting medieval stained glass windows. However most visitors come here to see the splendid series of wall paintings, especially the 14th-century specimens in the north aisle and elsewhere. These are regarded by Professor Tristram, the great expert on wall paintings, as quite outstanding, and they must have been the work of an artist far more sophisticated in style than those normally working at the time on most small parish churches. See especially *The Martyrdom of St Thomas á Becket* over the north doorway, and to the east of it, *The Martyrdom of Thomas, Earl of Lancaster.* This Thomas was beheaded at Pontefract in 1322 for leading a rebellion against Edward II, and was probably featured on South Newington's walls due to his friendship with a local family, the Giffards, one of whom perished with him at Pontefract. The whole series of paintings must have been a wonderful picture-book bible for the medieval peasants of this parish, and they are fascinating in every detail. Do not overlook the framed documents relating to compulsory burial in woollen shrouds; a popular measure in this sheep country, but one that was more to the advantage of the great sheep graziers rather than the peasants. It is possible to walk from here up the Swere valley to **Wigginton** and on to **Swerford,** or down to **Barford St Michael** and **Barford St John.** There is also a bridle road northwards over hill country to **Milcombe** and **Tadmarton.**

Norman Font, Southrop

SOUTHROP (1-2 J11) *2½ mi. N Lechlade.* Small village beside the willows and water-meadows of the lovely River Leach, with a fine manor house and a pleasant mill house nearby. There is a creeper-covered inn called the Swan, a pretty row of cottages, a gabled dovecot, and tucked away behind the manor an interesting little Norman church. This has a small bellcote, a Norman north doorway with geometric patterns in its tympanum, and a simple Norman chancel arch. John Keble was curate at Southrop between 1823 and 1825 (he was born in nearby Fairford) and it was he who was apparently responsible for rediscovering the Norman font, which for many years had been built into the south doorway. This font is a superb example of mid-12th-century craftsmanship, and in the view of most experts the finest specimen in the Cotswold area. Its subjects range from *Moses with the Tables of the Law to The Virtues trampling on The Vices.* Do not overlook the 16th-century effigies of Sir John Conway and his lady.

The nearby Old Vicarage was the home of John Keble during his short curacy (see above) and it was here, the first stirrings of the Oxford Movement must have taken place, for Keble used to invite friends from Oxford to come here for reading parties during vacations.

The manor house dates largely from the 16th and 17th centuries, but the discovery of a Norman archway appears to confirm the belief that it stands on the site of a very early building. The manor was purchased in 1612 by Dorothy Wadham, the founder of Wadham College, Oxford, and it formed part of her endowment, remaining in Wadham College's hands until as recently as 1926. Walk north from here beside the River Leach to **Eastleach,** or south-eastwards, also beside the river, to the hamlet of Little Faringdon, with its flooded gravel pits.

Spelsbury

SPELSBURY (1-2 F14) *1½ mi. N Charlbury.* There is a pleasant blend of stone and thatch in this quiet village looking over the Evenlode Valley towards **Wychwood Forest**. It has a pleasant row of gabled 17th-century almshouses and a Victorian drinking fountain. Its fine, largely 18th-century church has a handsome tower and a series of splendid monuments to the Lee Family, latterly the Earls of Litchfield, of nearby **Ditchley Park.**

SPOONLEY ROMAN VILLA (1-2 E8) *2 mi. SE Winchcombe.* Situated in Spoonley Wood, near the head of the 'Sudeley Valley' and about three quarters of a mile north-west of **Roel Gate,** are the remains of a Roman villa excavated in the late 19th century. This lies on private property, although there is a pleasant public footpath through the wood, passing close by. It is regrettable that the remains of this delightfully situated villa have been allowed to decay, although the deteriorating remains of mosaic pavements are in fact said to be only 19th-century copies of originals lifted during the initial excavations. Did the Romans' **White Way** from Cirencester extend as far north as this? The answer is far from certain, but it seems likely that the owners of the villa would have wished to make frequent visits to this thriving centre of local civilisation. Consult the Ordnance Survey's Landranger Sheet 163 to arrive at your own conclusions.

STANLEY PONTLARGE (1 D7) *2 mi. NW Winchcombe.* A hamlet beneath high Langley Hill, over which it is possible to walk to **Winchcombe.** The small Norman church has an original north doorway and chancel arch, but most of the remaining 'Norman' features are Victorian copies. As a result of this over-zealous restoration there is less atmosphere here than might have been hoped for.

Stanton

STANTON (1 C8) *3 mi. SW Broadway.* An outstandingly beautiful village situated below the wooded Cotswold edge, and tempting enough to have brought the course of the **Cotswold Way** down the steep slopes of Shenberrow Hill, through the village, and on to **Stanway.** The village was lovingly restored by its owner, the architect Sir Philip Stott, in the first quarter of the 20th century. The house he once owned, Stanton Court, is a fine Jacobean example and rather outshines the 16th-century manor house, but almost every building in Stanton is a delight to the eye.

The church has a well proportioned Perpendicular tower and spire and a very attractive two-storeyed porch complete with pinnacles and battlements. Inside, its Norman origins are revealed by the stout north arcading, and there are the remains of early 14th-century wall-paintings in the north transept. There are two pulpits here - a Jacobean one, and a late medieval one, no longer in use. The church was splendidly refurnished by one of the 20th century's finest restorers, Sir Ninian Comper, and his work has enhanced an already beautiful medieval interior. See especially the altar and communion rails, the gallery, the rood screen and the reredos, and above all, the 15th-century stained glass, which originally came from Hailes Abbey, and which was reset by Comper.

The young John Wesley often stayed at his *dear delightful Stanton* with the Reverend Lionel Kirkham and his sons and daughters, who were all his great friends. In the years before his departure to America in 1735, Wesley preached several times from the pulpit at Stanton, and also at nearby **Buckland** and **Broadway.** For more details read V.H. Green's *The Young Mr Wesley.*

Walk beyond the old wayside cross, up the quiet village street to the hospitable little Mount Inn, which awaits you on its small knoll below the wooded scarp. From here it is possible to walk up over the hills to **Snowshill,** passing a small car-parking area which straddles the **Cotswold Way.** Other walks from Stanton include a path over the fields to **Laverton,** and, using the **Cotswold Way,** either up to Shenberrow Hill (where there are the earthworks of a large Iron Age settlement) and eventually heading for **Broadway,** or through semi-parkland to neighbouring **Stanway.**

STANWAY (1 D8) *4 mi. SW Broadway.* This small village with its thatched, stone cottages, lies at the foot of the beautifully wooded Stanway Hill. The quiet crossroads well beyond the village is overlooked

by a handsome war memorial incorporating a bronze by Alexander Fisher of *St George and the Dragon*, mounted on a plinth designed by Sir Philip Stott of neighbouring Stanton, with lettering by Eric Gill. A short distance to the north of this crossroads stands the church, Stanway House and its splendid 17th-century gatehouse. Stanway church was over-restored in the late 19th century, but it has a Jacobean pulpit, a beautiful little bronze by Alexander Fisher and an altar made by Sir

Gatehouse, Stanway

Ninian Comper, who worked so extensively at neighbouring **Stanton.**

Stanway House is a handsome Jacobean manor house containing fine period furniture, including a working shuffleboard table and 'Chinese Chippendale' day-beds. The house stands in lovely gardens beneath steep, wooded parklands enhanced by an 18th-century stone belvedere called the Pyramid, from the base of which once descended a cascade similar to the one at Chatsworth in Derbyshire. There was once an ornamental canal between the base of the cascade and the house, but this was filled in many years ago and is now covered by a lawn.

Stanway's gatehouse is an enchanting piece of architecture, so beautiful that it was once attributed to Inigo Jones. However, it is now thought to have been the work of Timothy Strong of **Taynton,** one of the Cotswolds' outstanding masons and quarry-owners, and kinsman of Thomas Strong, who built the bridge over the Windrush at **Little Barrington.** Timothy also worked as a contractor at **Cornbury Park** under the direction of the great Nicholas Stone, and it seems likely that some of Stone's influence was at work in the design of Stanway. In the grounds is a fine 14th-century tithe barn, used by the abbots of Tewkesbury when they held the manorial rights here, and close by is a thatched wooden cricket pavilion set on staddle stones. This was presented to the village by Sir James Barrie, the author of *Peter Pan.*

War Memorial, Stanway

Stanway lies astride the **Cotswold Way,** and this can be used for walks to **Stanton,** or to **Wood Stanway,** both relatively level stretches of the Way. However, the best walk from Stanway is up through the great woodlands below

Lidcombe Hill and over to **Snowshill.** A glance at the Ordnance Survey's Landranger Sheet 150 will also indicate a fine circular walk, up through the same woods, down to Stanton by way of Shenberrow Hill, and back along the Cotswold Way to Stanway.

STEEPLE BARTON (1 E16) *5 mi. N Woodstock.* A beautifully quiet place in the valley of the little River Dorn, with a few houses and a church standing by itself at the end of a lane overlooking the parklands of Barton Abbey, a large house on a site once occupied by a cell

Men & Beasts of Steeple Barton

of Osney Abbey. There is no sign of a steeple here, but the church's stout Perpendicular tower dominates its sloping churchyard and its interior contains arcading ornamented with splendid medieval heads of both men and beasts. There is a bridleway south from the church and another starting out through the park and leading all the way to **Woodstock.** In a wood near Barton Lodge, the latter path passes close to the Hoar Stone, a long barrow with a long mound and the chaotic remains of its burial chamber.

STINCHCOMBE HILL (2 K2) *1 mi. NW Dursley.* Part of this area is used as a golf course, but there is parking space for cars, good walking opportunities and fine views over the Berkeley Vale, especially from Drakestone Point. Walk south from here, along the **Cotswold Way** to the **Tyndale Monument** and on to **Wotton-under-Edge.**

STONEHOUSE (2 J3) *3 mi. W Stroud.* A largely industrial town, with a church rebuilt, apart from its Perpendicular tower, in the mid-19th century. This is not of great interest to the visitor but it is

The Stroudwater Canal at Stonehouse

pleasantly situated, looking across a meadow to a pretty stretch of the **Stroudwater Canal** and it is itself overlooked by Stonehouse Court - a fine Elizabethan house.

STONESFIELD (1 G15) *3 mi. W Woodstock.* A charming, but confusingly complex village on a hilly site above the Evenlode valley, with distant memories of the quarries and mines that once provided the well known Stonesfield Cotswold-stone slates. One or two houses in the village have entries to old slate mines in their cellars or gardens, but it is not possible to view them. However, in the yard of Spratt's Barn, in Upper Witney Lane, at the western end of the village, by the road to North Leigh, there is an impressive circular shaft leading down to an extensive slate mine beneath the nearby hill slopes. *(It is possible that permission for interested groups may be obtained to view this, by phoning in advance to the owner, Mr John Lawton - Tel: (01993) 891539. The cost of ladder hire would have to be met.)* Spratts Barn has recently been re-roofed with genuine Stonesfield slates and is a fine example of craftsmanship, with the size of the slates gradually decreasing as they ascend the roof, in the true Cotswold style.

There are two inns in the village, the White Horse and the Black Head, and a minute village lockup. The church, which lies beyond the Black Head and the Post Office, has a Decorated-style chancel arch, south arcading with corbel figures, interesting medieval stained glass in the east window and a beautiful triptych reredos in its south aisle chapel. See also the Jacobean pulpit and the late-medieval wooden screen between the chancel and the north-aisle chapel. Stonesfield lies just to the north of the **Akeman Street** and there is a pleasant path southwards from here, which crosses this Roman road just before going over the River Evenlode. From here it is only a short way to **North Leigh Roman Villa.** The village also lies on the **Oxfordshire Way,** and this can be followed north-westwards to **Charlbury.**

Wall painting at Stowell

STOURTON (1 C13) *6½ mi. NE Moreton-in-Marsh* This is virtually a continuation of **Cherington,** but it lies closer to the Stour than its neighbour. There are several pleasant old houses, including two mills on the Stour. Walk north-east from here beside the banks of a small tributary of the Stour, to Lower Brailes.

STOWELL (1-2 H9) *2 mi. SW Northleach.* Here is a fine Elizabethan mansion (not open to the public) in a large park looking westwards over the Coln Valley to the Chedworth Woods. Behind the mansion there is a small Norman church, which has been over-restored externally, although the interior is still full of character. Its contents include some fascinating and very early 'Doom' paintings, which are believed to have been executed between 1150 and 1200, soon after the church was built. See also the two Norman piscinas, and the two 18th-century wall monuments in the chancel. This church lies within the bounds of the estate and it is suggested that visitors walk up the drive from the Northleach to Yanworth road. Parking on the roadside can be a problem, but the possibly long walk would be well justified.

STOW-ON-THE-WOLD (1-2 E11) *4 mi. S Moreton-in-Marsh.* This attractive little market town is the focal point of the northern Cotswolds, with no fewer than eight roads converging upon its windy site 700 feet above sea level. There was an Iron Age settlement here - an area of about thirty acres enclosed by earthworks, the partial remains of which are visible (but not worth searching for) in Camp Gardens on the north-eastern edge of the town. Later the Romans built a villa here, not far to the west of the **Foss Way,** which itself runs along the western edge of the present town.

Stow Cross

The best of Stow is centred upon its large Market Square, and a weekly market and two annual fairs, known as the Charter Fairs, have been held here since 1107, when Henry I granted Borough status to *Edwardstow,* as it was then called. The connection of Stow-on-the-Wold with 'St Edward' remains a mystery as there are three possible candidates to be considered - Edward the Hermit, a shadowy figure from early Christian times, Edward, King and Martyr, the young king stabbed to death at Corfe Castle, and the better-known King Edward the Confessor. The writer prefers the earliest candidate, Edward the Hermit, and likes to feel that this old bewhiskered saint spent his days in zealous prayer near the well below nearby **Maugersbury** that still bears his name.

Stow's fairs were renowned for the sale of wool and sheep, and Daniel Defoe, who once visited one of them, noted that over 20,000 sheep were sold. However, since Defoe's time they have become better known for the sale of horses, and until only a few years ago the official Stow Horse Fairs were held in fields just to the west of the town. Regrettably they have now had to be moved to **Andoversford.** The two Charter Fairs which are still held in Stow, one in May and one in October, are largely funfairs, although Stow is still visited by many gipsy horse traders at these times and much colourful buying and selling takes place.

Although undisturbed by any of the main roads entering the town, the Market Square is normally busy with visitors and local country shoppers. There are several antique shops, picture galleries, hotels, restaurants and inns - all facing into the Square - and most are traditional 17th- or 18th-century Cotswold buildings, apart from St Edward's House, a handsome building with Corinthian pilasters. There is a medieval cross here, although this has a headstone made in 1878, the year that St Edward's Hall was built a little to its north. This substantial Perpendicular-style building tends to divide the Market Square into two separate areas. It now houses the town's library. Beyond St Edward's Hall, the northern and more open half of the Square, known as the Green, has wide grass verges and the old town stocks which were once used for the punishment of evil-doers.

St Edward's Church lies well back from the Square, between this and the Foss Way. It is a large building with medieval origins, but much restored in the 17th century, following extensive damage caused whilst it was used to house prisoners during the Civil War. The last battle in this bitter struggle between king and Parliament was fought at nearby **Donnington,** although it is usually referred to as the Battle of Stow. The church's interior was again restored in the 19th century, when the roof was rebuilt. The work was carried out by J.L.Pearson, the architect best known for the building of Truro Cathedral, but Stow's restoration does not appear to have been one of his better efforts. However, do not miss the impressive painting of the Crucifixion in the south aisle, thought to be by the 17th-century Flemish artist, Gaspar de Craeyer, nor the floor slab in memory of Francis Keyte, one of the Keytes of **Ebrington,** who was killed at the Battle of Stow. Before leaving the town, explore the small streets leading from the southern end of the Square where there are further shops and hotels, all contributing something to Stow-on-the-Wold's qualities as an excellent touring centre for the northern Cotswolds.

THE STRATFORD AND MORETON TRAMWAY (Not shown on map.) This was the brainchild of William James of Henley-in-Arden, near Stratford-upon-Avon, and was part of an ambitious scheme to link his other transport and mining interests to London, by a projected line entitled the Central Junction Railway. However, James was only able to gain local support for a line as far as **Moreton-in-Marsh** with a branch to **Shipston-on-Stour.** An Act of Incorporation for this scheme was passed on 18 May 1821, six weeks earlier than the Act of Incorporation for that world pioneer line, the famous Stockton and Darlington Railway. It is interesting to speculate on what would have happened to Shipston-on-Stour and Moreton-in-Marsh if James's proposal for the Central Junction Railway had been accepted in full. As it was, the local scheme soon ran into difficulties, both with problems of civil engineering, and with the prevention by the authorities of the use of steam trains on at least the first six miles south of Stratford-upon-Avon. The line to Moreton was finally opened in 1826, but by then James had been declared bankrupt, and all passenger and goods traffic was restricted to horse-drawn wagons provided not by the company but by toll-paying local traders.

In 1836 a branch line was opened to **Shipston-on-Stour,** and when Brunel's main Oxford, Worcester and Wolverhampton Railway line was built in 1853, the tramway provided a useful link to it from **Moreton-in-Marsh.**

The Moreton-Shipston section was eventually converted to take steam trains, as a branch of the Great Western Railway, an arrangement that lasted until its final closure in 1960. The most enduring monument to the tramway is its mellow brick bridge over the Avon at Stratford-upon-Avon, The line of the tramway may be followed in several places, especially beside the Shipston Road out of Stratford, but its total disappearance in others is a reflection of the problems often facing archaeologists looking for signs of civilisation many hundreds or even thousands of years older. Read the most interesting story of this tramway in John Norris's book, *The Stratford and Moreton Tramway.*

STRATTON (1-2 J7) *1 mi. NW Cirencester.* Almost a suburb of Cirencester, most of old Stratton is situated astride the **Ermin Way,** although it has now largely been bypassed. The church, situated at its north-western end, was largely rebuilt in 1850, although the south wall of the original Norman building has survived, complete with one Norman window and, above a late Perpendicular doorway, a Norman tympanum with a Tree of Life. Apart from the white-painted chancel, the interior has been scraped and pointed, and this is relieved only by a few 18th- and 19th-century wall monuments. It is possible to walk north-westwards from here, up the Dunt Valley to **Daglingworth,** and on to the **Duntisbournes.**

STRETTON-ON-FOSSE (1 C11) *4 mi. NE Moreton-in-Marsh.* An unspoilt village on a little hill just to the west of the busy Foss Way. The 'e' added to the word 'Foss' in the village's name is evidence of continuing confusion over the correct spelling of one of

Britain's best-known Roman roads. The church here was entirely rebuilt in 1841, and is not of great interest to visitors, but the 'William and Mary' Old Rectory and the Georgian Court House both add interest to the village. From a distance, the unusually restrained 19th-century Manor House could easily be mistaken for a building some 300 years older. It overlooks the Foss Way, which crosses the line of the old **Stratford and Moreton Tramway** in the valley below. This was once the site of a small railway station, and the mellow-brick building that still stands here was once the Golden Cross Inn. This has been a private house for many years, but there is a welcoming inn in the village - the Plough. It is possible to walk south-westwards from Stretton, over the fields passing the site of the medieval village of Upper Ditchford, and on to **Aston Magna. A return** could be made eastwards to **Todenham,** and then north-westwards back to Stretton-on-Fosse.

STROUD (1-2 J4) *8 mi. S Gloucester.* Built on steep slopes at the junction of no fewer than five valleys, this busy town has retained considerable character despite its industrialisation in the late 18th and early 19th centuries. It had established itself as the pre-eminent centre of the Cotswold cloth industry as early as the 15th century, and the availability of Cotswold wool, of water for washing, and of minerals for dyeing and cleaning ensured that it remained so for several hundred years. At the height of its prosperity there were at least 150 cloth mills in the valleys centred upon Stroud; 'Uley Blue', 'Stroudwater Scarlet' and other West of England cloths were renowned throughout the world as the basis for a wide range of military and naval uniforms and high-class civilian wear - a reputation that has lasted almost to this day. As the 19th century progressed, more and more cloth manufacture moved to the mills of Yorkshire's West Riding, and competition from here and more recently from abroad has by now resulted in the closure of all but two companies. However, these two are still very active, many light industries have come here to replace the others, and Stroud and its surrounding valley country continue to thrive.

Most of Stroud's prosperous clothiers chose to build their houses in the countryside beyond, but many of its steep and often narrow streets retain a character formed by the town's early industrial success. Beside the Tudor Town Hall and to the south side of St Lawrence's Church is The Shambles, once a meat market, and now the site of a busy market on Wednesdays and Fridays. The nearby Subscription Rooms, in George Street, are housed in an elegant early-19th-century neo-classical building. Numerous local functions are held here.

Apart from its fine 14th-century tower, St Lawrence's Church was rebuilt in the 1860s, and although its interior contains some earlier monuments it is not of great interest to visitors. The interesting Stroud Museum is now located in Stratford Park (see below). It's contents is largely devoted to items of local interest, including a 20ft model of a dinosaur, a collection of early lawnmowers, and displays illustrating the story of Stroud's cloth industry.

The delightful Stratford Park, just to the north-west of the town, has a large lake and a fine Leisure Centre. Another of Stroud's features is the **Stroudwater Canal,** which runs up the Frome Valley, and which once formed a link here between the Severn at

Stratford Park, Stroud

Framilode and the **Thames and Severn Canal**. It is possible to walk along its towpath, and that of the **Thames and Severn Canal,** eastwards up the valley, most of the way from **Eastington** to **Daneway.**

Also of interest are the Stroud Civic Society's two *Wool Walks* booklets, also available from the Tourist Information Centre. *Wool Walk One* passes, amongst other features of the cloth industry, Lodgemoor Mill, which still produces fine West of England cloth, and its nearby Mill Shop. *Wool Walk Two* explores more cloth industry features in the Nailsworth Valley, which runs south from Rooksmoor to **Woodchester.** Both of these walks make part use of another excellent facility, the Stroud Valleys Pedestrian and Cycle Trail. This uses an abandoned railway track-bed between **Nailsworth** and **Stonehouse,** with a branch to Stroud. A leaflet describing this trail may also be available from the Tourist Information Centre.

STROUDWATER CANAL (Not shown on map.) This canal, linking the River Severn at Framilode with the busy industrial town of Stroud, was opened in 1779. Within ten years it had become part of a link between the Severn and the Thames, with the opening of the **Thames and Severn Canal,** between **Stroud** and **Inglesham** near Lechlade. The Thames and Severn was never a commercial success and the last recorded journey through it was made in 1911. However, the Stroudwater Canal was more successful and was not finally abandoned until 1954. Brave attempts are being made to restore sections of both canals, and parts of their towpaths make delightful walks, especially near **Stonehouse** and along the Thames and Severn Canal between Stroud and the western portal of the Sapperton Tunnel at **Daneway.** For further details read Ronald Russell's *Lost Canals and Waterways of Britain*, and Michael Handford's *The Stroudwater Canal.*

SUDELEY CASTLE (1-2 E8) *½ mi. SE Winchcombe.* This is beautifully situated just outside the little town of **Winchcombe,** and looks out towards the wooded slopes of **Cleeve Hill.** Sudeley was in royal hands from the time of King Ethelred the Unready, and it included a fine deer park which took up most of the valley running into the hills to its south, and of which many of the boundaries can still be traced today. Ethelred granted the estate to his daughter Goda, who was the sister of Edward the Confessor. Thanks to her distant relationship with the Duke of Normandy it was not confiscated by the Normans, and she was able to pass it on to her son, Ralph de Sudeley. His descendants held it until a new castle was begun in 1441 by the victorious Admiral of the Fleet, Sir

Sudeley Castle

Thomas Boteler, who was created Baron Sudeley by Henry VI.

No trace of the earlier castle or castles remains, but much of Boteler's magnificent building has survived, including St Mary's Chapel, the ruined Banqueting Hall, the Tithe Barn and the Portmare Tower. This tower is said to have been named after a captured French admiral, whose ransom money very largely financed the castle's rebuilding. In 1455 the Wars of the Roses broke out, and within six years Boteler's master, the Lancastrian Henry VI, had been succeeded by the Yorkist Edward IV. Boteler was soon forced to forfeit his beloved Sudeley, and it once more became royal property. Queen Catherine Parr, the only one of Henry VIII's six wives to outlive him, came with her court to Sudeley on his death. Within a short time the scheming Sir Thomas Seymour had secretly married Catherine and persuaded the young Edward VI to create him Baron Sudeley. In August 1548, while Sir Thomas was already making free with other ladies at court in London, Catherine gave birth to a daughter. A few days later she died of puerperal fever, and was buried in the beautiful little St Mary's Chapel, with the ill-fated Lady Jane Grey as one of the chief mourners.

Queen Mary granted Sudeley to Thomas Brydges and created him Lord Chandos of Sudeley. Her sister Queen Elizabeth visited the castle on three occasions and, as was the custom, was lavishly entertained. During the Civil War the castle was held by the Royalists, but in 1644 it was forced to surrender to the Parliamentarians after a siege. At the end of the war it was, like most castles which had been held by Royalists, 'slighted', or effectively ruined, by the victorious Parliamentarians, and a process of decay set in, which was only to be reversed after nearly 200 years had passed.

It was in 1837 that the estate was purchased by two highly successful glove makers from Worcester, the brothers John and William Dent. They immediately set about the massive task of restoring the castle, employing the distinguished architect Sir Gilbert Scott to restore the chapel. By the early 1840s Sudeley was again habitable, but sadly the two brothers had both died by 1855, and the estate passed to their nephew John Dent. He, however, had the good sense to marry Emma Brocklehurst, the daughter of a Cheshire Member of Parliament. Emma Dent, even when widowed, carried on the work of restoration and improvement, contributing much to this and to the community in general. She must have been a formidable figure - tireless, demanding, generous - in many ways resembling Queen Victoria in her later years, especially in her looks. She died in 1900, but the castle has remained in the same family ever since.

Today Sudeley is full of interest, its restored rooms containing many art treasures, including works by Constable, Turner, Rubens and Van Dyck, along with tapestries, needlework and armour. Moreover the powerful personality of Emma Dent still seems to linger here. Thanks to Gilbert Scott, the chapel's interior, including the tomb of Catherine Parr, is rather heavily Victorianised, but its lovely Perpendicular exterior has survived intact. There are craft exhibitions, regular falconry displays and an Elizabethan Garden. Restaurant and gift shop, plant centre and garden shop.

SUTTON-UNDER-BRAILES (1 C13) *7 mi. N Chipping Norton.* Most of this village is spread around a delightful green, once shaded by great trees, but now having to 'start all over again', due to the ravages of Dutch elm disease in the late 1970's. The church of St Thomas á Becket has a well proportioned Perpendicular south tower, but the austere interior appears to have never recovered from the harsh treatment inflicted upon it by Victorian restorers, and it is all pitch-pine pews and thoroughly scraped walls. Walk north-west from here, around the side of Brailes Hill, to **Shipston-on-Stour.**

SWALCLIFFE (1 C14) *5 mi. W Banbury.* Small stone village astride the Banbury-Shipston

Wall Paintings, Swalcliffe

road, with a massive tithe barn at its western end containing a collection of old farm wagons and carts. This fine barn is said to have been built by William of Wykeham, the founder of New College, Oxford, which also used to own the large manor house to the west of the house, a building which retains many of its medieval features. At the centre of the village is a pleasantly thatched inn called the Stag's Head, which is overlooked from the other side of the road by a most interesting church. This has a handsome 17th-century door within a Decorated style south doorway, and an old roof looking down on pleasing 17th-century seating, pulpit and lectern. These last two items were given to the church in 1639 by Anne Wykeham and there is a colourful monument to Anne and her husband Richard, with their kneeling figures in a wall frame. See also the monuments to John Hawten, John Duncombe and to an 18th-century Richard Wykeham. There is a 14th-century wall painting of St Michael in the south aisle, and also two figures on the west wall of the same aisle.

The small mansion of Swalcliffe Park is on the south-west side of the village, and there is a pleasant road southwards just beyond it, leading past Swalcliffe Grange, towards Tadmarton Heath. This is a largely open road from which there are outstanding views westwards to the distant line of the Cotswolds above **Chipping Campden** and **Blockley,**

with the outline of **Broadway Tower** just visible on a clear day. Walk northwards from Swalcliffe to **Shutford,** passing close to **Madmarston Hill,** or southwards beyond Swalcliffe Grange to **Hook Norton.**

SWERFORD (1 D14) *5 mi. NE Chipping Norton.* This village is situated near the head of the quiet valley of the Swere, a stream which flows east from here to join the Cherwell near **Deddington.** Swerford has a pleasant green by its church, which is set in a neat churchyard overlooking the earthworks of a long vanished Norman 'motte and bailey' castle. The church has a dumpy spire and a 13th-century porch enriched with

Swerford

a series of earthy gargoyles, but the interior is not very exciting. Swerford Park is an 18th-century mansion, with elegant early-19th-century alterations by a pupil of Sir John Soane, and is beautifully sited on slopes above the little River Swere. It is not open to the public. There is a delightful, but all too short field road over towards **Wigginton,** with glimpses of the Swere to its immediate south. The best walks from Swerford are north-eastwards down the Swere valley to **South Newington,** or north-westwards, up over wold country to **Hook Norton.**

SWIFT'S HILL (1-2 J5) *2 mi. NE Stroud.* This is a Nature Reserve and is a pleasantly scrubby, grass covered area, which should be left undisturbed as much as possible. There is an attractive minor road from **Slad** over to **Bisley,** passing Swift's Hill, with mouth-watering views back over to Slad.

SWINBROOK (1-2 H12) *2 mi. E Burford.* Delightful village with a rough, sloping green. It is enlivened by a small stream which flows into the River Windrush close to the Swan Inn, once Swinbrook's mill. The church with its small tower should on no account be missed. A fine Perpendicular window fills the whole of the east end and light floods in upon two splendid three-decker wall monuments, in which there are the effigies of no fewer than six male members of the Fettiplace family, all lying on their right sides, looking not upwards but outwards. The Fettiplaces once owned a great mansion, which stood between the church and the Windrush, but of this there is now no trace apart from vague grassy terraces and a fishpond. See the 15th-century choir stalls with their

Swinbrook

misericords (the carved undersides of their seats), the brasses of John Croston and his three wives, and of Anthony Fettiplace, and several other wall monuments including one by the celebrated sculptor, Richard Westmacott.

In the churchyard, in addition to the considerable number of handsome table tombs in the best Cotswold tradition, will be found the gravestone of Unity Mitford and her sister Nancy, whose childhood years at Swinbrook are so wonderfully described by their sister Jessica in her book *Hons and Rebels*. They lived at nearby **Asthall** for a time, and then at Swinbrook House, which was built by their father, Lord Redesdale, some way to the north of Swinbrook village. Read more about this fascinating family in Jonathan and Catherine Guinness's book, *The House of Mitford*. Walk westwards along the Windrush Valley to visit the attractive little church at **Widford,** then go up Dean Bottom and back down a quiet road to Swinbrook. It is also possible to walk eastwards down the valley to **Asthall.**

SYDE (1-2 H6) *7 mi. NW Cirencester.* A quiet hamlet looking across the deep, wooded valley of the upper Frome to **Caudle Green.** Its early Norman church has a small saddleback tower and a pleasing 15th-century, almost barn-like roof. Beyond the plain Norman chancel arch the church is Victorian, but considering its age, this is unusually pleasant. See also the 17th-century box pews, the octagonal 15th-century font, and the little 15th-century glass roundel of St James of Compostela in lovely muted colours. There is a tithe barn on the south side of the churchyard, and the cottage on the right-hand side of the road down towards **Caudle Green** has 14th-century windows, and is believed to be based on a chantry chapel founded here in 1344 by Sir Thomas Berkeley. Walk down into the valley and then northwards, up beside the infant Frome to **Brimpsfield,** or down the valley to **Caudle Green** and **Miserden.**

Cottages at Syde

SYREFORD (1-2 F8) *5 mi. S Winchcombe.* This hamlet north of **Andoversford** has a pleasant mill house, but few other special features. A Roman settlement was excavated here many years ago and amongst the articles recovered was a delightful four-inch-high statuette of the god Mars, which is now in the British Museum. Walk north from here beside the infant River Coln to **Sevenhampton** and **Brockhampton.**

TADDINGTON (1 D9) *2 mi. S Snowshill.* Small, windy upland hamlet with a few houses and a fine 17th-century barn with the date 1632 upon its porch. There are low earthworks to the north of the hamlet, the remains of a larger medieval settlement probably depopulated by sheep graziers. This is in high watershed country and under half a mile to its east is the substantial farmhouse, Field Barn, with a reed-bordered pool beside it which gives birth to what is arguably the loveliest of Cotswold rivers - the Windrush. Walk south from here, down the head of the Windrush Valley to **Cutsdean, Ford** and **Temple Guiting,** or westwards to the great woodlands above **Stanway.**

TADMARTON (1 C15) *4 mi SW Banbury.* Modest village of stone and thatch strung out along the Banbury to Shipston-on-Stour road, with a handsome manor house opposite a church, which is of Norman origin. The fine 14th-century font is richly ornamented, and in the nave there are some well carved bench ends about a century younger. Do not miss the little doorway to the original rood loft, behind the pulpit.

TARLTON (1-2 K6) *4 mi. W Cirencester.* This scattered little village has a small, largely neo-Norman church, the result of a complete rebuild in 1875. There is a simple Norman chancel arch retained from the original building, and the Norman tub font appears to have been recut in low relief in the 14th century. Tarlton lies on the **Macmillan Way** and this can be followed northwards to the **Tunnel House Inn** and on through the great **Hailey Wood** to **Sapperton.**

Taston Cross

TASTON (1-2 F14) *4 mi. SE Chipping Norton.* Small hamlet with the interesting base of a 14th-century wayside cross and a minute stream beside the road in a little valley below. Walk south from here to **Charlbury,** or west to **Spelsbury** to link onto the **Oxfordshire Way.**

TAYNTON (1-2 G11) *1½ mi. NW Burford.* Trim stone village in the Windrush Valley with views out towards the willow-bordered river. Yew trees line the wide path to the north door of the church, which has a slender Perpendicular tower. The 14th-century north aisle is a fine example of the Decorated style, with much ballflower ornamentation and rich stone tracery. Other notable features include an elaborate early 15th-century font, interesting corbel figures, carved roof bosses and an old alms chest. There is also a pleasant assortment of 17th- and 18th-century tombstones in the churchyard.

Stone has been extracted from the great Taynton quarries since medieval times, and it has been used in the construction or repair of Windsor Castle, St Paul's Cathedral, **Blenheim Palace** and most of the Oxford colleges. The Clerk of Works at Windsor during the reign of Edward III was named Richard Taynton, and he no doubt acquired his skills in his home village before moving on to greater things. In his fascinating *Natural History of Oxfordshire,* the eccentric Dr Plot relates that he once saw a wagon-load of Taynton stone being hauled by no fewer than twenty-one horses.

Taynton

It was probably being driven southwards to the Thames at Radcot Bridge or Lechlade, where it would have been loaded onto barges bound for Oxford or London.

Unlike the quarries at Windrush and Barrington, which were driven underground into the ridge which now carries the A40, the Taynton quarries have always been open to the sky. Now much overgrown, they lie on private land in a valley about a mile and a half to the north of the village.

TEDDINGTON (1 D6) *5 mi. E Tewkesbury.* Pleasant village beneath the steep, orchard-clad slopes of Oxenton Hill, an outlier of the true Cotswolds. Although Norman in origin, with a tall early Norman chancel arch, the church has much from the 13th, 14th and 15th centuries. The tower was built in 1567 and the fine Early English tower arch and west window were imported from **Hailes Abbey,** which was by then a total ruin following the Dissolution some thirty years earlier. The plastered nave walls are decorated with various paintings, including a handsome Royal Arms of William and

Mary. See also the 17th-century pulpit and reading desk. At Teddington Hands, on the main A46 road, half a mile to the north, there is an attractive stone guide-post, put up here in 1676 by a certain Edmund Attwood.

Temple Guiting

TEMPLE GUITING (1-2 E9) *4 mi. E Winchcombe.* This minute village shelters in the pleasantly wooded valley of the Windrush, with pools both above and below a small bridge over this delectable river. There is a small bow-fronted shop, and several attractive houses. These include the early 16th-century Manor Farm, which may have been one of the summer residences of the Bishop of Oxford, and the elegant 18th-century Temple Guiting House, which looks across the Windrush Valley to the church. This was once given to the preceptory of Quenington, itself owned by the Knights Templar, but only fragments of their Norman church remain. The architectural history of the remainder is most involved, and restoration and rebuilding have occurred many times. The fine tower was built as late as the 18th century, while its pinnacles are an even later (19th-century) addition. We are also indebted to the 18th-century builders for the Georgian classical windows, the pulpit, the tower arch, the reredos and the handsome Royal Arms of George II, in white plaster. See also the Decorated piscina and font, the early 16th-century stained glass and the 18th-century wall tablets. The best walk from here is northwards up the Windrush Valley to **Ford,** from whence it is possible to walk westward to Slade Barn Farm. By using the Ordnance Survey's Landranger Sheet 163, it is possible to plot a return to Temple Guiting via Pinnock Farm.

TETBURY (2 L5) *10 mi. SW Cirencester.* Situated on the busy A433, this largely unspoilt little market town is centred upon its delightful mid-17th-century Town Hall, or Market House. This is supported on three rows of dumpy Tuscan pillars, and has a stone roof and a handsome cupola topped by a weathervane with gilded dolphins. To the north of the Market House is the mid-19th-century Snooty Fox Hotel. Formerly the White Hart, this was rebuilt by Lewis Vulliamy, the architect of **Westonbirt,** with the large ballroom on its first floor specially designed to accommodate the junketings of the celebrated Beaufort Hunt, but now subdivided into bedrooms.

The Market House, Tetbury

Beyond the Snooty Fox is The Chipping, once a 'lesser market', which is still overlooked by a number of attractive 17th- and 18th-century houses. These, and many other buildings of the same period in other parts of the town, bear witness to the continuing prosperity of Tetbury, due largely to its importance as a wool collecting centre for the cloth towns and villages to its north and west. The Chipping Steps lead down from the Chipping's north-east corner to the foot of steep Gumstool Hill, up which it is possible to return to the Market House. Gumstool Hill is the scene of Tetbury's famous Woolsack Races, when the young men and girls of two local teams have to race down to the cattle market and back up this 1-

in-4 hill, from the Crown Inn to the Royal Oak, each carrying a 65lb sack of wool. This feat of endurance is part of the lively Tetbury Festival (or Woolsack Day), which takes place on each Spring Bank Holiday Monday, with stall-holders in medieval dress, a town jester, Morris dancers and other revivals of ancient revelry.

The Church of St Mary was built in the Gothic style in 1781, by the architect and builder Francis Hiorn of Warwick. He retained the fine medieval tower and spire, but these had to be rebuilt about a hundred years later. The tall, beautifully proportioned interior, with its panelled galleries, box pews and several pleasing monuments, is splendidly lit by tall Perpendicular-style windows. The two handsome 18th-century chandeliers add further elegance to a church which should on no account be missed.

Tetbury's interesting little Police Bygones Museum is in the Old Court House, at the far end of Long Street near the north end of the town. There is a pleasant variety of shops in the town, including several devoted to the sale of antiques. For a more detailed description of Tetbury's architectural gems refer to the Tetbury Society's interesting *Walkabout Guide and Map*, which should be available at the Tourist Information Centre.

TEWKESBURY (1 D5) *10 mi. NE Gloucester.* Not truly Cotswold in character or location, the delightful old town of Tewkesbury is just too good to omit from this guide. There is some evidence that there were monks here as early as AD 715, but the great Benedictine abbey from which the town drew its medieval prosperity was founded by the Norman, Robert Fitzhamon, who imported stone from Caen for its construction. Fitzhamon died in 1107, fourteen years before it was consecrated, but on his death his patronage was continued by his son-in-law, the bastard son of Henry I, Robert Fitzroy, Earl of Gloucester. The 'Honour of Tewkesbury', as this patronage was known, then descended to the powerful de Clare family, and thanks to their endowments and

Tewkesbury Abbey

support, the abbey grew into one of the country's most powerful religious houses, owning great tracts of land on the Cotswolds, and several large tithe barns including the one that still stands at **Stanway.** The abbey remained the focal point of the town for over 400 years, but at the Dissolution of the Monasteries in 1539, its great abbey church was sold to the town for what must even then have been the very modest price of £ 453.

It was in the meadow off Lincoln Green Lane (known from that day forward as 'Bloody Meadow'), to the south of the abbey, that one of the bloodiest and most decisive battles of the Wars of the Roses took place, when on 4th May 1417 the Lancastrian army of Margaret of Anjou, wife of the imprisoned Henry VI, was massacred by the Yorkist army of Edward IV. Some of the defeated troops sought sanctuary in the abbey itself, but despite the protests of the abbot, they were still put to the sword in the aisles. The queen's illegitimate son Edward was slain during the battle, but Margaret escaped, only to be imprisoned later in the Tower, until ransomed by her father, the King of France.

The town that grew up in the shelter of the great abbey was confined by the Rivers Severn and Avon, which join just to its west (and which were, and still are, very vulnerable to flooding), and by the abbey's lands to its east and south. But within these confines it continued to grow - not in size, but in density. In the 17th and 18th centuries especially, the areas behind the three main streets, Church Street, High Street and Barton Street, were threaded with a fascinating but no doubt insanitary series of alleys and courts. Several of these have survived to this day and bring a special quality to this town of timber-framed and mellow-brick houses, which also has a pleasing number of genuine country-town shops amongst the inevitable chain stores.

Exploration of the town is best started from one of the two car parks close to the abbey, one at the end of Church Street on the road out to Gloucester, and one in Gander Lane just to the east of the abbey itself. First visit this great Abbey Church of St Mary, with its massive 132ft-high and 46ft-square Norman tower. From the top of the tower there are fine views over the town and the two rivers beyond, to Bredon Hill and the Malverns, and in the other direction, towards the long scarp face of the Cotswolds. The west front has a 65ft-high Norman recessed arch, one of the largest ever built, and light floods in through the window it surrounds, which is a 17th-century replacement. This illuminates the fourteen massive Norman columns which support the splendidly vaulted 14th-century roof of the nave, with its fifteen bosses illustrating the life of Christ. From the ambulatory behind the apsidal choir, also 14th-century, six chapels radiate outwards, and in this area there are a number of beautiful monuments, including several to the de Clares and to members of the family with whom they became linked by marriage, the Despencers; here also is the lovely Warwick Chantry Chapel, endowed by the Beauchamp family, many of whose members are buried in the abbey. Perhaps of even greater beauty are the choir's seven 14th-century stained-glass windows. However, this is only a brief summary of some of this great abbey church's outstanding features. To enjoy it to the full, purchase one of the detailed guides available at the abbey's well stocked bookstall, and take time to explore it in detail.

Tewkesbury

Now go down Mill Street, passing the richly timbered Bell Hotel, to 'Abel Fletcher's Mill', a restored water-mill thought to have provided inspiration for Mrs Craik, the Victorian writer who used Tewkesbury as the model for *Nortonbury* in her novel *John Halifax, Gentleman*. From here it is possible to walk out over the wide water-meadows of Severn Ham to look at the weir and lock on the Severn at Upper Lode. It is also possible to walk beside the Avon, passing an attractive row of timbered cottages, and into St Mary's Lane. However, it is probably better to return to the Bell Hotel and turn left into Church Street, where there is soon an alley or court down to the left leading to a delightfully unspoilt Baptist Chapel. With origins in the 15th century, this was skillfully converted into a chapel in the 17th, and it still retains the flavour of this era. Almost opposite the turn to the chapel there is a restored row of medieval merchants' cottages, one of which houses 'The Little Museum', which is furnished to illustrate the life of the original occupants. Another is the John Moore Museum, a countryside museum which commemorates the local author John Moore, who died in 1967, and whose books were very largely based on Tewkesbury and the surrounding countryside. Read his *Portrait of Elmbury* for a flavour of Tewkesbury in the first half of the 20th century.

From here continue along Church Street, to the Georgian-fronted Hop Pole Hotel, where Charles Dickens's Mr Pickwick and his friends did so well on 'ale, Madeira and five bottles of port'. From here it is a short distance to The Cross. This is now the War Memorial, but it stands at the point where the medieval High Cross stood before its demolition by the Puritans in 1650. Here is the true centre of the town, where its three streets meet - Church Street, High Street and Barton Street. First go down Barton Street for a short way to visit (on the right-hand side) the interesting Tewkesbury Museum, an 'architectural heritage centre', with its local history items including a model of the Battle of Tewkesbury.

Walk back to The Cross and turn right into the High Street. Soon turn left into Quay Street, near which it is possible to hire a boat on the River Avon. For other boating opportunities from Tewkesbury, please enquire locally. It is also possible to walk over the bridge leading to the large flour mills (do not trespass into the mill area), and to follow the right-of-way immediately to the right, on a riverside path leading past the last lock on the Avon before it joins the River Severn. From here it is a short way to the main road which crosses the Avon over the rebuilt King John's Bridge. Turn right, cross the bridge, turn right into High Street and head back for the Cross, passing on the right, The Roses Theatre and the Shopping Centre on the way. From here it is not far to walk back to either of the starting car parks.

THAMES HEAD (1-2 K6) *3 mi. SW Cirencester.* This is at Trewsbury Mead, the true source of the River Thames. There are pleasant paths across the fields, either southwards from Coates, or northwards from the Thames Head Inn, on the **Foss Way.** In his Itinerary, Henry VIII's antiquary John Leland states, *Wher as the very head of Isis ys, in a great somer drought apperith very little or no water.* Things appear to have changed but little, and visitors will probably still find no more than a muddy depression beneath a tree, relieved only by a granite slab declaring this to be the true source of the Thames. This modest stone replaces a handsome statue of Neptune, which was removed in 1974 to St John's Lock below **Lechlade,** as it sadly became the subject of vandalism soon after its installation here by the Thames Conservancy in 1958.

The Thames Head Bridge, some distance to the south-east, once carried the **Foss Way** over the **Thames and Severn Canal.** The canal has long been abandoned, and the bridge is now on a lay-by just to the west of the road, with a plaque fixed to its parapet. The group of buildings (now converted into a private house) just to the south-east of the Foss Way is all that remains of the old Thames Head Pumping Station, where a pumping engine drew water from a deep well to top up the summit level of the canal. Use the Ordnance Survey's Landranger Sheet 163 to follow a path from the **Foss Way** south-eastwards and then south towards **Kemble,** to come to the first appreciable flow of Thames water - probably at Lyd Well. Leland appears to have missed this.

THAMES PATH (Not shown on map.) This is a 180-mile long-distance path following the course of the River Thames from its source at **Thames Head** to the Thames Barrier. The best long-distance paths to link with it in the Cotswolds, are the **Macmillan Way** and the Wysis Way, both of which come past **The Tunnel House Inn,** which is about a mile from **Thames Head,** along the towpath of the **Thames and Severn Canal.**

THAMES AND SEVERN CANAL (Not shown on map.) Designed by Robert Whitworth, this was opened in 1789 to link the **Stroudwater Canal** at **Stroud** with the head of the navigable Thames at **Inglesham,** near **Lechlade.** Unlike the Stroudwater it was never a great success. There were no fewer than forty-four locks between Stroud and the western end of the tunnel. The tunnel at **Sapperton** was a constant problem, and there were often water shortages on the summit level, despite the pumping station at **Thames Head.** The Upper Thames navigation was also never good, and the **Oxford Canal,** which opened only one year after the Thames and Severn, provided a better link between London and the Midlands. Both were soon to be overshadowed by the Grand Junction Canal, which opened in 1800.

The last recorded journey on the Thames and Severn was made in 1911 and it was finally abandoned in 1927. Its closure was one of the great tragedies of English canal history, and although brave efforts are being made to restore certain sections of both this and the **Stroudwater Canal,** it is hard to believe that this outstandingly beautiful link between our two great river systems will ever be reopened in its entirety. See also **Daneway** and the **Tunnel House Inn.**

Several sections of the old canal course may still be walked, including a length from the western end of the Sapperton Tunnel to the Daneway Inn and beyond, down beside a long flight of sadly empty locks. Much of the canal's course can be traced on the Ordnance Survey's Landranger Sheets 162 and 163, and it is interesting to note the clumps of trees at intervals between Sapperton and Hailey Wood, to the north of the Tunnel House Inn, which neatly conceal the mounds of spoil around the top of each ventilation shaft. See also Ronald Russell's excellent *Lost Canals and Waterways of Britain*, and for a more detailed study of the canal's history read Humphrey Household's *The Thames and Severn Canal*.

Canal Tunnel's Eastern Portal

TIDMINGTON (1 C12) *2 mi. S Shipston-on-Stour.* Here is a 17th-century bridge carrying the still busy A3400 over the River Stour, and overlooked by an old water-mill. Well to the north, beside the garden of Tidmington House, a largely 17th-century building with a handsome 18th-century front, is one of Warwickshire's smallest churches. This has a late 12th-century tower with pyramid roof, and a 16th-century chancel; the rest was rebuilt in about 1875. However, the early Norman font has an interesting carving of Christ upon it, and makes a visit here well worthwhile. It is possible to walk beside the Stour northwards to **Shipston.**

TOADSMOOR VALLEY (1-2 J5) *3 mi. E Stroud.* (Not shown on map.) A deep wooded valley running up from the larger **Golden Valley** at **Brimscombe,** almost as far as **Bisley.** There are old cloth mills here, but these are now long closed. There is an interesting account of the once thriving cloth industry in this valley in Jennifer Tann's *Gloucestershire Woollen Mills.*

Monument at Toddington

TODDINGTON (1 D8) *3½ mi. NE Winchcombe.* This village is divided into two halves. The old village extends northwards from the B4077, with a farmhouse and several pleasant houses before the church is reached in a well wooded area on the edge of parkland. This is an impressive 19th-century building, the creation of G.E. Street, one of most talented of Victorian architects and perhaps best known for his work on London's Law Courts in the Strand. It has a handsome tower topped by an elegant spire, and its interior, in neo-Decorated style, is a formidable combination of starkness and extravagance - qualities that are typified by the splendid white marble tomb of Charles Hanbury-Tracy, 1st Lord Sudeley of Toddington, and his wife.

To the immediate west of the church is the ruined gatehouse of the Tracy's largely Jacobean manor house, which was inhabited until the early years of the 19th century. Toddington Manor, the massive Victorian Gothic mansion just visible in the park beyond, was designed by the owner, Charles Hanbury-Tracy. He was an amateur architect who was considered capable enough to be appointed chairman of the commission which adjudicated on the designs for the new Houses of Parliament. The massive mansion was built between 1820 and 1835 and many of its features were inspired by various Oxford colleges, Hanbury-Tracy having been an undergraduate there in the closing years of the 18th century. It is not open to the public. It is possible to walk south from the old village, to **Greet** and on to **Winchcombe.**

The new part of the village, New Town, extends in three directions from the roundabout on the B4632, and lies about a mile to the east of the old village. There is a large garden centre here, and next to it, are the headquarters of the fascinating **Gloucestershire Warwickshire Railway.**

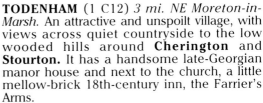

G.W.R. Toddington Station

Todenham

TODENHAM (1 C12) *3 mi. NE Moreton-in-Marsh.* An attractive and unspoilt village, with views across quiet countryside to the low wooded hills around **Cherington** and **Stourton.** It has a handsome late-Georgian manor house and next to the church, a little mellow-brick 18th-century inn, the Farrier's Arms.

The church of St Thomas of Canterbury is largely 14th-century in origin and has a fine tower and octagonal, broach spire. There are many pleasing items in the Decorated style here, including the east window, the sedilia, and the little priest's door on the south side. On the north side of the chancel will be found Perpendicular windows, which were added by the Greville family when they built a north chapel and north aisle in the early 16th century. Victorian restoration was carried out here with a very much lighter hand than at neighbouring **Lower Lemington**, and the interior of Todenham church is well worth a visit. See especially the 13th-century font with the names of the churchwardens of 1773 inscribed upon it, the brass to William Molton and his wife (1614), and outside, the memorial tablet on the south wall complete with skull and crossed bones. Walk north-west, over the fields, to **Stretton-on-Fosse,** or eastwards to **Little Wolford,** in both cases back from Gloucestershire into Warwickshire.

TORMARTON (2 P3) *4 Mi. SE Chipping Sodbury.* Modest village astride the **Cotswold Way** and just to the north of the M4 motorway, which is fortunately in a cutting here and not too obtrusive. The church was heavily restored in the 19th century and even its Norman chancel arch has been re-worked to such an extent that it lacks any feeling of antiquity. The chancel is almost entirely Victorian, but there is a wide 'walk-through' squint, a slender 13th-century font, a Jacobean pulpit, a 15th-century brass in the floor of the nave and several wall monuments - all of which makes a visit here worthwhile.

TRAITOR'S FORD (1 C14) *6 mi. N Chipping Norton.* A beautifully cool place in the lightly wooded valley of the infant Stour. A normally tranquil spot, it could become crowded on a summer Sunday afternoon. Who was, or who were the traitor or traitors? We have still to solve this mystery, but like to imagine some small, but inevitably violent encounter in medieval times, perhaps during the Wars of the Roses. Or was this place once known as Traders' Ford - astride a route used by wool traders with their pack animals. This theory is strengthened by the fact that Traitor's Ford lies on the border between Warwickshire and Oxfordshire, and

Traitor's Ford

there is an ancient trackway called Ditchedge Lane, which leads north from here, along the line of this boundary between the two counties. Traitor's Ford is also on the line of the **Macmillan Way** on its way between Epwell, Ditchedge Lane and Whichford.

TREDINGTON (1 B12) *2 mi. N Shipston-on-Stour.* An elegantly beautiful village in the valley of the Stour, with wide, well-mown grass verges and several interesting old

Tredington

houses. However, everything has been so polished and tidied up that Tredington's real character has been somewhat eroded, and to the west of the busy A3400 there is also considerable modern housing development. But do not let this description deter you from exploring Tredington, for it is still very pleasant to walk along the small roads leading to the church of St Gregory, which is itself well worth visiting. It has a tall tower topped by a noble 15th-century spire - a landmark visible from many points of the delightful south Warwickshire countryside. It also has a Norman south doorway and a Perpendicular two-storey north porch, beyond which will be found old stone floors, beautiful old benches, a handsome Jacobean pulpit, a Perpendicular rood screen, lovely roofs of the same period in nave and transepts, and several interesting brasses. Architectural enthusiasts will also note evidence of St Gregory's Anglo-Saxon origins, but everyone who comes here will soon sense the atmosphere of the past that lingers in this fine building.

TRESHAM (2 L3) *3 mi. SE Wotton-under-Edge.* This is a rather scrappy village but it is gloriously situated, with views south-westwards along the hilly edge to the **Somerset Monument.** The little neo-Norman church is very severe outside, but some of the sculptural details within are rather pleasing. There is a attractive walk south-westwards down a wooded valley to **Hillesley.**

TUNLEY (1-2 J6) *5 mi. E Stroud.* Minute hamlet in a deeply wooded combe thrusting northwards from the Frome Valley. The attractive thatched cottage, Sherwood Hill, was once the home of the potter Alfred Powell, a friend of Ernest Gimson (see **Daneway**). There is a delightful walk continuing up the combe to Sudgrove and over to **Miserden.**

THE TUNNEL HOUSE INN (1-2 K6) *4½ mi. W Cirencester.* A pleasant 18th-century building close to the south-eastern end of the **Thames and Severn Canal's** two-mile tunnel under the Cotswolds. During the canal's heyday this inn, like the **Daneway Inn** at the other end of the tunnel, must have been a popular port of call for the thirsty leggers at the end of each journey. For many years the tunnel's portal with its handsome Doric columns, stood neglected at the end of a long canal 'ditch' shaded by massive beech trees, but happily it has now been restored. Near the southern end of this section of canal will be found one of the delightful little 'Gothic' round-houses which were built to accommodate the canal's lengthmen (maintenance men).

The inn lies on the **Macmillan Way** and this can be used to approach it through part of **Hailey Wood** and on to **Tarlton.** Please ask the landlord if you wish to use

The Tunnel House Inn

the inn's car park. Permission will almost certainly be given to those making use of the inn's facilities. It is also possible to walk south-east from here, following the course of the canal, to the source of the River Thames at Trewsbury Mead (see **Thames Head**).

TURKDEAN (1-2 G9) *2 mi. N Northleach.* This small village is pleasantly sited on a hillside, with the hamlet of Lower Dean in the valley below, the two being joined both by a road leading down through a magnificent avenue of beech trees and also by a shorter, but steep little path. The Norman church, situated in a large churchyard bordered by chestnut trees, has some interesting items of early sculpture built into the lower stages of its tower. There is also a blocked-up Norman doorway in the south wall of the chancel. The Perpendicular north doorway is sheltered by a porch of the same period, and opens into an interior which contains a Norman chancel arch and a stout Perpendicular stone pulpit. Do not overlook the interesting photograph of the vaulted undercroft, or crypt, of nearby Rectory Farm.

Turkdean lies midway between **Hazleton** and **Cold Aston,** both of which may be reached by pleasant bridle roads. The one from Cold Aston is known as Bangup Lane and is used by the **Macmillan Way.** A glance at the Ordnance Survey's Landranger Sheet 163 will indicate a good circular walk from Turkdean, making use of both these sections of bridle road and also taking in the village of **Notgrove.**

North Door, Turkdean Church

TYNDALE MONUMENT (2 L2) *2 mi. SW Dursley.* This 111ft-high tower above the little village of **North Nibley** was built to the designs of S.S. Teulon in 1866, in memory of William Tyndale, the first translator of the New Testament into English. There are fine views to the Severn Estuary from the gallery near its top, and there is an inscription here, part of which reads: *Born near this spot* (a fact disputed by the inhabitants of **Slimbridge**) *he suffered martyrdom at Vilvorde in Flanders on 6th October, 1536.* Ask for the key to the tower in the village below.

TYSOE (1 B13) *8 mi. NW Banbury.* A long straggle of a village, consisting of Lower, Middle, and Upper Tysoe; all beneath the scarp face on which the Red Horse was carved (see below), and on the edge of wide valley country, the Vale of Red Horse, through which a series of little streams flow lazily north and west to join the River Stour. There is much modern development, but the little 'old' fire station, with its thatched roof, still stands next to the Peacock Inn, which ironically was largely destroyed by fire some years ago. The handsomely pinnacled church has a Norman south doorway and a fine 14th-century font with sculptured figures of the Virgin and saints. The walls were scraped and pointed by over-enthusiastic Victorian 'restorers'. However do not miss the medieval and Jacobean seating nor the three interesting brasses.

Upper Tysoe is overlooked by a well restored stone tower windmill, which stands on a hill to its south, part of the **Compton Wynyates** estate. For many generations this mill was worked by the Styles family of Tysoe, and in the mid-nineteenth century, there were no less than three windmills in the area, which were being worked by three Styles brothers. Sadly the last milling Styles was killed during the 1914-18 War. For a wonderfully evocative account of life in Tysoe in the latter half of the 19th century, and the early years of the 20th, read *Joseph Ashby of Tysoe*, by his daughter, Miss Ashby. In his youth, Joseph was much influenced by Joseph Arch, the founder of the National Union of Agricultural Workers, who lived at Barford near Warwick. The giant hill figure, The

Countryside above Tysoe

Red Horse, has long since disappeared, a victim of the enclosure of the village's open fields. It was originally cut into the red soil of the hillside above Tysoe church, probably in medieval times and possibly by Richard Neville, Earl of Warwick, known as the 'Kingmaker', in memory of the horse that he killed at the Battle of Towton, on Palm Sunday 1461, in an attempt to assure his wavering troops that he had no intention of retreating from the field. At first sight this seems an unlikely story, but it is interesting to note that the Red Horse was preserved for centuries by an annual scouring ceremony that took place on each Palm Sunday, the very anniversary of the battle where Neville killed his horse.

Walks from Tysoe are numerous: from Middle Tysoe, north-east across the fields and up to the woods near Sun Rising Hill; from Lower Tysoe, up past Old Lodge Farm, over the scarp, and down a valley south-eastwards to Shenington; from Upper Tysoe, up the hill to the south, past the windmill, and on to **Winderton,** skirting well to the west of **Compton Wynyates.**

ULEY (2 K3) *2 mi. E Dursley.* Situated in a deep valley this large village has many delightful 18th-century houses - evidence of Uley's prosperity as a cloth centre in the years immediately prior to the Industrial Revolution. Uley also possesses its own brewery, which is noted for a rather special beverage called *Old Spot Ale.* Beautifully sited above the valley, Uley's handsome Victorian church was designed by the talented architect, S.S Teulon, who also designed the **Tyndale Monument.** Beside the churchyard there is a path leading steeply up the hill to the Iron Age settlement of Uleybury, from which there are spectacular views in almost every direction.

Uley

ULEY LONG BARROW *(See Hetty Pegler's Tump.)*

UPPER COBERLEY (1-2 G6) *4 mi. SE Cheltenham.* (Not shown on map.) Attractive hamlet overlooking the upper Churn Valley, not far from the source of the Churn at **Seven Springs.** There is a pleasant circular walk taking in **Seven Springs** and **Coberley.** There is also a good walk north-eastwards, passing Needlehole, and turning right onto an unfenced road running southwards through Pinchley Wood. To return to Upper Coberley, either turn right at **Hilcot,** or walk further southwards on a minor road, before turning sharp right to return via Pinswell Plantation. A brief study of the Ordnance Survey's Landranger Sheet 163 will clarify these rather complex directions, and also reveal a host of alternative walks in this delightful area.

UPPER KILCOTT (2 M3) *4 mi. SE Wotton-under-Edge.* Tidy hamlet near the head of a deep wooded valley running up into the Cotswold edge.

UPPER SLAUGHTER (1-2 F10) *3 mi. SW Stow-on-the-Wold.* This village is situated on the banks of the little River Eye, less than two miles from its source below Eyford Hill. It is fortunately rather less visited than its neighbour **Lower Slaughter,** but is equally delightful. Its gabled manor house is perhaps one of the finest examples of Elizabethan domestic architecture in the Cotswolds, and has a beautiful two-storeyed porch with Doric and Ionic pilasters. Although it is not open to the public, there is a tantalising glimpse down its front drive from a minor road. Further into the village will be found the pleasant Lords of the Manor Hotel, which used to be owned by the Witts family, rectors and later lords of the manor. Beyond this is

The River Eye at Upper Slaughter

a small square overlooked by a group of eight trim cottages much restored by the distinguished early 20th-century architect, Sir Edwin Lutyens. The passing of time and the genius of Lutyens have together ensured that this group blends in perfectly with its tranquil surroundings.

Just to the north of the square is Upper Slaughter's late Norman church, with its attractively pinnacled tower. This church was largely rebuilt in 1877, when the results of earlier tinkering with its Norman features were to a large extent rectified. Despite the care taken, the interior is inevitably Victorian in feeling, and this effect is increased by the presence, in a specially built mortuary chapel to the north of the chancel, of a very grand monument to F.E.Witts, the local rector and lord of the manor, who died in 1854. The diary of this most energetic of country parsons was published in 1979, and anyone wishing to gain insight into life in the Cotswolds and the towns of Cheltenham and Gloucester between 1820 and 1852 should read this, *The Diary of a Cotswold Parson.*

Beyond the church there is a small road leading down to a minute bridge over the River Eye, here no more than a modest stream. This is itself sheltered by a massive tree and overlooked by a mound just to its east, on which are the none-too-obvious earthworks of a long-vanished motte and bailey castle. Explore both Upper and Lower Slaughter, which are linked by a pleasant footpath beside the little River Eye. There is also a fine walk northwards up the Eye Valley to the B4068, and by using a short length of this (with great care) it is possible to move north again skirting part of **Eyford Park.**

UPPER SWELL (1-2 E10) *1 mi. NW Stow-on-the-Wold.* This small village overlooks the valley through which the little River Dikler runs. This is crossed by a small 18th-century bridge, above which is a moss-covered weir retaining an extensive mill pool. The water-

The Weir and Mill at Upper Swell

mill still has its wheel, and waterfowl are usually to be seen on the pool. Do not try to park here, but use the small lay-by beyond on the road to Stow-on-the-Wold.

Above the mill there is a fine manor house with a two-storeyed porch, an outstanding example of late 16th- or early 17th- century Cotswold domestic architecture. This was built by the Stratford family of **Farmcote** and **Hawling,** after they had acquired land here, which had previously belonged to Evesham Abbey.

The little church nearby is largely Norman in origin and has a good Norman south doorway within its 15th-century porch. Inside will be found a 14th-century piscina and sedilia and a handsomely carved Perpendicular-style font.

UPTON HOUSE (1 A14) *7 mi. NW Banbury.* Given to the National Trust by the 2nd Viscount Bearsted, this fine William and Mary mansion is built of local Hornton stone and stands at the end of a long grass-bordered driveway, off the main A422, Stratford-

upon-Avon to Banbury road. It is situated less than half a mile behind the Edge Hill scarp, and from its south front there are is a pleasant view over wide grassy terraces and beautiful, steep sloping gardens to its Temple Pool. This is enhanced by a little temple at the far end in the Tuscan style, said to have been designed by Sanderson Miller, squire of nearby Radway, and gentleman-architect extraordinary (see also

Upton House

Adlestrop, Radway and **Wroxton**). Miller may also have carried out improvements to the house in the 1730s, but there appears to be some doubt about this.

The interior of the present house is largely the work of the 20th-century architect, Morley Horder, who created a series of fine neo-Georgian rooms in about 1927. These provide a perfect setting for the remarkable collection of works of art presented by Lord Bearsted to the National Trust in 1948. This includes 18th-century furniture, Brussels tapestries, and 18th-century porcelain, both English and European. But of outstanding interest is the superb collection of pictures, with works by Bosch, the Brueghels, Holbein, Rembrandt, Van Dyck, Canaletto, Goya, El Greco, Tiepolo, Tintoretto,

Constable, Hogarth, Reynolds, Romney and Stubbs. On no account should a visit here be missed, for it provides, in the heart of the English countryside, a sparkling insight into the rich diversity of European culture - an experience that many wrongly believe can only be achieved by visiting one of the great art capitals of the world. However, visitors should not allow the wealth of art treasures to prevent them from seeing Upton House's extensive gardens. Time should be allowed for both.

UPTON ST LEONARDS (1-2 G4) *3 mi. SE Gloucester.* Situated below the scarp on which **Prinknash Abbey** stands, this is a rather scattered village, with its timber-framed farms and cottages now greatly outnumbered by modern houses. Gloucester is not far away and the noisy M5 motorway is depressingly close to Upton's church. This has a handsome Perpendicular tower, but is now largely the result of Victorian rebuilding. However, there is a handsome monument to Sir Thomas Snell in the north chapel, and some pleasant table tombs in the churchyard.

WADFIELD ROMAN VILLA (1-2 E7) *1½ mi. S Winchcombe.* This Roman villa was excavated in the 19th century, thanks no doubt to the enthusiasm of Mrs Emma Dent, the formidable chatelaine of **Sudeley Castle. The Cotswold Way** passes close to a small shed which still houses a small mosaic pavement, but it should be stressed that this is private property. Strangely, the best pavement taken up during the excavation, well documented and removed to Sudeley Castle, has since vanished without trace. It is thought that it lies hidden under the turf in a quiet part of Sudeley's garden, but this theory has yet to be proved.

THE WARDENS' WAY (Not shown on map.) A 14-mile walking route between Bourton-on-the-Water and Winchcombe which has been established by members of that most helpful of organisations, the Cotswold Voluntary Warden Service. It passes through Lower and Upper Slaughter, Naunton, and Guiting Power. The Wardens' Way runs approximately parallel with the **Windrush Way** and parts of both them can be combined to form circular walks. Use the Ordnance Survey's Outdoor Leisure Map No. 45 to plan these circular walks.

Warmington Church

WARMINGTON (1 A15) *5 mi. NW Banbury.* Herbert Evans, the author of that most delightful early guide book, *Highways and Byways in Oxford and the Cotswolds,* found that this village, *nestles umbrageously at the foot of the hill* and we must assume that, travelling by bicycle, he came here on a hot summer day, and found many shady trees in its cool churchyard, perched high above the village. Since Evans came here in about 1900, Warmington has happily changed little, apart from suffering noise from the not far distant M40. The village still has its lovely sloping green complete with pond and sheep dip, all overlooked by a series of charming Hornton stone houses and cottages, including an early-l7th-century manor house and an elegant little Georgian rectory.

The church is approached up a long flight of steps, and in its steeply sloping churchyard there is a series of table tombs beneath pines, probably the very trees that inspired Evans's use of the delightful word *umbrageously*. Despite his possible fatigue,

Evans was able to note a gravestone in memory of a Captain Alexander Gaudin, dated October 1642; no doubt one of the many who fell on Edgehill Field, or who died from their wounds soon after.

Like the rest of the village, the church is of toffee-coloured Hornton stone, and its Norman origins are revealed by the substantial north and south arcading within. There is much Decorated work, and the priest's door, the sedilia and the piscina are all headed with delightful little ogival arches. The vestry is two-storeyed and the upper storey must have been the priest's room, and is still complete with fireplace and little window looking down into the chancel.

THE WELSH WAY (1-2 J8) *3 mi. NE Cirencester.* (Not shown on map.) There are several rough tracks across the Cotswolds which were used by Welsh cattle drovers to take their beasts to the London markets before the coming of the railways. The section of the Welsh Way running westwards from **Barnsley** probably had its origins in prehistoric times, but it is still used as a minor road and provides a pleasant contrast to the busy B4425, as it winds across country towards the **Foss Way.** Much of its course must have been used by the prosperous wool merchant Sir Edmund Tame, on his frequent journeys between his estates at **Fairford** and **Rendcomb.**

For more details of this and other Cotswold roads and trackways read G.R. Crosher's *Along the Cotswold Ways.*

WESTCOTE (1-2 F11) *3½ mi. SE Stow-on-the-Wold.* Made up of Church Westcote and Nether Westcote, this small village has fine views eastwards over the broad Evenlode Valley to the distant wooded slopes of **Wychwood Forest.** It has a handsome 16th-century manor house and several pleasant old houses nearby, but its church is the result of several 19th- and 20th-century reconstructions and is not of great interest to visitors. However, in the churchyard, which is colourful with primroses and daffodils in early spring, can be seen the sculptured base of a 13th-century cross.

Here, at least until the 1960s, on land to the west of the A424 just north of the Hunter's Lodge Inn, were to be found the last vestiges on the Cotswolds of the medieval farming practice of the open field - the division into strips of land, the produce of which was originally shared between the peasant renting the strip and the lord of the manor. Open fields still survived in many Cotswold parishes in the early 19th century, although the process of enclosure was by then gathering momentum. Walk north-westwards from Westcote to link onto the **Oxfordshire Way** at nearby Gawcombe, or north-eastwards across the valley to **Bledington.**

WESTINGTON (1 C10) *To immediate S of Chipping Campden.* This is the quiet and somewhat over-trim south-western part of Chipping Campden, with some bewilderingly beautiful houses and cottages, many of which are thatched. On Westington Hill, on the B4081 south of the village, there is a little stone conduit by the roadside, built by Sir Baptist Hicks in 1612 to supply water to his almshouses below **Chipping Campden** church.

WESTONBIRT ARBORETUM (2 M4) *3 mi. SW Tetbury.* The magnificent neo-Elizabethan Westonbirt House was designed by the architect Lewis Vulliamy for Robert Holford, for whom he had also designed Dorchester House in London's Park Lane (now the Dorchester Hotel). The mansion is now a girls' boarding school, and for most visitors to the Cotswolds, Westonbirt is perhaps better known for its splendid arboretum - the creation over the years of Robert Holford, his son Sir George Holford, and Sir George's nephew, the fourth Earl Morley. Since 1956 it has been owned by the Forestry Commission (now Forest Enterprise), who have continued to develop the woodlands and to provide visitor facilities.

This world-famous collection of over 13,000 trees and shrubs covers 116 acres, and includes an unrivalled variety of different species in carefully contrived harmony, with maples, rhododendrons, azaleas and camellias in great profusion, all linked by woodland paths and grassy glades. The Silk Wood, a very extensive area of semi-ornamental woodland to the immediate south-west of the car-parking area, should not be missed. One of the great features of the Silk Wood is its long Broad Ride and this is used by the **Macmillan Way** as it heads southwards to Sherston. Westonbirt has a visitor centre, cafeteria and picnic areas.

WESTON-SUB-EDGE (1 B9) *3 mi. NE Broadway.* There are several attractive stone houses in this village and at least one with a timber frame upon a stone base, emphasising Weston's position on the borders between the Cotswolds and the Vale of Evesham. The church is at the upper end of the village looking across the earthworks of a medieval moat towards the steep, wooded slopes of the hills above. Its attractively pinnacled tower is Perpendicular, and although the rest of the building has been heavily 'Victorianised' its interior does contain several items of interest, including a handsome late Jacobean pulpit, a brass to a very smart Elizabethan gentleman named William Hodges, and several other monuments.

The Roman **Ryknild Street** runs just to the west of the village, and its course up part of the Cotswold scarp is followed by a well defined bridle road ending up just above neighbouring **Saintbury.**

WESTWELL (1-2 H11) *2 mi. SW Burford.* A delightful and still totally unspoilt village in open wold country with church, rectory and manor house looking across a rough green complete with duck-pond. The impressively simple war memorial consists of a great block of stone into which has been set a figure 'I' rescued from the shattered Cloth Hall at Ypres - a poignant reminder of the 'War to end all Wars'. The nearby Norman church stands amongst a fascinating array of beautifully lettered 17th- and 18th-century table tombs and is overlooked by an exquisite

The Rectory, Westwell

late-17th-century rectory. Amongst several interesting features within the church will be found a charming 17th-century monument to Charles Trinder, his wife and their fourteen children.

WHATCOTE (1 B13) *3½ mi. NE Shipston-on-Stour.* A remarkably remote little village in the Vale of Red Horse (see **Tysoe**), flat farming country between the Stour valley and the scarp face of the Oxfordshire Cotswolds. John Leland, the 16th-century antiquary wrote of the area, *Corn is the cheapest commodity grown in the county, whereof the Vale of Red Horse yieldeth abundantly.* The church tower is Perpendicular, but a Norman doorway and two windows are evidence of its much earlier origins. The south porch and part of the nave were damaged by a bomb in the 39-45 War, but all has been made good and the interior is well worth visiting. See especially the three finely carved 15th-century benches, the brass to William Auldyngton, a fifteen-inch-long, headless figure in mass vestments dated 1511 and the shaft of a medieval cross in the churchyard, crowned by an 18th-century sundial. See also the tablet in the church in memory of William Sanderson Miller, at one time rector of Whatcote, and the last Squire Miller of Radway, a descendant of the 18th-century architect, Sanderson Miller (see **Radway**). There is a much visited inn here, the warm and lively Royal Oak.

WHICHFORD (1 C13) *5 mi. N Chipping Norton.* Here is a wide green overlooked by the little Norman Knight Inn and surrounded by houses and cottages of almost every age - not outstandingly beautiful, but one of the most comfortable villages in southern Warwickshire. It is enfolded in lovely wooded hill country, not far from the Oxfordshire border, but well sheltered from the winds that blow around Great Rollright, on the hills to its south. The 18th-century rectory in mellow stone is one of the most elegant country buildings one could wish to encounter, and the church close by is equally attractive. This has a Norman south doorway, a rugged early 14th-century tower, and in contrast a finely built Perpendicular clerestory. The white-painted interior was restored in 1845, when neo-Gothic pews were installed, and these now blend in well with their surroundings. Do not miss the medieval stained glass in some of the window heads, nor the coffin lid, thought to be that of Sir John de Mohun, who fought at the Battle of Boroughbridge in 1322, and who died shortly afterwards. See also the alabaster relief of John Merton, and the tomb chest with brass of Nicholas Asheton, both men rectors of Whichford in the 16th century. Whichford lies on the **Macmillan Way** and this can be followed along the southern edge of Whichford Wood, and south-west, down over the fields to **Long Compton.** It is also possible to walk eastwards round the flank of Whichford Hill, to **Hook Norton,** or northwards to **Brailes,** past Whichford Mill and New Barn Farm.

WHITEWAY (1-2 H5) *6 mi. SE Gloucester.* A community was founded here in 1898 by a group of idealists from a sect called 'The Brotherhood Church of Croydon', who wished to follow the principles of the writer Tolstoy. Their original ideas, based on shared land and resources, had to be drastically modified, and the bleak hill farm they had purchased had to be split up into self-contained smallholdings, each with its own small house or bungalow. The architectural results are hardly inspiring, but the courage that it must have required to espouse a philosophy of life and follow it through in practical terms, even modified ones, is still unquestionable. For a fuller account of Whiteway read Joceline Finberg's most revealing book, *The Cotswolds.*

THE WHITE WAY *North from Cirencester.* (Not shown on map.) This was a minor Roman road, the purpose of which appears to have been the serving of the numerous villas that lay between **Cirencester** and the Cotswold edge in the vicinity of Winchcombe. See **Chedworth, Spoonley** and **Wadfield.**

WHITTINGTON (1-2 F7) *4 mi. E Cheltenham.* Small village not far to the south of **Cleeve Hill** and **Cleeve Common.** It has a pleasant row of cottages, a Victorian wayside well succinctly inscribed *Waste not, want not* and, away from the village, a small church sheltering beneath the high walls of the romantic 16th-century Whittington Court.

Whittington Court

The church, which has some Norman details, has a small bellcote and a pretty little north porch. However, the most interesting treasures here are the three 14th-century effigies - two of knights and one of a lady. There is also a brass (dated 1556) of the builders of Whittington Court, Richard Cotton and his wife, with the unusual wording *in the reign of King Philip and Queen Mary* included in its inscription. Do not miss the two little figures used as headstops to the arcading - a gentleman and a lady, who both look quite Chaucerian. There are small but convenient access roads to Cleeve Common northwards from here. If possible use the Ordnance Survey's Landranger Sheet 163. Also walk northwards from here to **Cleeve Common,** West Down, **Belas Knap** and down to **Winchcombe.**

WIDFORD (1-2 H12) *1 mi. E Burford.* Situated just above the water-meadows of the Windrush Valley, this hamlet consists of a pleasant 16th- and 17th-century manor house and a minute 13th-century church. This was built on the site of a Roman villa and at one time a small portion of mosaic floor lay exposed amongst the old stone flags of the chancel floor. This has now been covered over, but quite apart from this most interesting feature, the interior is delightfully unspoilt, with Jacobean pulpit, early 19th-century box pews and 14th-

Church in the fields, Widford

century wall-paintings. It is possible to walk from here, up Dean Bottom, down a quiet road to **Swinbrook,** and back along the Windrush Valley to Widford.

WIGGINTON (1 D14) *6 mi. SW Banbury.* Quiet village above the little River Swere, with

Cottages at Wigginton

pleasing views over the valley to the wooded ridge along which the Banbury to Chipping Norton road runs. There are a variety of Banbury-stone houses and cottages, including a handsome 18th-century house at its centre, which was once the Dolphin Inn. The church has a late-13th-century nave, and a Perpendicular tower. In the 14th-century chancel will be found a stone seat with a swan on the arch above it, and also two 14th-century effigies, one of a knight and one of a civilian complete with minute effigies of a wife and child. Do not miss the lovely 15th-century roof to the nave, well lit by the accompanying clerestory.

The Waterfowl Sanctuary and Children's Farm is situated close to a cross-roads just over a mile to the north of the village. Here are over 2000 creatures including a large selection of birds and rare farm breeds and children are encouraged to handle chicks, ducklings and baby rabbits.

WILCOTE (1-2 G14) *3 mi. SE Charlbury.* A deliciously quiet, tree-shaded hamlet with several large houses withdrawn from the road and a small, partly Norman church, with little of interest for the visitor. The River Evenlode is only a short distance to the east of the hamlet and the course of the Romans' **Akeman Street** runs just to its north. There is an attractive walk north-westwards up the Evenlode valley to **Charlbury.**

WILDFOWL TRUST *(See Slimbridge.)*

WILLERSEY (1 B9) *1½ mi. NE Broadway.* Situated just below the steep Cotswold scarp, this modest village sits astride the still-busy B4632. The little Bell Inn looks across to handsome 17th-century Pool House, with its stone gate-pillars standing between the house and a lively village duck-pond. Opposite this pond there is a quiet cul-de-sac leading to the church, which lies on the eastern fringes of the village looking up and across to Saintbury church, itself poised half-way up the Cotswold edge. Willersey church has an imposing Perpendicular tower, almost certainly built by Evesham Abbey, which then owned this parish. It is complete with pinnacles and gargoyles and inside there is fine vaulting beneath it, installed as late as 1859. Other features that make this church worth visiting include a small north porch, a pleasantly shaped Norman tub font, and the Royal Arms of George III. Walk eastwards from here beneath the Cotswold edge to **Saintbury,** and onwards up to **Dover's Hill,** from where it is possible to walk to **Chipping Campden** along the **Cotswold Way.**

Pool House, Willersey

WINCHCOMBE (1 D8) *6 mi. NE Cheltenham.* This surprisingly unspoilt town lies in a fold of the Cotswold edge and is sheltered on three sides by partly wooded hills. One of the seats of Mercian royalty, it was the capital of its own shire until it was incorporated into Gloucestershire in the early years of the 11th century. It prospered greatly in medieval times, due largely to the presence of an abbey founded here in AD798 by King Kenulf of Mercia, and dedicated soon after to his martyred son, St Kenelm. Although this event is now believed to be the fabrication of a later period, it brought pilgrims to the shrine of St Kenelm in great quantities, and stood the monks and the citizens of Winchcombe in good stead for several hundred years. A great Benedictine abbey was established here in the 13th century, and this continued to grow in power, thanks not only to the number of its pilgrims but also to the prosperity of its very extensive Cotswold sheep runs. The town must also have derived some benefit from its proximity to **Sudeley Castle.**

To explore the town start from the main car park behind the Library. It is only a short walk from here to the Parish Church. This fine Perpendicular 'wool church' was built jointly by the parishioners, by Sir Ralph Boteler of Sudeley Castle, who provided the nave, and by the abbot, who provided the chancel. But despite this connection with the abbey, it survived the Dissolution unscathed.

Winchcombe Pottery

Its fine west tower is in the best 'wool' tradition and is today crowned by the gilded weathercock which once graced the tower of St Mary Redcliffe, Bristol. Inside the broad, beautifully proportioned, but rather severely restored interior will be found a number of wooden 15th-century screens, a 17th-century holy table, the Royal Arms of George III and, displayed on a wall, an old door and floor tiles from the abbey. There are also a number of interesting monuments, including a rather sad one in the chancel with a lonely Sir Thomas Williams of Corndean kneeling at a prayer desk, opposite an empty space reserved for his widow - a lady who eventually remarried and who apparently had no wish to join the lonely effigy of her first husband.

Winchcombe's great abbey, unlike the church, did not survive the Dissolution. It was destroyed so thoroughly by Lord Seymour of Sudeley that no single trace remains above ground. The only reminder of its past glories is the medieval George Inn in the High Street, which was once the abbey's hostel for pilgrims. Carved on its doorway are the arms of Richard Kidderminster, a 16th-century abbot, whose efforts on behalf of the abbey were so successful that it was claimed to have been 'equal to a little university'. Almost opposite the George Inn is the Tourist Information Centre, which is housed in the Old Court Room on the upper floor of the little Town Hall, together with the Simms Collection of Police Memorabilia, while the adjoining Judge's Room houses the interesting Winchcombe Folk Museum. In the little fenced enclosure below are the town's old stocks.

There are several pleasant old houses, some timber-framed, in narrow Hailes Street, but having walked down there, it is then best for visitors to retrace their steps, back past the George Inn, into Abbey Terrace. Here, extending to the left down Dent Terrace, will be found the pretty Sudeley Almshouses. The work of Sir Giles Gilbert Scott, they were built at the expense of Emma Dent of Sudeley Castle in 1865. Also to the left, a little further on and almost opposite the church, is Vineyard Street, which is lined with regularly pollarded trees and a series of delightful cottages, each with its own rustic porch. Beyond the cottages there is an old stone bridge over the little River Isbourne, carrying a small road which leads to **Sudeley Castle.**

Beyond the turn to Vineyard Street visitors will again pass the Parish Church and go beyond to explore the length of Gloucester Street, which contains a number of attractive old buildings. On the right, at No. 23, will be found the interesting little Winchcombe Railway Museum, where visitors are encouraged to operate some of the working exhibits. Well beyond this, also on the right-hand side, is the pleasant 16th-century Old Corner Cupboard Inn.

Follow the **Cotswold Way** north-eastwards over the fields to **Hailes Abbey,** or southwards to **Belas Knap Long Barrow** and beyond to **Cleeve Common.**

WINDERTON (1 B13) *4 mi. E Shipston-on-Stour.* Beautifully sited on the steep southern slopes of a hill, with views over the tree-lined fields of the Feldon countryside to the tower of Brailes church. Here are farmhouses and cottages, some thatched, and almost all on different levels. The handsome Victorian church, built in 1878 by a certain Canon Thoyts, stands just above the village and its slender spire is a well known local landmark. It has a very grand apsidal chancel enriched with

Winderton

alternative bands of red and white stone, and lancet windows with deep coloured glass. This is Victorian architecture at its best, and should on no account be missed. Non-enthusiasts will at the very least enjoy the splendid views from the churchyard.

WINDRUSH (1-2 H11) *4 mi. W Burford.* Prettily sited above the Windrush meadows, this delightful village has a small triangular green around which are several pleasant houses and cottages. The green is also overlooked by the handsome Perpendicular tower of Windrush church - an attractive and most interesting building. Its outstanding feature is the beautiful Norman south doorway with its double row of grotesque beak-heads - one of the finest in the Cotswolds. There is also a lovely 15th-century roof to the nave, a medieval screen, a fine Jacobean pulpit, a 15th-century font, some interesting medieval floor tiles and a charming little sheep's head above the arcading. The churchyard

Windrush

contains an impressive series of 18th-century table-tombs.

Windrush was once noted for its stone quarries, or to be more precise its mines. These were driven up to a quarter of a mile in length, into the valley slopes between the village and the line of the present A40, and were worked until the 1890s, when safety regulations became too stringent for them to continue profitably.

There are the earthworks of an Iron Age settlement, Windrush Camp, about a mile to the south-west of the village, beside a bridleway leading over open country beyond the A40. However, the best walks from Windrush are up the valley to **Sherborne** or down to **Little Barrington.**

THE WINDRUSH WAY (Not shown on map.) This is a 14-mile walking route between Winchcombe and Bourton-on-the-Water. Like the **Warden's Way,** this was created by members of the Cotswold Voluntary Warden Service. It runs almost parallel with the **Warden's Way** and parts of both them can be combined to form circular walks. Use the Ordnance Survey's Outdoor Leisure Map 45 to plan these circular walks.

Winson

WINSON (1-2 H9) *2 mi. NW Bibury.* Situated on the lovely River Coln, this minute village has a handsome 18th-century manor house and a small Norman church. The latter stands in a neat churchyard with some 18th-century table tombs, and overlooks a fine group of farm buildings. It has a typical Cotswold-style bellcote and a Norman south doorway. Its simple interior contains a Norman chancel arch, a 15th-century stone pulpit (so ruthlessly restored that it looks more like a 19th-century reproduction) and some quaint Victorian wall-paintings in the chancel, with vine and honeysuckle in profusion. There are pleasant walks up the Coln Valley to **Coln Rogers, Coln St Dennis** and **Fossebridge,** or down it to **Ablington** and **Bibury.** It is also possible to walk southwards over the wolds to **Barnsley,** going through Barnsley Park.

Winstone

WINSTONE (1-2 H6) *6 mi. NW Cirencester.* A rather scattered village with an unusually large number of farms, but little of special interest apart from its church. This is attractively situated at the eastern end of the village, looking south and east over open farmland. It has a saddleback tower, but it has been ruthlessly restored both inside and out, and tantalising glimpses of medieval wall-paintings on stonework show what the Victorian restorers must have scraped away. The blocked north doorway and the chancel arch, both with their massive jambs, are late-Anglo-Saxon, but the south doorway is more Norman in character. It would therefore appear that much of this church was built at about the time of the Norman Conquest. Do not miss the base and broken shaft of a 14th-century churchyard cross near the south porch. There is a good linear walk southwards to **Duntisbourne Abbots,** and down the Dunt valley towards **Cirencester.** It is also possible to walk across the deep Frome valley to **Miserden.**

WITCOMBE ROMAN VILLA (1-2 G5) *4 mi. SE Gloucester. To reach this, follow signs from the A46 between Brockworth and Painswick.* (Not shown on map.) In the care of English Heritage, this is a large 1st-century Roman villa built around three sides of a courtyard.

Witcombe Roman Villa

There is a small mosaic pavement with dolphins and sea-horses, and various items from the excavation are displayed in a small building on the site. It is situated on a terrace beneath high woodlands and there are fine views over the Severn Plain - proving once again how adept the Romans were in their choice of villa sites.

WITHINGTON (1-2 G8) *5 mi. W Northleach.* An exceptionally pretty village situated near the head of the Coln Valley, less than six miles below the river's source near **Brockhampton.** Its manorial rights were once held by the bishops of Worcester, and both the manor house and Halewell Close were once used by them. Both have 15th-century origins, but have been much altered and added to in the following centuries. There are several other very pleasant buildings including the busy Mill Inn, which has the River Coln flowing through its gardens.

The Mill Inn, Withington

However, the village is very much centred upon its stout-towered church. The tower itself is partly Norman and there is a blocked Norman north doorway, as well as a fine Norman south doorway still in use. The interior was ruthlessly scraped by the Victorians and lacks any great feeling of antiquity. However, there is a fine wall monument to Sir John and Lady Howe of nearby **Cassey Compton,** complete with their eight children, and several other interesting monuments. The east window of the south chapel is by Sir Ninian Comper, one of the 20th century's most capable church decorators. There is no trace above ground of the large Roman villa which once stood to the south of the village, but a mosaic pavement from here is in the British Museum. One of four known villas in this vicinity, its farm area is believed to have amounted to about 4000 acres. Walk south from here, through the extensive Withington Woods to **Chedworth** village, or down the Coln Valley to **Cassey Compton** and **Chedworth Roman Villa.**

WITNEY (1-2 H14) *7 mi. E Burford.* This pleasant old cloth town astride the River Windrush prospered from the days of Edward III through the making of blankets, an industry which is still exists in Witney today. Dr Plot, in his *Natural History of Oxfordshire* (published in 1677), claimed *that no place yields blanketing so notoriously white as is made at Witney.* The coming of the Industrial Revolution, which removed most of the Cotswold woollen industry to Yorkshire, with its supplies of cheap coal for fuel, might have been expected to put an end to Witney's blanket weaving, but it continued to prosper because by then it had become noted throughout the trading world for the quality of its products. These were even popular with the Red Indians, who are said to have even purchased Witney blankets at the remote trading posts of the Hudson's Bay Company.

Witney

The mills here, which are certainly not cast in the 'dark Satanic' mould of William Blake, were founded by the Early family over three centuries ago. This family was part of a group of wealthy weavers who were granted a charter for their Company of Blanket Weavers in 1711 and who built the Blanket Hall in the High Street in 1721.

Witney's most attractive streets run south to the Market Square. Here is the quaint little 17th-century Butter Cross, with its clock turret beneath a cupola, and also the 18th-century Town Hall, which incorporates the town's Tourist Information Centre. In Court Mews, off the High Street, is the Witney and District Museum with its contents illustrating the story of Witney and its surrounding countryside. Beyond the Market Square is Church Green, an unusually large tree-bordered green overlooked by lovely 17th- and 18th-century houses and, at the far end, by the massive tower and tall spire of Witney's largely 13th-century Parish Church. Viewed from the green, the exterior is most impressive, but the interior was unfortunate enough to be restored by the over-enthusiastic Victorian architect, G.E. Street, and lacks the sense of antiquity that might have been expected. However, there is a wealth of interesting detail including several fine windows of the Decorated period and a number of monuments. Woodgreen, on the north-eastern edge of the town, grew up in the 18th century, and there are many pleasant houses of this period looking out across it. The 19th-century blanket mill on its south side has been turned into flats.

There is a fascinating Farm Museum at Cogges Manor Farm, to the immediate south-east of Witney, off the B4022. This is equipped as an Edwardian farm and is complete with period machinery and tools. There is also a working kitchen with a dairy, and some livestock. The farmhouse, with its kitchen and series of charming period rooms, and its walled garden, is delightfully set out and very much part of the farm. In addition there are nature and history walks beside the River Windrush, a cafeteria, and shop. Nearby Cogges church is also well worth visiting, with its handsome monument to members of the Blake family, who used to live in Cogges Manor farmhouse, and above it a primitive frieze of monsters, some with human heads. Walk north and west from Witney, up the Windrush Valley to **Crawley** and **Minster Lovell.**

WOODCHESTER (1-2 K4) *2 mi. S Stroud.* Modest village on the steep western slopes of the Avon Valley between Stroud and Nailsworth, with several 18th- and 19th-century mills in the valley bottom. The new church of St Mary, designed by the talented Victorian architect, S.S. Teulon, contains a few monuments taken from the old church, which was abandoned in 1863. The remains of this building, situated to the north of the village, consist of a Norman chancel arch and north doorway and a Perpendicular window. However, its churchyard is the site of Woodchester's greatest treasure - the remains of a luxurious Roman villa, the principal feature of which is a splendid mosaic pavement featuring *The Myth of Orpheus* with Orpheus playing a lyre in its centre, surrounded by animals in two circles. First excavated systematically in 1796 by the Gloucestershire antiquary Samuel Lysons, it used to be uncovered every ten years in comparatively recent times. This is unlikely to occur again in the foreseeable future, but plans have been in hand for many years for a beautiful full-sized replica to be put on permanent display. *(Stroud Tourist Information Centre should have the latest news.)* The churchyard also contains monuments to the prosperous mill-owning Paul family, including the tomb of prison reformer, Sir George Onesiphorus Paul (see also **Northleach, Doughton** and **Rodborough**). The best walk from Woodchester is westwards up onto the ridge occupied by the open spaces of **Selsley Common,** and on through winding Stanley Wood, to **Frocester Hill.**

Woodchester Roman Pavement

While in Woodchester, do not miss a visit to Rooksmoor Mills, a 19th-century stone woollen mill, which now sells cane and pine furniture, and floor coverings. There is also a resident potter at work here.

Woodchester Park

WOODCHESTER PARK (1-2 K4) *4 mi. SW Stroud.* The ambitious mid-19th-century mansion of Woodchester Park, well to the west of the village, was designed by local architect Benjamin Bucknall, in a neo-Gothic style much influenced by the work of the great French architect, Viollet-le-Duc. Regrettably it was never completed although it still stands as a substantial ruin, parts of which are being restored. There is now limited access to the mansion on certain days and the surrounding wooded parkland in the long, narrow valley, with its string of lakes, is in the care of the National Trust, which has a car park off a minor road between **Nympsfield** and the **Coaley Peak Picnic Site,** just short of the latter. This delightful valley is open every day and stout footwear is advised.

WOODMANCOTE (1-2 H7) *5 mi. N Cirencester.* Substantial hamlet on a ridge to the north-west of **North Cerney** with a number of attractive 19th-century houses and cottages. Woodmancote is on the **Macmillan Way** and this can be followed south-westwards to **Duntisbourne Rouse** and on to **Sapperton.**

WOOD STANWAY (1 D8) *3 mi. NE Winchcombe.* This delightful hamlet beneath the steep Cotswold scarp has several beautiful houses and farms, and a number of good walks. It is possible to walk over the fields to **Hailes Abbey,** then up a track above the abbey, and back to Wood Stanway via **Beckbury Camp** and Stumps Cross - making a fine circular walk. It is also possible to walk northwards over the fields to **Stanway,** following the course of the **Cotswold Way.**

WOODSTOCK (1 G16) *7 mi. NE Witney.* This prosperous and beautiful little town was already a royal manor before the Norman Conquest. From these early times the story of the town is indivisible from that of the manor and the great park in which it stood. This was first enclosed by Henry I, in the early years of the 12th century, and he built a palace or hunting lodge here and even maintained a menagerie in the park, the contents of which included lynx, leopard, camel and even porcupine. It is not recorded whether or not these exotic beasts were kept for the purpose of hunting, but if replacements were available they would certainly have been released and pursued.

Woodstock

Henry I's grandson, Henry II, came here both for the hunting and for the company of his mistress, Rosamund Clifford - the 'Fair Rosamund' of many a legend. Henry II enlarged the palace and built the town of New Woodstock to house his court. The medieval palace of Woodstock was used by a succession of monarchs until the 17th century, when it was besieged and damaged beyond repair in the Civil War.

In 1704 the manor and its park were presented to John Churchill, first Duke of Marlborough, as a reward for his great victory at the Battle of Blenheim. The remains of the old royal palace were soon swept away and work commenced on the massive **Blenheim Palace.** Ever since then the town's prosperity has been greatly influenced by the affairs of the palace and its great estate. From medieval times it was also noted for its glove-making, but although this trade lasted well into the 20th century, tourism must now be Woodstock's most important activity.

If possible make use of the Main Car Park off the Hensington Road, to the east of the A44, and then call at the adjoining Tourist Information Centre, which is in the Library. Now cross the very busy Oxford Street, the A44, and walk up the High Street, passing the wonderful assortment of 17th- and 18th-century houses, shops, restaurants, hotels and inns, towards the dignified Town Hall. This was built by Sir William Chambers in 1766 at the Duke of Marlborough's expense, and makes a perfect foil to the cosier charms of the much older Bear Hotel, which is on the left at the beginning of Park Street. St Mary Magdalen's Church, also on the left and not far beyond the Bear, has a splendid tower, built in the classical style in 1785, which stands above a church medieval in origin, but almost entirely rebuilt about ninety years after the tower's construction. The interior is not of great interest, largely because this church was until the 18th century only a chapel of ease under the parish of **Bladon** (where the body of Sir Winston Churchill lies in the churchyard); the Dukes of Marlboroughs and their immediate family being buried in their own magnificent chapel at Blenheim.

Opposite the church, behind the Town Stocks, is Fletcher's House, a 16th-century merchant's house which now houses the Oxford County Museum. This contains a series of very interesting displays depicting life and work in Oxfordshire. The museum has pleasant gardens, a coffee bar and a bookshop. At the far end of Park Street is Nicholas Hawksmoor's massive Triumphal Arch, known as the Woodstock Gate, and the best pedestrian entrance to the park from the town. The view of the park and its great lake from a point just beyond the Woodstock Gate should on no account be missed (see **Blenheim Palace**). Much of the park is open to pedestrians for 364 days a year on payment of a modest fee.

It is suggested that on their return journey to the main car park, visitors fork left by the Town Hall and go down Market Street, before turning right into Oxford Street (A44), and then left into Hensington Road. Take time in Woodstock as there are several other little streets which are also well worth exploring.

WOOTTON (1 F15) *2 mi. N Woodstock.* Attractive village whose steep narrow streets climb up from its bridge over the River Glyme. St Mary's church has a pleasingly plain tower and a beautiful 13th-century south porch.

Why is one of the inns at Wootton called *The Killingworth Castle?* It appears that a 17th-century owner named Killingworth decided to perpetuate his name by changing the title of the inn - so please do not search for fortifications hereabouts!

WOTTON-UNDER-EDGE (2 L2) *3 mi. S Dursley.* This was burnt to the ground in the reign of King John by the king's mercenaries, who were bitter enemies of the Berkeley family

Wotton under Edge

of nearby Berkeley Castle. However, it was soon rebuilt and became a borough in 1253. Now an attractive little market town, it still shows signs of its prosperity as a cloth centre in the 17th and 18th centuries, and in recent years it appears to have come alive again after a long sleep. See especially the little Tolsey House in Market Street, the Wotton-under-Edge Heritage Centre, which is a museum in a converted fire station, the 17th-century Hugh Perry's Almshouses in Church Street and, of course, the imposing church of St Mary the Virgin. This has a fine Perpendicular tower and a large over-restored interior, the contents of which include several interesting monuments and the splendid late 14th-century brass of Lord and Lady Berkeley. This is not normally viewable, but there is an excellent glass fibre replica on display.

The Cotswold Way passes through the town and this can be used for walks northwards to **Dursley,** passing the **Tyndale Monument** and **Stinchcombe Hill,** or southwards to the **Somerset Monument** and **Horton.** There is also an attractive walk north-eastwards up the wooded Tyley Bottom.

WROXTON (1 B15) *3 mi. W Banbury.* This is a delightful village, much of it around a sloping green with a pretty pond usually lively with ducks. Here are many of the thatched stone cottages so typical of the Oxfordshire Cotswolds, where the local ironstone is less suitable for splitting into tiles than the true Cotswold stone further to the south and west. Each roofing method has its own merits, but how attractive these cottages look with their climbing roses and small trim gardens. There are two lively inns here, the White Horse, and the Lord North, and a hotel and restaurant, Wroxton House.

Wroxton Village Pond

An Augustinian priory was founded here in the early 13th century, but only fragments of this remain in the present Wroxton Abbey, a fine 17th-century mansion with 18th- and 19th-century modifications. The 17th-century house was built by Sir William Pope, but it passed to the North family soon after. Many improvements were made in the 18th century by Lord North, Prime Minister during the time England lost her North American colonies. He appears to have been not only a client, but also a great friend, of Sanderson

Miller, the architect-squire of **Radway,** and Miller carried out work for him not only on the house, the chapel and the park, but also on the village church. Wroxton Abbey is now a college for students of Farleigh Dickinson University, New Jersey. Its lovely gardens and park, with their sweeping lawns, rich woodlands and series of lakes, are often open, having been extensively renovated in recent years. Do not miss the early 18th-century ice-house and the octagonal dovecot, nor the distant views of the Gothic arch on a wooded ridge to the east. These features are probably also the work of Sanderson Miller.

The largely 14th-century church has a west tower designed by the same architect, and built in 1748. See the series of elaborate tombs to various inhabitants of Wroxton Abbey, especially the beautifully canopied tomb of the builder of Wroxton, William Pope, Earl of Downe, and his wife; and the handsome monument to George III's Prime Minister, Lord North, by the brilliant sculptor, John Flaxman. Thomas Coutts, the founder of the famous private bank still bearing his name, is also buried here.

WYCHWOOD FOREST (1-2 G14) *To immediate SW Charlbury.* From as early as Saxon times this was a royal forest, with the royal hunting lodge at **Woodstock** and its great woodlands extending from the Glyme Valley near **Enstone** southwards to the Thames

near Stanton Harcourt, and from **Taynton** in the west to the Cherwell Valley in the east. Every English king from Ethelred the Unready to James I is said to have visited the forest, and even as late as the 17th century Charles I started to build a wall round the whole forest - a process completed by Cromwell in 1655. The area was subject to the extremely harsh Forest Law, but although it was sometimes said that Oxford gaol was built largely to house those caught stealing game from here, this

The edge of Wychwood Forest

does not seem to have deterred the more determined poachers. The reputation of **Burford's** coaching inns for great meals, known locally as 'Burford bait', appears to have been due to their ability to acquire large quantities of venison - certainly not all the result of their one day's permitted hunting per year and the town's ancient right to two bucks annually.

Although this state of affairs did not wholly cease until as late as 1856, several great parks had by then been carved out of the forest - **Ditchley, Blenheim, Cornbury** and Eynsham - and most of the remainder had been cleared for farming. Wychwood is therefore now confined to a modest triangle between **Charlbury, Finstock** and **Leafield,** and most of this is part of the strictly preserved **Cornbury** Estate. There is one footpath across the forest (see **Cornbury Park**) and the road south from Ranger's Lodge to **Leafield** has great woodlands on its east side for almost three miles and is very pleasant. For a detailed account of Wychwood Forest and its history, read Joceline Finberg's excellent book, *The Cotswolds.*

WYCK RISSINGTON (1-2 F11) *1½ mi. NE Bourton-on-the-Water.* This unspoilt little village has a wide rough green, complete with Victorian drinking fountain. Several attractive houses and cottages are situated around this green, the most pleasing of which is a substantial farmhouse fronting on to a well stocked duckpond. The delightful road sign on the green asking motorists to 'beware of the ducks' should of course be heeded at all times.

The church of St Laurence, which once belonged to the monks of Eynsham Abbey in Oxfordshire, has a squat 13th-century tower and a chancel of the same period with two unusual lancet windows at its east end. There was once a strange maze, with religious significance in the old vicarage garden close to the church. Although this has now been cleared away its creator, Canon Harry Cheales, who died in 1984, is fittingly remembered with a well lettered wall-tablet, beneath which is a reproduction of the maze itself in a beautifully designed mosaic. See also the colourful fragments of 14th-century stained glass and an interesting series of 16th-century wooden plaques, which are believed to be Flemish in origin.

Wyck Rissington

The composer Gustav Holst, was organist here in 1892 at the early age of seventeen. In the lovingly tended churchyard will be found the grave of *James Loveridge, Gypsy - of no fixed abode* - a travelling man whose final journey ended at Wyck Rissington. This village is astride the **Oxfordshire Way,** and it is possible to use part of this long footpath to walk eastwards over Wyck Beacon to **Bledington** in the Evenlode Valley.

THE WYSIS WAY (Not shown on map.) This 55-mile pathway links the southern terminus of Offa's Dyke Path with the start of the **Thames Path** at Thames Head and the **Macmillan Way** at the **Tunnel House Inn.** It passes through **Gloucester, Robins Wood Country Park, Bisley** and **Daneway** before following above the tunnel of the Thames and Severn Canal to arrive at the **Tunnel House Inn** and **Thames Head,** just beyond.

YANWORTH (1-2 G8) *2 mi. W Northleach.* This modest village overlooks the beautifully wooded Coln Valley. The small Norman church stands among a fine group of farm buildings to the east of the village. It has a Norman south doorway with chevron

Yanworth

moulding, a Norman chancel arch and a stout tub font of the same period. From a much later period, probably the late 16th century, there is a wall-painting of Father Time complete with his scythe. Yanworth is astride the **Macmillan Way** and this can be followed southwards, then west to **Chedworth Roman Villa** and, beyond extensive woodlands, to **Chedworth village.** It is also possible to follow it north-eastwards to **Hampnett.**

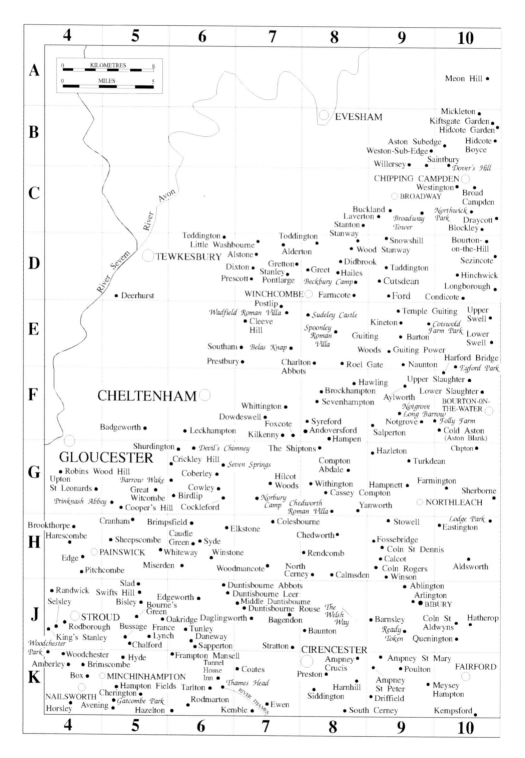

Radway • • Ratley Warmington •   **A**

• Quinton

• Edgehill

Sunrising Hill •   *Upton House*

• Admington

Lark Stoke • Armscote • Oxhill • Hornton

Ilmington • Tredington • Idlicote • • Whatcote • Tysoe Alkerton Horley •   **B**
Foxcote •   • Honington *Compton* • Shenington Wroxton •
Darlingscott •   *Wynyates*   • Drayton

SHIPSTON-
Ebrington ON-STOUR Barcheston • Epwell • Shutford   BANBURY

• Charingworth • Willington • Winderton *Madmarston* North
Hill Newington • • Bodicote

• Paxford • Stretton- • Tidmington Brailes Sibford • Swalcliffe • Broughton   **C**
on-Fosse Burmington Gower • • Sibford *Broughton Castle*
Aston Todenham Little Sutton-under- Ferris • Tadmarton
Magna Wolford Brailes
Lower Great • Stourton *• Traitor's Ford* Bloxham •
Batsford Lemington Wolford *Weston* • Cherington *Waterfoul* • Milcombe
Arboretum *Park* • Ascott HOOK *Sanctuary*
• Batsford Long Compton • NORTON • South Newington

MORETON- *Four* • Barton-on- • Whichford • Great Rollright • Wigginton • Barford St John   **D**
IN-MARSH *Shire* the-Heath • Barford St Michael
Stone *• Rollright Stones* • Swerford • Deddington
Little Compton • • Little Rollright • Nether Worton

• Chastleton • Over Worton
Donnington • Evenlode • *Chastleton* • Great
Barrow • Salford Little Tew Tew • Duns Tew

• Broadwell • Ledwell
STOW-ON- • Cornwell • Over Norton Heythrop • • Sandford St Martin   **E**
THE-WOLD Adlestrop CHIPPING NORTON Westcott • • Middle Barton
• Daylesford Barton • Steeple Barton
Heythrop
• Oddington *Park*

Maugersbury • Kingham Lidstone • • Gagingwell
• Churchill Enstone • *• Rousham House*

• Icomb Sarsden • *Hawk* • Kiddington
Stone Spelsbury *Ditchley*
Wyck • Dean • *Park* • • Glympton   **F**
Rissington • Bledington Chadlington • Taston

• Westcote *Bruern Abbey* Shorthampton
• Little • Idbury Ascott-under- CHARLBURY Wootton •
Rissington Lyneham • Wychwood *Wychwood* *Cornbury*
Forest *Park*
• Fifield • Milton-under-Wychwood
• Shipton-under- • Fawler • Stonesfield
• Great Rissington Wychwood Finstock • • Combe WOODSTOCK   **G**
• Wilcote *Blenheim Palace*
Ramsden • *North Leigh* • Bladon
Great *Roman Villa*
Barrington • Taynton Leafield • • Long Hanborough
North Leigh •

• Windrush • Asthall • Delly End • Church Hanborough
Little • BURFORD • Fulbrook Leigh • Hailey   **H**
Barrington • Swinbrook • Minster • Crawley
Widford • Lovell
• Westwell Asthall • Charterville • WITNEY
• Holwell • Shilton *Cogges Farm Museum*

Cotswold • Brize Norton
Eastleach *Wildlife Park*
Martin • Carterton
Broughton Poggs OXFORD   **J**
Eastleach • Filkins • Alvescot
Turville • Kencot • Black Bourton
• Southrop Broadwell BAMPTON

• Langford
• Clanfield River Thames
• Little Faringdon
LECHLADE Kelmscot   **K**
• Radcot Bridge
Inglesham Buscot
• *Buscot Park*

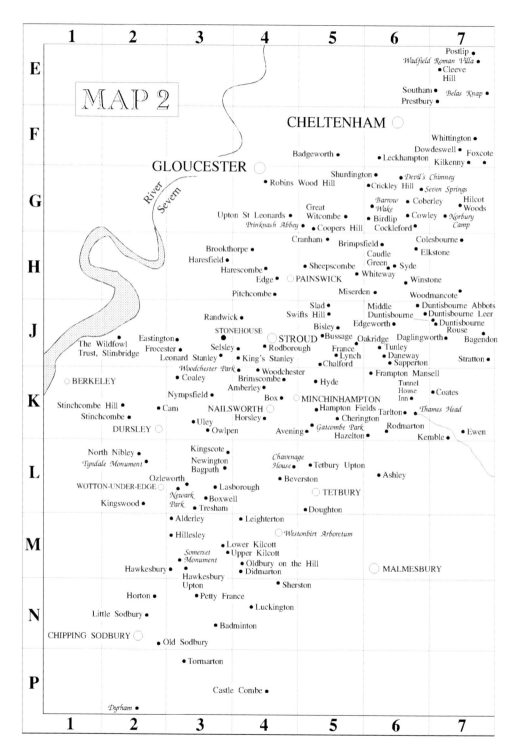

MAP 2

	1	2	3	4	5	6	7

E — Postlip •, *Wadfield Roman Villa* •, • Cleeve Hill, Southam • *Belas Knap* •, Prestbury •

F — CHELTENHAM ○, Whittington •, Badgeworth •, Dowdeswell • Foxcote •, • Leckhampton Kilkenny •, GLOUCESTER ○

G — River Severn, Robins Wood Hill •, Shurdington • *Devil's Chimney* •, • Crickley Hill *Seven Springs*, Great Witcombe • *Barrow Wake* • Coberley • Hilcot Woods, Upton St Leonards •, *Prinknash Abbey* • • Birdlip • Cowley • *Norbury Camp*, • Coopers Hill Cockleford •

H — Cranham • Brimpsfield • Colesbourne •, Brookthorpe • Caudle • Elkstone, Haresfield • Green • Syde, Harescombe • • Sheepscombe Whiteway • Winstone, Edge • ○ PAINSWICK, Pitchcombe • Miserden • Woodmancote •

J — Slad • Middle Duntisbourne Abbots, Randwick • Swifts Hill • Duntisbourne • Duntisbourne Leer, STONEHOUSE Bisley • Edgeworth • Duntisbourne Rouse, Eastington • ○ STROUD • Bussage Oakridge Daglingworth • Bagendon, Frocester • Selsley • • Rodborough France • • Tunley Stratton •, Leonard Stanley • • King's Stanley • Lynch • Daneway, • Chalford • Sapperton

K — The Wildfowl Trust, Slimbridge •, *Woodchester Park* • Woodchester • • Frampton Mansell, • Coaley Brimscombe • • Hyde Tunnel House Inn • Coates •, ○ BERKELEY Amberley •, Nympsfield • Box • ○ MINCHINHAMPTON, Stinchcombe Hill • • Cam • Hampton Fields Tarlton • *Thames Head* •, Stinchcombe • NAILSWORTH ○ Horsley • • Cherington Rodmarton • Ewen, DURSLEY ○ • Uley • Owlpen Avening • *Gatcombe Park* Hazelton • Kemble •

L — Kingscote • North Nibley • Newington *Chavenage House* • • Tetbury Upton, *Tyndale Monument* • Bagpath • • Beverston • Ashley, Ozleworth WOTTON-UNDER-EDGE ○ • Lasborough ○ TETBURY, *Newark Park* • Boxwell • Doughton, Kingswood • • Tresham

M — • Alderley • Leighterton, • Hillesley ○ *Westonbirt Arboretum*, *Somerset Monument* • Lower Kilcott, • Upper Kilcott, Hawkesbury • • Oldbury on the Hill ○ MALMESBURY, Hawkesbury Upton • Didmarton, • Sherston

N — Horton • • Petty France, Little Sodbury • • Luckington, CHIPPING SODBURY ○ • Badminton, • Old Sodbury

P — • Tormarton, Castle Combe •, *Dyrham* •

	1	2	3	4	5	6	7

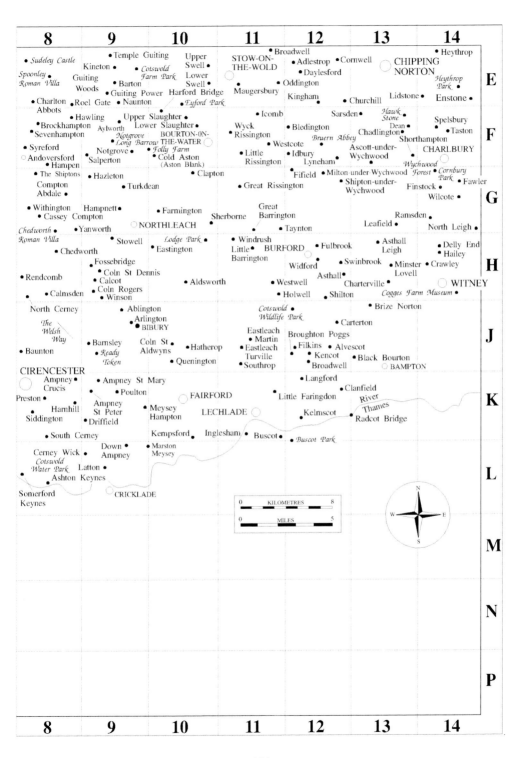

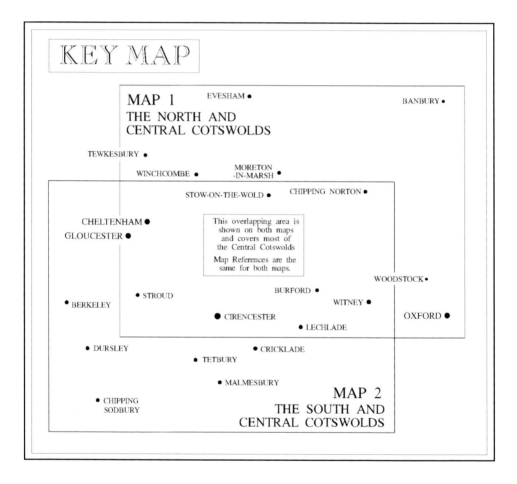

KEY MAP

MAP 1
THE NORTH AND
CENTRAL COTSWOLDS

EVESHAM ●

BANBURY ●

TEWKESBURY ●

WINCHCOMBE ●

MORETON
-IN-MARSH ●

STOW-ON-THE-WOLD ●

CHIPPING NORTON ●

CHELTENHAM ●
GLOUCESTER ●

This overlapping area is
shown on both maps
and covers most of
the Central Cotswolds

Map References are the
same for both maps.

WOODSTOCK ●

● STROUD

BURFORD ●

WITNEY ●

● BERKELEY

● CIRENCESTER

● LECHLADE

OXFORD ●

● DURSLEY

● CRICKLADE

● TETBURY

● MALMESBURY

● CHIPPING
SODBURY

MAP 2
THE SOUTH AND
CENTRAL COTSWOLDS